GULAG TO SPITFIRE

GULAG TO SPITFIRE

A POLISH SERVICEMAN'S FIGHT TO SURVIVE IN THE SECOND WORLD WAR

ANDREW HUBERT VON STAUFER

First published 2024

The History Press
97 St George's Place, Cheltenham,
Gloucestershire, GL50 3QB
www.thehistorypress.co.uk

© Andrew Hubert von Staufer, 2024

The right of Andrew Hubert von Staufer to be identified as the Author
of this work has been asserted in accordance with the
Copyright, Designs and Patents Act 1988.

All rights reserved. No part of this book may be reprinted
or reproduced or utilised in any form or by any electronic,
mechanical or other means, now known or hereafter invented,
including photocopying and recording, or in any information
storage or retrieval system, without the permission in writing
from the Publishers.

British Library Cataloguing in Publication Data.
A catalogue record for this book is available from the British Library.

ISBN 978 1 80399 521 2

Typesetting and origination by The History Press
Printed and bound in Great Britain by TJ Books Limited, Padstow, Cornwall.

To the memory of my father,
Kazimierz Tomasz (Tomek) Hubert:
17 September 1921–1 January 2006
and
My remarkable mother Angela (née Oakeshott):
24 August 1923–19 March 2022
Who remained faithful and endured so much, yet was the repository
of so many memories

And to the thousands of other Poles who suffered atrocities,
betrayal and disappointment.
Sadly, even at time of writing, others are treading a similar
path in Ukraine.

Nihil novis sub solum!

('There's nothing new under the sun!',
one of Tomek's favourite sayings.)

Contents

Author's Note		9
Foreword by Andrew Jelinek		11
Prologue: The Bird's Eye View		13

Part One: Capture!   **17**
1. The Realities of War — 19
2. Torture — 31
3. Vorkuta – The City Built on Skulls — 40
4. Break-up! — 51
5. Rape and Abuse — 61
6. The Criminals Take Over — 65
7. Another Year of Misery — 72

Part Two: Escape!   **81**
8. Saved by an Ancestor? — 83
9. Where Are Your Papers? — 93
10. Disappointment in Tashkent — 114
11. Frustration and Fever — 143
12. Iran and the *Aviateur* — 160

Part Three: Spitfires!	**175**
13 Scotland to Brighton	177
14 Life-Changing Tea and Cake	187
15 The Hazards of Fire	196
16 Marriage and Disappointment	204
17 Spitfires at Last!	221
18 Dogfights and Rockets	236
19 The Sting in the Tail	248
20 Aftermath	261
Postscript	271
Appendix: In His Own Words	274
Acknowledgements	281
Further Reading	282
Notes	283

Author's Note

War is a shared trauma and what is frequently overlooked is that trauma is not just shared laterally across the same timeline but sequentially, with the effects of historical failures and individual PTSD being passed on to future generations. Their suffering, often undocumented by those who were its victims with no access to paper, pen or film, is seared into a collective memory, often ignored, suppressed or dismissed as the fantasy of plainly damaged veterans with a bitter axe to grind. This simply leaves their families to bear the brunt of frustrated anguish.

This is not an official history. It is just a single account from the perspective of one man who endured extraordinary suffering during the Second World War and its effects on him. He was by no means unique, but it is a story that has been largely glossed over since 1945.

He never had the literary and linguistic gifts of Joseph Conrad, who wrote so effectively in an alien tongue. Instead, my father Tomek lashed out with often heart-rending and occasionally terrifying accounts of what happened to him.

His memory was photographic and his often broken English created an almost high-definition ongoing documentary in his older children, of whom I was the eldest. He would quote verbatim, first in Polish or Russian, never varying his subsequent translation of who said what to whom and its effects.

In many ways his trauma became our living nightmare. As so often happens, the wounds opened by war endure to be passed on to children and grandchildren living with the consequences of lives burned in the wildfires of war. The pain, distress, hopelessness and frustration had become contagious.

The Second World War generation has largely passed. We, their children, were brought up on the memories of veterans who only had personal experience to go on, often without understanding the broader view or the political realities and compromises that are the inevitable legacy of war. We are now in our late sixties and seventies and are the remaining custodians of their experiences.

The one advantage of my own creeping *Anno Domini* is that subsequent personal experiences in Eastern Europe, where the Russian threat has been very real, have reinforced many of the fears and opinions my father passed on to me decades earlier.

Please read on and hopefully see, through his eyes, the bitterness, cruelty and sheer indifference of Stalin's Russia, via the brief hope of being an effective operational Spitfire pilot, to the ultimate betrayal of a pre-war Poland Tomek knew and loved.

Where possible, Tomek's accounts have been cross-referenced with service records, pilot's notes and logbooks together with extensive reading of the few official histories on the subject of Stalin's deportations, General Anders' recruiting of Polish forces in Tashkent, Uzbekistan, and the Polish Air Force in exile.

Conversations are based exclusively on Tomek's frequently quoted memories, which hardly varied over more than sixty years.

Andrzej Roman Hubert
(aka Andrew Hubert von Staufer)
2023

Foreword

by Andrew Jelinek

Andrew Jelinek is a former Captain in the Household Cavalry, who was severely injured in Afghanistan. He has since trained Local Defence Volunteers in Tomek's hometown of Lwów (modern-day Lviv).

In setting down the story of his father's remarkable life, Andrew Hubert von Staufer has given us a personal lens through which to view a profoundly dark chapter of Polish and Eastern European history.

We first join Tomek as he glides above the Tatras Mountains, the tranquil and serene vista stretching away from the cockpit analogous to a young boy's future about to be derailed by cataclysmic events. As Poland is savagely torn apart from both east and west, we follow Tomek as he is catapulted along dusty roads, choked with refugees, under screaming air attacks, and into his panic-stricken home city of Lwów. Poland falls, Tomek goes into hiding, is arrested and transported into the depths of Siberia. Throughout his ordeal, he is repeatedly beaten and questioned in a Kafkaesque nightmare of pseudo-justice, where his only 'crime' is to be of a class and nationality which is to be liquidated.

This brutal story is told without sentimentality, and is the more powerful and impactful for it. In an almost throwaway sentence we learn early on that Tomek will never, ever see his home again. There is almost no time to appreciate the deep sadness of this before we are bundled into the depths of Soviet Russia.

This is a tale of a man subjected to all the punishments of a violent, tyrannical regime, of the sadistic and desperate men such systems create, and of nature's own cruel capacity to imprison, injure and kill. But through this unrelentingly bleak odyssey shines humanity, humour, and the extraordinary capacity of man to endure, survive, and ultimately fight back.

Gulag to Spitfire is a cautionary tale, but sadly not one from a Europe of a dim-and-distant past. The themes of invasion, annexation, deportation, ethnic cleansing, atrocities and violence are, sadly, 'live' ones. Indeed, the very same sirens that Tomek would have heard in Lwów warning of air raids are wailing again today, heralding the approach of Russian cruise missiles.

Prologue

The Bird's Eye View

It was a warm afternoon in late August 1939. Before him the rolling foothills of the Tatra Mountains gave way to the wide open plains of south-eastern Poland. Seventeen-year-old Tomek was aloft in a very low-performance Salamandra[1] glider, which surprised him, as following a bungee launch, where two teams of volunteers ran down the slope pulling long elastic ropes to catapult him into the air, his normal flights always resulted in, at best, a five-minute glide to the bottom of the green valley below.

Something had happened this time and the brisk breeze blowing up the slope had not only allowed him to soar along, waving to the other Boy Scouts lining the ridge, but to gain several hundred extra metres.

It looked peaceful below, but as he already knew, following the death of his father more than a year before, all was not well. A cousin had been shot by the Russians trying to smuggle Polish literature to those still cut off from their homeland, despite the territorial gains by Poland in 1921.

His father, Kazimir, had been a friend of the father of modern Poland, Josef Piłsudski,[2] and was a pallbearer at his funeral in 1935, a singular honour for those few who had served in the legions with him up to the war of 1919–21 against the Russian Bolsheviks. Kazimir had been one of the instigators, organising the revolt of those Polish officers who had been forced to serve the Tsar up to his overthrow in 1917.

Everyone knew that Russia was a permanent threat. Its revolutionary chaos resulted in what would now be described as war crimes. Several of Piłsudski's men had been captured and tortured, with one unfortunate crucified and skinned alive by Tatar tribesmen.

Small wonder that Tomek's father, who was effectively the military governor for south-eastern Poland, was a hard, uncompromising martinet at home. He was no longer able to calm his fractured nerves by playing the piano, his scarred hands being in constant pain from shoving burning charcoal in the face of the Tatar chieftain who had committed that atrocity. A mad action that had caused enough shock and awe to allow his men to escape.

He may well have loved his long-suffering wife Stefania, but home life under his thunder cloud was difficult. She had borne him two girls older than Tomek and a younger son, Bartek, who had been killed in infancy when their Ukrainian maid dropped him on a stone-flagged floor. Tomek remembered the screams of anguish from his mother, followed by the wailing and screams of the maid as his father whipped her.

No, Tomek's life was easier now since the old man had died of a stroke. His family never called him Kazimierz, or the diminutive Kazik, as it was probably a reminder of his very difficult and overbearing father. Tomasz was his second name, Tomek being the affectionate pet name that somehow allowed more informality and a more relaxed atmosphere among the family.

Without fear of censure or over-expectation from a father who was determined that his son should become a surgeon, Tomek could now indulge his passions for skiing, radio and flying, as the *de facto* man of the family. His life was now so much better.

From his exposed, lofty perch in the creaking wood-and-canvas glider with its open cockpit, Tomek looked down at the club with amusement. Someone, probably the chief flying instructor, had rigged the sleek high-performance Orlik,[3] obviously in the hopes of gaining yet another badge or record. If something so basic as Tomek's

Salamandra could stay aloft for so long, surely the Orlik could do so much better.

To his sheer delight the Orlik was catapulted off, and despite weaving left and right in a frantic search for lift, it was soon stranded in the long grass of the valley floor. Tomek was going to revel in this later. If he kept this up, he might even get his long desired 'C' badge to wear on the lapel of his Scout's tunic, the envy of his mates.

It was then that he noticed something was going on next to the clubhouse. Everyone was mustering round and pulling out long canvas sheets that they arranged into a large 'O'. That meant: Land Immediately! Tomek grinned to himself; he was certain it was sheer jealousy. If the advanced pilots couldn't stay up, they were not going to stick around for a cheeky Boy Scout with a sense of his own superior abilities. No, he would risk their wrath and land when he felt like it.

All good things had to come to an end eventually. The sun had moved inexorably down to the horizon as the shadows of the clubhouse and windsock lengthened. Besides, his bladder was hurting now.

Reluctantly he made a reasonable approach and landed a short distance from the clubhouse. To his disappointment, none of his mates came out to greet him, it looked quite deserted. Surprised, he made to tie down the glider, but as he looked for the pegs and rope the CFI came out with another of the older pilots. They did not look at all happy.

'You stupid young fool. Think you're a god? You should have come down over two hours ago. There's been a general mobilisation. You're to report to your nearest military reserve unit!'

This was the end of Tomek's youth. Everything now had changed.

PART ONE
CAPTURE!

1

The Realities of War

Getting back to his home in distant Lwów[1] turned out to be far more complicated for Tomek than his arrival at the gliding club. The instructors were going in a completely different direction and Tomek soon discovered that if he was going to get home, it would be entirely by using his own resources.

He had been dropped by what passed for a main road and pointed in the general direction of his home town nearly 200km away. The weather was hot and he was thirsty. He saw a couple of military lorries going in the opposite direction and his wave was met with little response. The faces that stared out looked strained and resigned. For the first time his natural self-confidence was beginning to ebb away.

A policeman on a bicycle stopped Tomek and asked for identity papers. This was unusual and he argued back. The policeman just shrugged: 'It's war.' He pointed out that, having given his name as Tomek, his identity card recorded him as Kazimierz Tomasz Hubert: 'Stick with Kazimierz, whatever they call you at home. Some of the militia are very nervous, shooting at anything that worries them. There are all sorts of stories going about infiltrators and German soldiers parachuting down dressed as nuns. Everyone is in a panic. Keep your story simple. You don't want to be shot by accident.'

Tomek was now beginning to get very worried.

A farmer took pity on him, giving a lift in a hay cart. He had no idea what was going on, but told Tomek that he reckoned that the war had either started already or would begin in a matter of hours. He passed that first night in an outhouse having eaten black bread and quenched his thirst with flat yeasty beer.

The next day he fared slightly better at hitching lifts but even so the journey was tiring, depressing and often lonely, with no chance of phoning ahead to let his mother know he was OK. He had never thought of it before, but the countryside was so empty. Not all the hamlets were Polish as some of the poorer farms were owned by Jews, who clustered together for mutual support and, unlike the polyglot population of his home town, tended to be insular and fearful of strangers. For the first time Tomek had the uncomfortable feeling that maybe those in charge, like his late father, should have been more open to the realities of this part of Poland and not so obsessed with rallying nationalist feeling behind the shield of a Polish version of Roman Catholicism, where national identity, statehood and religion made an uncompromising and probably toxic mix.

He was tired, smelly and in pain by the time he reached his home, thirty-six hours after leaving the club. If he had hoped for a warm and sympathetic welcome, he was out of luck as his older sisters were already in uniform and, far from listening to him as the man of the house, they were preoccupied with orders they had received by phone.

His mother wasn't really bearing up to the strain. Still unsure what was going on, he turned on the radio the next morning hoping to hear a news bulletin. Instead there was static, interrupted occasionally by what sounded like grid references, and what he guessed to be coded movement orders.

Things were not much better when he reported to the city hall. There were queues of young men and women. Nobody seemed to know what was going on. Finally his old Scout master spotted him and pulled him out to join a few younger lads who looked terrified. Within an hour they boarded a bus that took them westwards to a tented camp, where they drew very uncomfortable, ill-fitting uniforms.

Tomek might have expected to be given some sort of enhanced training or fast track, given his family background, but any hope of being an officer cadet, trainee pilot or even using his experience in ham radio disappeared within a matter of days. He was told he would be assigned duties once he reached a forward position.

It was now obvious that the only training was that of surviving in the crucible of war.

In that late summer of 1939, Germany was well prepared for invading a Poland that Hitler argued should not exist. Even his arch rival and equally cruel despot, Stalin, could agree with that. Stalin was once quoted as saying: 'The death of one man is a tragedy. The death of millions is a statistic.' There was little doubt that an independent Poland would not be allowed to survive.

Hitler's '*experten*' were pilots who had the advantage of lessons learned supporting Franco in the Spanish Civil War. The Poles had no chance of achieving air superiority over their home soil. Their PZL P.11s were at least 30mph slower than many of the German bombers and too lightly armed to knock them down with anything less than a very long machine-gun burst at very close quarters. When it came to taking on the Messerschmitt Bf 109 fighters, the P.11s, known as Jedenastka by the Poles, were almost 100mph slower.

Tomek didn't really appreciate how badly equipped the Polish Air Force was until his reserve training unit was surprised by a P.11 landing in a rough field near their tents. The heavily muffled pilot got out, took off a helmet and unwrapped a scarf to reveal it was a girl not much older than himself, who asked to see their maps as she had lost her way and had no radio. He watched her take off again and for the first time realised that they probably wouldn't win.

The next day, he was given a map and a grid reference and told to take a group of younger lads in leading several horse-drawn waggons to another camp about 30km away. It was now obvious that they were heading towards where the war was being fought.

He had heard the German Stuka dive bombers in the distance, their sirens shrieking as they bombed villages and columns of both soldiers and refugees. Their sirens, known as Jericho Trumpets, were designed to cause fear and panic. Even at this distance, the effect made his unit's horse-drawn transport scatter. Many of the reserves were nervous, diving into ditches at the sound of any approaching aeroplane, then spending anything up to an hour trying to re-muster the horses and set off again along the road before the whole chaotic carousel began again.

Tomek was shocked the first time he came across a column that had been bombed. As he later told my mother, the smell made him gag and retch. Horses lay on either side of the road, some with limbs blown off or almost eviscerated by the blast, while others plainly had been put out of their agony by a single bullet wound to the head. Wounded men had already been removed and temporary graves littered the surrounding field. From now on things changed rapidly.

A very worried-looking man in uniform, who announced he was a medical officer, arrived in a large car and asked for volunteers. Tomek was among the first, thinking he was about to see action at last. To his surprise he and five others were taken off to the east, away from the still very distant fighting, in the direction of Lwów. They had barely gone a few kilometres when a farmhouse in the distance seemed to mushroom, instantly exploding into an expanding boletus of mud, dirt and clouds of smoke. The blast hit a second later. Tomek had never experienced anything like this before. It slammed the breath out of his body. The officer continued driving and didn't appear to flinch. One of the younger boys on the back seat was now crying.

The officer turned to Tomek. 'Can you drive?' Tomek shook his head. 'I suggest you watch me, you'll have to learn quickly.'

The next week was spent moving to one place then another without being sure where they were or what they were supposed to be doing. This was complicated by columns of refugees blocking the roads as they moved east. Many of them were orthodox Jews, women with their heads covered in scarves or something that looked a bit like a turban, while the men wore long black coats and wide-brimmed hats, despite the heat, and curls in ringlets down the side of their faces. Those who were not showing signs of fear were stone-faced. Women and children were crying; from a distance it sounded like a constant, nerve-jangling, keening wail.

An old sergeant at a crossroads looked grim. 'Poor bastards, I've heard stories of mass executions by the Nazis. They'll be the first to go.' Tomek later heard that some of the younger men had shaved off their curls, ditched their wide-brimmed hats and headed into the forests, saying they'd fight the Germans. This was greeted by the dismay of their parents, who were afraid it would only make matters worse for them.

Not yet knowing how far the Nazis were prepared to go in their hatred of the Jews, this didn't make a lot of sense to Tomek. Sure the Jews were always a people a bit apart, but by and large they were no threat. They usually played the best music at weddings and sold the best bargains at the market. Although they spoke Polish, they preferred to converse in Yiddish or even Russian. Tomek wasn't too sure about this, as sometimes he thought they were talking about him. Even so, he never met one in the Scouts or among the reservists.

His first field hospital was another shock: one doctor, two orderlies and more than 200 patients, many of them dying with horrendous injuries. He had not realised before, but blood and spilled guts smelled.

Not having any real medical experience, his first task had been to bury the dead in their makeshift graves. Every morning there were more, every afternoon ever greater numbers of wounded appeared. Those capable of walking were sent on while the worst were given morphine, if available, to kill the pain and wait either for them to get better or die. There were no operating facilities at all.

He lost all sense of time or place. He was now dog tired, numb and utterly bewildered. There were a couple of older men who seemed to know what they were doing. Most days were spent obeying the last order, emptying slops, digging new latrines or occasionally being called over to hold down a screaming, struggling man as disinfectant was sluiced into an open wound, then bandages wound tightly.

He saw gangrene for the first time and was horrified at the look and stench of it. Fortunately they had no bone saws, so he didn't have to assist or witness any amputations. Those poor sods were wheeled outside for collection as and when any transport of any kind passed by.

By his second week (or so he thought) he began to notice aircraft flying from the north-west towards the Rumanian frontier that lay approximately to the south and east of his latest field hospital posting. He had no means of knowing, but from 14 September orders had been given for the evacuation of all Polish Air Force units to neutral Rumania. The air battle over Warsaw and Western Poland was already lost.

On 17 September (the day before his 18th birthday), the Polish Commander in Chief and his staff evacuated to Rumania as well.[2] Although it had not been recorded, it is probable that Polish intelligence were aware that the Russians had agreed on the 14th to initiate an immediate attack on Poland from the east.

Tomek was completely unaware of any of these developments. The first he knew of it was seeing, in the distance, some very large and slow unfamiliar aircraft that seemed to hang just above the horizon for ages. They were, most likely, Russian transports being used to move troops to forward positions. What is known is that on the 18th, Russian aircraft were engaged by a few Polish stragglers among the few airworthy Polish P11s, with a couple of Polikarpov I-16s and I-15bis being claimed as shot down. These were followed by Tupolev SB-2 bombers carrying out raids on targets untouched by the Germans.

From Tomek's perspective matters had quietened down on his uncelebrated birthday and everything had almost gone silent. The stream of casualties had all but dried up and nobody knew what was happening. It was then that the rumours began. There were no messages or radio contact. Traffic was few and far between, seemingly heading south to Rumania rather than the usual east or west.

The older orderlies were looking very worried and began hurrying anyone capable of moving under their own steam out from the tents and away to the south as well. When asked by Tomek or any of the younger boys what was going on, they were greeted with the one word, 'Russians', and nothing more.

Finally one of the more senior orderlies suggested that Tomek ought to find his way back home without suggesting how he could do it.

The question was answered later that same day. A commandeered van arrived and Tomek was offered a lift. Unsure what to do, the sound of machine-gun fire made his mind up for him. As he jumped in he saw a soldier running towards them with what looked like a missing foot. He was screaming at them to get away, before he collapsed in a heap on the recently ploughed field.

The driver hesitated, then moaned as he doubled over and fell out of the cab. Tomek leaned across to help and to his horror was waved away as the driver appeared to be trying to stuff his own intestines back into his body. Terrified, Tomek slid over to the driver's seat and drove off, crunching the gears. He heard shouts from the back of the van and guessed that others were jumping in.

His last view of the field hospital was as he breasted a ridge. Two tanks were driving rapidly over the field hospital tents. He had no idea what happened to the wounded who couldn't move. He guessed they were crushed. Fortunately, as he was driving east, the Russian tanks seemed not to be interested in him.

Initially, upon the advice of his passengers, he joined a stream of other vehicles that shared petrol as they drove south to the Rumanian border, crossing it at night. Not knowing what to do, they waited around for instructions, only to be told that all military vehicles and weapons were to be surrendered to the Rumanians. Any officers or men would be moved further into Rumania and interned awaiting a decision as to their fate. Rumania's neutrality was already under threat.

Tomek wasn't at all happy about this, as he didn't really qualify as military personnel, so he slipped away once more and recrossed the border back into Poland, in the hopes of finding out what had happened to his mother and sisters.

He was very lucky in being picked up by a mixed group of students and service veterans, who announced that they were going to stay behind and start a resistance movement. To his surprise he recognised a face from his college who had got hold of a heavy machine gun, announcing to all that he was going to find a church tower somewhere and pick off any Russians or Germans. That was the last Tomek saw of him.

He got to Lwów early the next day and found his mother alone in the house. Everything seemed almost normal, if unusually quiet. She had no idea what was happening. The local police had been replaced by Ukraine-speaking militia wearing Russian uniforms who directed traffic. Nobody was keen to engage with them.

A curfew was imposed and anyone picked up after hours disappeared. There was a rumour that all churches were closed and locked by the new Russian-appointed officials. Tomek thought about going to Rumania again but his mother thought it was too risky.

Within a few days a general order went out ordering the population to report to their schools, colleges and places of work. Tomek, in common with many, was reluctant, especially as over the next few weeks the most popular teachers were replaced by others who were either dedicated socialists or, in a few cases, did not seem to speak much Polish, lapsing into Ukrainian, which was just about understandable, if accompanied by technical drawings on the blackboards. Lectures in philosophy and history had been stopped for those who had not yet matriculated.

Tomek had sat his exams before the summer and was hoping to go on to greater things. Instead he was back at his old college marking time, while technical subjects such as engineering and the sciences that preceded entry into university or technical institutes were peppered with communist propaganda and speeches on political theory.

Rumours were beginning to circulate about secret meetings and more than once a note had been passed to Tomek telling him to stay at a particular street corner, noting any military vehicles or squads of Russian soldiers. He would report back in the bustle between lectures, when he would have a tap on the shoulder and be told not to turn round. Any initial excitement paled with a growing sense of menace as groups of civilians were rounded up and loaded into lorries. New faces speaking Ukrainian started to appear, taking over shops and

The Realities of War

businesses. Tomek had never heard the term 'ethnic cleansing' but he was witnessing the beginnings.

Tensions were racked up when notices went up announcing that elections would be held to choose spokesmen for each class, workshop and so on. Everybody was suspicious of this order, but few saw any sense in disobeying it.

Tomek was soon to find out the reality of what the Russians planned.

When he duly reported to his college class, he quickly heard that the Russians were indeed carrying out elections and those voted in were promptly arrested and disappeared. His worst fear now bore out the stories his late father had told him about how the Russians in the Tsarist times did exactly the same thing in the past, using what was then the *Cheka* (Secret Police).

This rerun of elimination was now being carried out, with even greater efficiency, by Stalin's head of the NKVD, Lavrentiy Beria. His agenda was to eliminate all political leaders, intelligentsia and officer class, an action that would ultimately culminate in the Katyn massacres, where thousands were shot in the back of the head and shoved into mass graves. Beria would later complain to Stalin that such mass executions were exhausting for his men!

Tomek's class refused to hold any such election. They were soon confronted by a uniformed officer who would only speak to them in either Russian or Ukrainian, insisting that the students would understand him. This resulted in uproar, which had already begun elsewhere in the college. The numbers were such that even if the Russians present had drawn their weapons, they would have been overrun in seconds. The chaos was a successful diversion for Tomek, who made his escape in the confusion and hid until nightfall.

His first inclination was to make for his home, but recognising a friend of his in the street, he risked talking to him. The news was not good. His friend was walking out of town that night as he didn't think it was safe. Tomek thought this was a crazy idea as his friend had no real idea of where he was going beyond saying he would make for Rumania. Even when Tomek told him what he had found when he got there, his friend wasn't to be dissuaded.

Tomek never saw him again and never knew if the lad ever got to his stated destination.

More by good luck than judgement, a friend of his mother took Tomek in, having found him hiding among some bins on a street corner. Bewildered, tired and hungry, he was still debating whether to risk going back to his own family home.

'You'll be safer in my house. We have a secret room hidden behind a wardrobe.' It sounded like a better bet.

Having given him some tea and hard-boiled eggs, she introduced him to her daughter, who had only been married a couple of weeks. Her new husband had been spared military service, though it was never explained why.

They gave him a bottle of water and took him up to the secret room. It was more like an attic just off the top bedroom. There was a chair, a mattress on the floor and two blankets. Tomek was shut in there. Once settled in, he could hear the large and ornate free-standing wardrobe being pushed across the floor and up against the door. It sounded as if it took the efforts of mother, daughter and new husband to make everything secure.

The only problem was that in the dead of the night, Tomek could hear giggles and the creaking of a bedstead coming from the bedroom. He vowed that whatever happened he wouldn't disturb them in the night.

At first everything went well. At about 5 a.m., the wardrobe was pulled back, the door opened and, after relieving himself, Tomek was able to stretch his legs, have a wash, and eat a substantial breakfast before being reinterned. The same happened around 9 p.m. every evening. He realised that this could only be a temporary measure and was fearful of what would happen to his hosts if the NKVD ever found out. The woman's own husband had already disappeared and nobody had any idea if he was alive or dead.

It all fell apart late one evening. The food and drink routine had been varied and for some reason the usual chamber pot had not been returned to the attic room. Tomek had no wish to interrupt the sounds of amorous activity coming from the bedroom beyond the door and wardrobe, yet his bladder thought otherwise.

Finally, out of desperation, he opened the little attic window and relieved himself. To his horror, he heard shouts in furious Russian from below and, quickly retreating and pulling the window quietly shut behind him, he was horrified to see an NKVD guard emerge from the shadows into the street light below. He was looking directly up at the top-floor windows. Tomek could not have chosen a worse person to widdle on. He realised that the game was up.

As soon as the guard walked away to report it, Tomek banged on the door. He had to leave at once. Interrupted lovemaking would be the least of his hosts' problems if they were found to be sheltering him.

Very scared, hungry and thirsty, he made his way carefully, under the cloak of darkness, keeping to unlit alleyways avoiding patrols looking for anyone breaking the curfew. He needed shelter but was out of ideas.

Reluctantly he returned to his home, where his mother, with an almost psychic maternal intuition, opened the door before he knocked. She looked pale, drawn, anxious and unwell. Holding back any questions, she fed him before he collapsed into an exhausted sleep.

The next day she explained that the NKVD had been to the house several times over the past week. She had not understood at first what they were after, until she realised that they were looking for Tomek's father, who had been dead for two years. She wasn't sure if they had realised that she had a son of the same name. Tomek thought that her optimism in believing that they did not yet know about his existence was misplaced.

Reluctantly, he agreed with her insistence that he should hide in yet another wardrobe during the day. He managed it for a short while, coming out to sleep in his own bed at night then stripping it before dawn to give the impression that he wasn't staying there. So far there had not been any more raids in his street and his mother retained an almost faith-driven optimism that they had got away with it.

That all changed after one midnight, when Tomek was woken by being prodded with a rifle barrel. There were several uniformed men in his bedroom, while his mother was protesting loudly outside, asking why it took so many men to arrest one boy.[3]

After a brief interrogation, he found himself outside, then bundled into the back of a lorry with half a dozen other men he didn't recognise. He finally caught sight of his mother running down the road with a pot of jam that she tried to throw to him. She was pushed back roughly by a couple of rifle butts. This would be the very last time in his life that Tomek saw his home, his street and his city.

2

Torture

There is a book in Polish that details all those deported from Lwów. It is based simply on research among those interviewed, underground documents and what few of the original public records survived.

This will surprise many historians who are prepared to troll exhaustively through reams of paperwork, trying to get to the facts of what happened in the past. The problem with Lwów and almost all of south-eastern Poland is that, as far as the Russians were concerned, it should never have existed as Polish territory.

Ethnic cleansing purged all such records.

Poland had gone from a vast commonwealth in the fifteenth and sixteenth centuries that went from the Carpathian Mountains to Estonia and from almost the Oder River in the west to beyond Smolensk in the east, covering much of what would be Belarus and Ukraine today.

Through mismanagement, poor administration and internal bickering instead of having a dynastic monarchy, they elected kings from the royal families of other countries. Inevitably they all had their own agendas. Through this political dog's dinner of conflicting political and strategic stresses, Poland all but disappeared under a series of partitions between Russia, Prussia and the Austrian-Hungarian Empire. Interference by the Swedes trying to invade from the north did not help either.

Part of the problem was that, beyond a few rivers, Poland did not really have any natural borders running east to west, while the south was only guarded by the Carpathian Mountains. Although forests and the Pripet Marshes occasionally slowed up some invading forces, they were not natural bastions against the enemy. For instance, as the Mongol hordes under Genghis Khan had discovered, a great deal of the country was sparsely populated, open and ideal for cavalry, and in much later years, tanks.

The Poland that Tomek knew was relatively modern, having been won back after the chaos of the First World War and the Russian Revolution. The Poles, under Josef Piłsudski, had defeated the Red Army in 1921. They had been aided by the fighting between White Russia and the Bolsheviks. The simultaneous intervention of the British Expeditionary Force sent by Churchill to attack from the north of Russia all helped to dilute Bolshevik forces' efforts in the west against the Poles. The Poles succeeded in winning back territory that had a mix of races and languages, much to the horror of such Western Allies as Britain, France and the USA, who wanted the Poles to adhere to the far more conservative and Russia-friendly Curzon Line drawn far to the west of their recent gains.

All in all, Tomek had grown up against a background of tension that had involved his father, Kazimir Hubert, who as a colonel was in a position of extraordinary power and influence, as there was no higher rank in the peacetime army. Regarded as a hero of the legions and recipient of the Virtuti Militari, the ultimate medal for bravery, he was frequently summoned, with a chartered aeroplane laid on by the government in Warsaw, for conferences about the state of Poland's armed forces and political stability. Against this background, the whole family well understood that a strong military presence was the only thing that stood between them and another partition.

Sadly, Poland's economy could not sustain the modernisation of its armed forces of any size to compete with a rearming Germany and a steadily industrialising Russia under the vicious iron fist of Stalin. Few Poles of Tomek's father's generation had any illusion that the war clouds were gathering. Their only hope was a series of alliances that would pull in France and Great Britain, should the worst happen. The reality was that neither country had the appetite for taking advantage of Germany's attack on Poland to invade the now unprotected Rhineland in the west. This indecision sealed Poland's and Tomek's fate.

He was about to learn the difference between 'official' and 'unofficial' Russia. Officially Russia had not invaded Eastern Poland, it had simply mounted a special operation of sorts to stabilise the situation and allow refugees to go home. This was not unlike the situation today with Putin's 'denazification' of Ukraine, and like its counterpart of 1939 is a cover for a great deal of cruelty and war crimes that they hoped would never see the light of day.

The Russian invasion involved no charm offensive, or attempts to win hearts and minds, but simply the crushing of opposition, the transportation of others to undisclosed fates and the complete dismantling of civil authority. Basically, it used brutal criminals, gave them weapons, and told them they could do what they liked. Behind them lay the NKVD, the dreaded secret police, which was there to make sure that were no exceptions, humanity, or deviations from the master plan. They were to take over all occupied territory and expunge any memory of Poland from the historical record.

Tomek, inevitably with his background, was possibly in line to be expunged, if he did not co-operate.

Interrogation began with no clue as to what he was accused of. The entrance to his interrogator's office had a tapestry of *Our Lady of Częstochowa* laid on the floor and he was ordered to wipe his feet on it. He refused, which resulted in the first of many clubbings by rifle butts.[1]

This was how they intended to change Tomek's heart and mind.

He was dog tired, he had not been allowed any sleep, and every time he closed his eyes he had been prodded awake. Once a bucket of water had been thrown over him. He had lost all sense of space and time. He had been blindfolded, moved from one building to another and even taken in a lorry somewhere. He wasn't even sure if he was still in Lwów.

He had been kept in solitary confinement and, although he could hear other prisoners shouting in Polish, he saw nobody as he was blindfolded and taken off to yet another interrogation.

Most of the time he was screamed at in Russian, then punched or beaten when he either didn't or couldn't answer.

Once he was denounced in badly accented Polish. He couldn't see who it was, as he was still blindfolded. The same statement was made again and again. He was an enemy of the proletariat, his father had oppressed the Ukrainian peasants, and he had been a war criminal. All Tomek had to do was accept that his Catholicism was wrong, his father was wrong, renounce God and accept that Marx and Engels were right. Religion was the opiate of the people, communism was unstoppable. It would take over the whole of Europe, he was a fool to resist.

This was followed by more beatings. His cell stank; there wasn't even a bucket for him to relieve himself. There was no schedule or mealtimes; when he least expected it, he would be given coarse black bread and a tin mug of water. Occasionally a hose was turned on his cell to sluice out the filth and urine. The subsequent soaking was bitterly cold but a relief from the stink.

He heard shooting and women screaming. After a while the number of Polish voices diminished. If he asked the guards what was going on, they said nothing and more often than not pointed their weapons at him, cocking them as if they intended to shoot. At first he was terrified, but after a while he became inured to it. His next punishment was to be put into something they called the *Karza*: a very small cell, too low to stand up in and too narrow to lie or sit down. His body was cramped and painful.

It was after that he was brought in to his final interrogation before being moved on. A weaselly man with a bald head had started the interrogation. He seemed to be enjoying it. That all changed when a tall woman walked in and said something in Russian. The man looked worried and immediately left the room. She was wearing a black uniform Tomek had not seen before. She looked as if she might have been Jewish, or even Georgian, but there was no glint of compassion or sympathy in her eyes. Her manner was that of someone who was out to prove unswerving loyalty to the Stalinist terror machine. Previous interrogations had been brutal; this, for a change, was cold, efficient and almost robotic.

She asked, in clipped Russian, Tomek's name, address and about his immediate family. Tomek refused to answer, so she just shrugged and made a note before reading out what sounded like an indictment. She handed him a large document printed in Russian, before giving Tomek a pen, indicating a space at the bottom of the page. She said just one word in Polish: 'Sign!' He shook his head. She snatched it back then signed it for him.

He was then dragged to his feet, hurried outside past a wall that had bullet marks on it and shoved into the back of a lorry. There were several other unkempt men all shackled together. A young armed guard climbed in after them and they drove off.

Tomek, by now, had no idea of his fate, what he was accused of, how long he had been confined or even if he would stand trial. He was now in that twilight world of 'unofficial' Russia. What little can be deduced from post-war research reveals that he was officially arrested on 27 October. It is almost certain he was never told he had been formally arrested. This pattern was to be repeated over the next two years.

There is now some confusion as to where Tomek was taken next. The pattern was the same, shouts and threats followed by interrogation then thrown in a lorry, or marched off in the middle of the night, with no idea of where he was or what he was charged with. This was deliberate.

Disorientation is a stress technique used even today to make prisoners amenable to interrogation, prone to agree to anything and, of course, to break any vestiges of spirited resistance. In his book *Spare*, Prince Harry describes enduring similar treatment in training exercises designed to toughen up officers, should they ever be captured. Tomek had no such preparation.

Even today, volunteers and Ukrainian PoWs have described similar treatment, having been taken in eastern Ukraine during the Russian invasion.

Often Tomek was reliant on other prisoners telling him what was happening, but of course there was no guarantee that this was anything more than guesswork. There are, however, a few stories he told that have been since repeated in similar form by others who survived.

It might have been in Kiev where Tomek was thrown, quite literally, into an already overcrowded cell. Nobody had washed, probably in weeks, and lice crawled everywhere. Some of the men were already quite ill, probably with typhus.

After a few hours they were taken out in groups, stripped naked then doused with paraffin and left standing outside in a bitterly cold courtyard. Their clothes were burned. Other prisoners who had already been shaven were then ordered to shave all body and head hair from each of the new batch of prisoners. For the first of what would be many times, Tomek felt violated, as this treatment didn't spare the pubic and anal areas. It was painful as the shaving was inexpert, done with already well used razors of various descriptions, and many of the men, my father included, had areas of their body that were left as an untreated, bloody mess.

They were then hosed down with freezing water and given a coarse, evil-smelling soap, which didn't lather, to wash off the paraffin. They were then issued with a *kufeika* (a sort of padded jacket), padded trousers, coarse socks and ill-fitting boots. They were then herded into trucks and sent off elsewhere. There were rumours that the sick men were all shot.

At their new destination, they were put into small cells with a single bucket serving as sanitation for upwards of a dozen prisoners. They were allowed out into an open courtyard once a day to be hosed down again, but beyond any small rags they had secreted about their bodies, there was nothing in the way of toilet paper or flannels.

Tomek was later convinced that he was taken to Kharkiv, then Gorodnya, before being taken to Moscow.

That was the last that Tomek saw of anything approaching natural daylight. Now the interrogations happened at any time with no warning. Sometimes they were left in total darkness, possibly for days, as there was no way of telling the time. This would change, as a single bulb might go on, then be extinguished after just a few minutes, or a few hours, often when they were all trying to sleep. There was no sense of day or night, and being denied any view onto the outside world simply confused their body clocks.

The pattern of interrogation was the same. The Russians called Tomek 'Gubert Kazimir Kazimirovich', mistaking the Western 'H' for the Cyrillic equivalent of 'G'. A whole list of spying charges (or so it sounded to Tomek), followed by a denunciation and a beating. Any answer at all resulted in more beating, usually with rifle butts, lengths of rawhide with a knot on the end, which the Russians called a *knout*, or wooden battens, which Tomek ruefully said made a pleasant change, as they often had a break mid-beating.

On one occasion, Tomek's left jaw was smashed with a rifle butt. The interrogator looked up and said, 'We must do something about that,' and one of the guards smashed his right jaw. His face would have a slight twist to it for the rest of his life.

He believed that he was taken to the Lubyanka jail in Moscow just before Christmas 1939. What is certain is that now the beatings and interrogations were carried out by the NKVD rather than Russian militia or regular soldiers. For one thing, the rifle butts were gone and this time it was almost exclusively the use of what are almost laughingly called rubber truncheons. These rarely broke limbs but caused severe internal bruising, sometimes with fatal consequences.

The Russian dissident lawyer Sergei Magnitsky, after trying to pursue the theft of public money through the state courts, was beaten to death with rubber truncheons on the night of 16 November 2009. Evidently these are still the weapons of choice in 'unofficial' Russia.

Tomek could see the effects of severe beating for himself when a young naked man, bound hands to feet, was thrust unconscious into his cell. He had been beaten to an ugly purple and black, from his kidneys and around the exposed testicles and buttocks, through blue to yellow, down the back of his legs and up his spine. Tomek had no idea if he survived as he also had a beating due shortly afterwards.

One evening, someone, somewhere, who bravely thought it must be Christmas Eve, started singing Polish Christmas carols – a refrain that was taken up almost immediately by other Poles whom Tomek couldn't see. His cell soon joined in, and despite the guards taking off individuals for further beatings, the singing continued, blocking out the sounds of thuds, shouts, screams and occasional shots.

Soon afterwards, in severely freezing weather, Tomek was taken out with a few other Poles, and after a brief journey to some marshalling yards was herded into cattle waggons. Others told him that any doctors, lawyers, teachers and university graduates had been left behind, probably to be shot.

Russia, under Gorbachev, admitted the massacre of 22,000 Polish officers and intelligentsia in the Katyn Forest during April to May 1940. Another 10,000, mostly civilians from the professions, disappeared at the same time and were never accounted for. To this must be added countless thousands who were about to disappear into the gulags, most of whom had been summarily picked up and deported without any idea as to why.

Tomek may have been spared liquidation, but his journey to Siberia had begun. He was well aware that he was following in the footsteps of his father, grandfather and great-grandfather. The difference was that they had endured political exile under various tsars. Tomek was now part of a systematic programme of elimination, promulgated by Josef Stalin, the most brutal Russian leader since Ivan the Terrible, who, it is now reckoned, may have had up to 20 million of his own citizens starved to death or liquidated.

Poland was to suffer, at the hands of Hitler and Stalin, the loss of around 20 per cent of its pre-war population – a larger percentage than any other country during the Second World War.

The situation across Eastern Poland was confused and difficult to understand from a Western perspective. The distances are vast, which meant that even with such a dedicated and ruthless force such as Beria's NKVD, maintaining control of any kind, let alone discipline over widely scattered villages masked by forests and marsh, allowed 'bandit' groups to take advantage of the situation. Many Ukraine, Belarus and local Russian allegiances changed in order to be on the winning side or, more often than not, settle old vendettas.

Torture

This was one such tragic atrocity that befell the family of Tomek's future brother-in-law, Alex Smirnoff. Unbeknown to Tomek, Alex was based not far from him in Lwów. Unlike Tomek, Alex stayed in Rumania when the order to evacuate was given and, already being in the Polish Air Force as a technician, was eventually shipped out via Beirut to join the RAF.

Sadly, his parents were isolated in a remote part of Eastern Poland with their young teenage daughter, Tatiana. As they had both German and Russian ancestry, living in St Petersburg at the time of Alex's birth in 1918, they fled south and west during the wars of 1919–21. That marked them down as being of the old Tsarist regime and it was only a matter of time before rumour, resentment and opportunity resulted in Tatiana being abducted, raped then murdered with bayonets. Such are the traumas caused by war.

No responsibility was ever claimed. The aggressors were variously described as Ukraine bandits, Russian deserters and rival villagers across the whole of Eastern Poland, where other such atrocities abounded.

The reality is that once Stalin had unleashed his poorly trained, undisciplined, barely literate and often unsupervised hordes on the course of invasion, other groups of predators joined in.

The same is happening now in eastern Ukraine where the Wagner Group is fighting today. They are nominally under Putin's control but they are a law unto themselves, flying their own flag and guilty of many atrocities.

This was the background of brutality into which Tomek found himself pitched. Only the NKVD maintained any discipline when they turned up from time to time. Their policy was simple: any complaint, shoot the complainer and the one they complained about, beat up a few others and if any of them complained, either shoot them as well or put them on a cattle truck to Siberia, where they could disappear for good.

It was admin by terror and what was about to happen to Tomek was part of this wider context.

3

Vorkuta – the City Built on Skulls

Tomek was on a train, not one passenger carriage, just a long procession of cattle trucks with no sanitation or provision for food or water. Occasionally the train stopped in the middle of nowhere and the prisoners were let out to forage for anything they could eat or to melt snow to quench their thirst.

Sometimes the train would stop for more than a day at a remote and bleak yard before another train laden with coal and tanks full of almost frozen slush pulled up alongside to feed the steam engine. The boiler had to be refilled before the firebox went out and the boiler cooled.

Obviously there was a temptation to escape, but pretty soon everyone realised that it was a question of escape to where? None of them had any idea of where they were or where they were headed. All they could see was endless forest and they would occasionally hear wolves, whose howls broke the oppressive and bitterly cold silence of grey skies that drizzled a constant fine spindrift of tiny, icing-sugar-like crystals that drifted down. Hunger, cold, thirst and fear smothered all of them with the deep gloom of Slavonic depression born of a fatalist history that stretched back to Ivan the Terrible and beyond. Even the guards had given up chatting as they sat round improvised pine- and larch-fed braziers that flared up, but made little impression on the cold.

Vorkuta – the City Built on Skulls

Somewhere – it might have been Kotlas, as there was a big frozen river nearby – a few desperate men made a break for it, resulting, at first, in a chase and a few shots. But as the journey dragged on, occasionally alongside the Pechora then Usa rivers, frozen and bleak, the guards couldn't even be bothered to waste bullets. The extreme cold was an efficient killer.

Many of the prisoners were lawyers, accountants and teachers, unable to cope, often rocking miserably and moaning to themselves. If any of them failed to get up after a stop, the guards might club them half-heartedly, but usually left them behind to meet a bitter and pointless end in the interminable snow. Wolves, bears and lynx would take care of the bodies – provided the ravens didn't get there first.

Tomek was surprised to find that the women, who may have made up as many as a third of the deportees, were much better organised. They arranged who had to collect wood, make a fire, melt snow and cook whatever they could forage or beg off the guards, sometimes in return for sexual favours. It was degrading but when faced with that or a cold, lingering death, other rules applied.

The women asked around if there were any doctors, which would have singled them out for special attention. At first Tomek couldn't think why, but after one stop was interrupted by screams, then the cries of a newborn baby, he realised what had been going on.

Although he never saw it, there were rumours that the doctors would tend to any guards who had health problems, probably in return for concessions for mother and baby. He never knew what eventually happened to them, as once they had arrived in Vorkuta he saw no sign of any babies.

The Vorkuta[1] of 1940 wasn't really a town, let alone a city. It already had an evil reputation of being the site of several coal mines, manned by what was essentially slave labour.[2] The mortality rate was astronomical, with no provision for safety equipment in any shape or form. There was no possibility of digging anything more than shallow graves as the ground was permanently frozen even in summer, with only the first 10cm or so thawing out. It took mechanical equipment to dig out mass graves, provided it was possible to get the machinery started!

The gulag compounds were scattered over a very wide area. The whole countryside was bare tundra with distant birch forest. In winter it gave an aspect of a slightly undulating landscape of snow, followed by squelching bog and swarms of mosquitoes in summer. Daylight in midwinter was almost non-existent, while summer days went on for twenty-four hours. They were well north of the Arctic Circle. The area was nominally populated by the Samoyeds, an Arctic tribe, first cousins of the Sami from Scandinavian Lapland. Being nomadic, they were only seen occasionally, being allowed to do odd contract work for the coal mines. One Samoyed even had a barge he used in summer on the Pechora River, and was, according to Tomek, the only free man he ever saw.

The two main rivers, the Usa and Pechora, were highways in both summer and winter, allowing reindeer sleds and the occasional tractor to use them in winter and barges in summer. Spring thaw and break-up held everything up for weeks, while the autumn usually allowed some barge traffic until the ice floes became too dangerous. The railway was really the only year-round access, delivering ever more prisoners who would be marched off, often never to be seen again. These were exchanged for coal that would be shovelled on by teams of exhausted men, blackened by coal dust that froze into icy grime in winter.

Tomek's waggon, along with a dozen or so others, was pulled off to a siding alongside miles of barbed wire, and what looked like watchtowers in the distance and a couple of huts. They were told that they could stay in the waggons until their huts were built, which they were expected to build.

Many of the men objected and went on a sit-down strike. Some just moaned, as it was obvious that they had no practical skills whatsoever. Tomek was afraid that the guards would shoot them but instead, after a couple of half-hearted blows from rifle butts, they were left to sit in the snow and freeze.

The women had other ideas and, after some negotiations, were directed to a mound of snow that concealed stacks of planks and baulks of wood. They must have found some nails and other tools, but Tomek never saw them. Instead, he was taken along a sort of lane with wire on either side, past a couple of unmanned watchtowers to a large compound that enclosed a long ramshackle shed open on both ends, giving at one end scant shelter to a large single-cylinder donkey engine that rose out of the blown-in snow. To one side was a large iron bowl of what looked like tar. With a number of prods from rifles, shouts and threats, Tomek was directed to light a fire under the bowl. He realised after a while that the tar was in fact frozen low-grade diesel oil.

He was next given a large blowlamp that took a lot of pumping and priming, and then, having stuck the barrel of the blowlamp into the wood fire under the bowl, he managed, after much more pumping and hissing, to get the blowlamp lit. He realised what the Russian guards wanted as they pointed to the cylinder head. Through trial and error, plus the eventual provision of another blowlamp, Tomek managed to get the top of the cylinder head to glow dully. By then the tar had softened to the consistency of runny honey. He wasn't at all sure what to do next. Despite the intense cold, he was sweating and his perspiration had frozen on his clothing in a dusty white hoar frost and a lumpy white beard that ran down the first few centimetres of his *kufeika*. His breath even froze around the hairs in his nostrils.

He knew enough to rub snow over his nose and cheeks as they lost sensation. He noticed that some of the guards and other prisoners were wearing rimed cloths over their faces as a precaution against frostbite and even their eyelashes were crusted in ice. The terrifying cold lay around him: a pervasive threat, just waiting for a single opening, the merest hint of vulnerability to smother in the killing numbness of the Arctic winter.

An enormous Russian appeared, with tattoos that led over his neck and up to his shaven pate. His fearsome bulk seemed to defy the snow and frost. In him, King Winter had met his match. This mountainous troll in human form reminded Tomek of the Mountain King from the *Peer Gynt* production that had scared him as a child at the Opera House in Lwów. This hideously scary figure barely grunted at Tomek, then indicated that he should spoon the oil into what looked like an open hopper to one side of the donkey engine. As Tomek did so, the Russian grabbed hold of the flywheel, which must have been more than a metre across, throwing his weight against it in trying to make it spin, without much success, as it just kicked back.

He grabbed one of the blowtorches and played it under the donkey engine for about five minutes, before handing it back, pointing once more at the cylinder head, and making a couple of other attempts to swing the flywheel. Eventually, with a dull thud, the engine burst into life with a slow, rumbling *thump, thump* that reverberated through the shed. Tomek reckoned it was making about one revolution per second. He had never come across such a slow-revving and ponderous engine.

The Russian pointed to what looked like a long frozen belt on the floor and between them they wrestled it up and over the flywheel, at great risk to their fingers, before going to the other end of the shed to see if everything was working. The belt must have been about 5m long and was looped at the other end over a huge unguarded circular saw that spun in a blur of vicious teeth from a slit in a long scarred wooden table that ran almost to the opposite opening. Two frozen men were standing just outside beside a large pile of ice-covered logs. Accompanied by grunts and words that Tomek could not understand, they wrestled one log off the pile and offered it in lengthwise to the saw blade. The screeching noise deafened Tomek as frozen wood chips flew everywhere.

It looked very dangerous and it was then that Tomek noticed the huge tattooed Russian was missing two fingers off his left hand. Tomek decided to be very careful and if possible spend his time attending to the engine rather than cutting the logs into planks.

He didn't realise at the time, but this was his first encounter with the notorious *Dzhuliki*: dangerous criminals who lived in the gulags, extorting food, favours and obedience from other prisoners and occasionally the guards, who were terrified of them. Each tattoo meant something: a crime, a murder, a sentence served. They even had their own language and they had no love for the Poles. Life for them consisted of threats, extortion and violence. There was no hint of humanity in their eyes.

Tomek knew he was caught between the Devil of the *Dzhuliki* and the Deep Blue Sea of the Russian guards, who answered to nobody, or so it seemed. He didn't know it at the time, but almost 20,000 of his compatriots were to disappear into the cruel white gaping maw of Vorkuta.

The huts went up fairly quickly, born of necessity as the real ferocity of the Arctic winter had yet to hit them. There was at first no heating at all and several prisoners died every night. Tomek's job first thing in the morning was to help gather up the frozen bodies and take them outside the barbed wire to dump into an open pit.

There was no bedding in the huts when they first arrived, so they just huddled together for warmth for the first few days. The rail waggons disappeared one night and any prisoners still sheltering in them were turfed out into the snow.

One enterprising Pole managed to smuggle out a small stove from one of the guards' vans. He installed it in his hut but the other occupants, though glad of the warmth, were terrified of any consequences. They were lucky as before long more stoves arrived and it was up to the prisoners how to install them with no guidance at all from the guards, who more often than not stayed in a smoky, filthy hut that doubled as a guardroom. Most seemed drunk and it was rumoured that they had an illicit still somewhere outside the camp.

Sanitation was pretty well non-existent, as it was impossible to dig holes in the frozen tundra. The women had built a hut with a raised plank floor that covered about four-fifths of the space and ended in a long gap that led down to the snow below a single plank, which was fixed as a sort of communal seat that allowed one's bottom to poise over the gap.

It wasn't organised in any official way, but more by an unspoken convention. The women used it first in the morning then the men afterwards. Most of the time the men urinated outside, their pee freezing in mid-air. Frostbite was a continual threat, with blackened fingers and noses being an occasional sight. The few imprisoned doctors improvised blades for amputations in the event of gangrene, but few patients screamed as by then the affected digit, or even limb, was beyond any feeling.

Where possible, anything that could be used as a surgical instrument was seared with flame, and if there was no fire then the next best way of sterilising a blade was by urinating on it!

There were stories of babies being born, but Tomek never saw any as he was now categorised as *Katurga*, which meant that he would be singled out for special treatment. Most with this categorisation were either shot or starved to death.

They were fed twice a day on a freezing-cold fish soup, heads, tails, bones and all, if they were lucky, but most of the time it was black bread and a boiled potato once in a while. Prisoners were paid in food, based upon their work output either in the makeshift sawmill or opencast coal mines. If the guards reckoned that any particular prisoner had not worked hard enough, their food ration was cut and as they got weaker that allowance was cut further, until they died of starvation or malnutrition.

Any decision as to who was productive and who was not seemed arbitrary and entirely within the gift of the guards. The risk of having one's paltry rations stolen by the *Dzhuliki* was a constant threat. There were occasional stories of cannibalism.

Things changed slightly when one day several NKVD officers visited. Tomek could hear a lot of shouting and screaming coming from the guard house. A little later a foraging party came back and, according to the NKVD, one prisoner was missing. They made one of the guards strip off his brown militia uniform and join the prisoners in his underwear. Several other guards were marched out and later shots were heard. Only the NKVD returned.

Now the camp became restless and the NKVD left without ceremony, leaving only a handful of guards to try to maintain order over several thousand internees. For a while the *Dzhuliki* were in charge as the guards realised they could not control the camp. A couple took refuge in one of the watchtowers during the day, until it was burned down one night.

The next morning Tomek was marched out; he had no idea where he was going. He realised that most of the remaining guards were overseeing his work party, leaving almost none back at the camp. This made him very afraid that they were being taken out for summary execution.

To his relief, they were taken to a hole dug at one end of what looked like a shallow quarry. The bottom of it had been waterlogged but was now frozen solid. They were herded into the hole, which turned out to be the gallery of a drift mine. Further along the water had melted slightly with some small coal trucks stuck on a rail just beyond. Another prisoner, who was acting as foreman, told them they had to unload the trucks and form a human chain to pass the coal up and out to be stacked near the entrance. Tomek was now up to his knees in icy water with a few thin panes of ice that bumped, cut and bruised him as he worked. He had no idea how long he was down there as it wasn't even a gloomy dawn when he arrived and pitch black when they finally left.

The next few days passed in much the same way. Once there was a small rock fall, trapping one man whom they managed to dig out. He was barely able to walk, needing to be half carried and dragged through the snow back to the camp.

One of the guards shouted that he was unproductive labour, ordering that he should be put in an open compound with no access to food or heating. This caused a minor riot that only stopped when an old machine gun on a tripod was brought out and pointed at them. Reluctantly the crowd dispersed and the poor injured wretch was thrown into the compound.

The next morning, on the single thermometer that hung on the latrine wall, which only went down as far as -40ºC, there was no red alcohol showing anywhere outside the bulb at the bottom. That meant it was really deathly cold, capable of killing within minutes. When Tomek looked, there was no sign of the injured prisoner in the compound.

Tomek tried to get the donkey engine to work, but it was so cold that everything mechanical had seized up. The cold was intense. No work parties were sent out and everyone was staying in their huts. The whole camp was silent. On his way to the latrine, Tomek noticed that, as the skies had cleared for the first time in weeks, he could see the Aurora Borealis. It was a fascinating, coruscating curtain of green and lilac. He imagined he could almost hear a slight hiss and pop as the scene changed overhead. Another prisoner passed him and said: 'You wouldn't be the first to die standing outside watching the Northern Lights. It must be minus fifty now.' It was only when he tried to move on that Tomek realised he ached with cold and his feet were frozen into the snow.

Back in the hut, he couldn't get warm and kept nodding off, even when he lay in front of the stove. To his annoyance, whenever his eyes closed he was shaken awake. Only much later did he realise that his companions were ensuring that he did not die from hypothermia.

That's when the suicides really began. When Tomek was handed over more bodies to toss into the pit, at first he thought that they had died of cold. Then the rumours began. People said the *Dzhuliki* were getting rid of rivals, and certainly tattooed bodies were now cropping up occasionally. Sometimes the bodies were naked, others having stolen their clothing or felt-lined boots. In theory everyone should have had a pair – not necessarily in the right sizes, but swapping with others, to get some kind of comfort and insulation against the cold was the rule. The exception seemed to be when it came to the Poles. He had heard of Polish officers hanging on to their cherished cavalry boots, but he had not seen a single uniform or pair of leather riding boots since he had arrived.

Any doubts about whether it was murder or suicide were cast aside the first time he was called to the latrine to remove the body of a man dangling from a beam with a small piece of cord tied around his neck. The woman who found him wasn't crying or looking particularly shocked, just numb. His boots and clothing were intact. She sniffed: 'That's no murder, there'll be others.'

She was right. The cold had slackened slightly and the days were getting longer. Others had told Tomek that meant they would be working longer hours. The next time there were two bodies, blue in the face with one still breathing and rasping … just. Tomek lifted the man's kicking legs while two other Poles loosened the makeshift noose. The badly tied knot gave way and they fell in a heap on top of the piss and shit that had puddled below. Although it was a damp cold that morning, the crap had not yet frozen.

The other man was stiff, quite dead. Rigor mortis had set in with one arm extended and a finger pointing to who knew where. Someone had called a doctor as Tomek, wincing with the effort, lifted the dead weight. The lifeless corpse's buttonless flies brushed against his neck, leaving a cold sticky feeling. The doctor nodded, without any expression of sympathy, and just commented, 'They often ejaculate when hanged.' Tomek felt numb and a little bit sick. He was to have nightmares about this for decades afterwards.

Dealing with this hopeless misery of almost daily corpses did not spare him from working on the donkey engine, which was in a vindictive mood, stalling every time someone tried to cut a log. They sweated trying to get the beast started again: the drive belt was slippery and the circular saw would not run freely. The air was milder and the snow slightly softer, but now the blizzards were starting with large, clinging snowflakes that clogged up everything.

It didn't look as if spring was going to be any better.

There was a rumour that any government officials, family of senior officers and others with links to either Polish regional government or the Catholic Church were to be moved. Tomek saw several groups being herded together and marched off. He had no idea of their fate and for weeks he feared he would be next, but nothing happened.

During another ferocious cold snap, the guards stayed inside their hut making no attempt to marshal or beat the prisoners. There were no working parties and no attempts to muster the survivors for a roll call.

To his surprise, he saw an old Samoyed woman come up to the wire fence and push something through. There was a rush as about a dozen prisoners scrabbled to pick it up. This was repeated several times over the next couple of weeks, whenever the guards were too slack or too drunk to patrol.

Whatever it was, Tomek didn't know until much later. As the Samoyeds migrated with their reindeer herds, this same old woman would appear and push cigarettes through to the prisoners. Nobody ever knew her story and she never spoke, but it happened at the beginning of spring over the two years that Tomek was interned.

Tomek could not understand why there was such a rush for the few cigarettes. One old Pole assured him that when the food ration was cut, smoking helped kill the pangs of hunger. Besides, the Russians would occasionally trade their cigarette hoard for extra favours from the guards.

There was to be a cost for the Samoyed though, as a deputation turned up one miserable day with wet snow and biting winds. They had run out of salt for the reindeer, many of which were showing signs of stress and illness. This time the guards were under orders not to help the Samoyeds in any way as Stalin did not like nomads. He wanted them settled where he could control them.

In later years, many would find themselves working those same coalfields that had been the graveyard of so many prisoners.

Even in neighbouring Finland, Sweden and Norway, efforts were made until well after the war to assimilate the Sami through abduction of children into boarding schools, where speaking their language was forbidden, and menfolk were forced away from their herds and into the mines. Stalin's Russia simply starved them into submission.

4

Break-up!

It sounded like gunfire, a loud *crack* that stopped Tomek in his tracks. He couldn't understand where it was coming from. Nobody else seemed bothered. Soon there were several other loud reports and they sounded as if they were coming nearer.

When he asked one of the Russians what was happening, he just shrugged and muttered the single word 'spring'.

The snow had been melting during the middle of the day and freezing overnight. Tomek's boots were soaking and his feet were a mass of rubbed skin and sores. He couldn't get them dry during the day and slept barefoot at night despite the cold in the hope of toughening up the skin.

One of the Polish doctors managed to get hold of some rock salt, which he pounded up and rubbed into Tomek's sore feet.

'Don't limp, don't let the guards know that you're in pain. They'll categorise you as *Katurga* and that will mean slow starvation. The bad times are coming.'

Tomek had no idea what the doctor meant but he noticed that as the weather got milder there were more anxious faces.

The loud explosions were more frequent and it wasn't long before Tomek realised that he was hearing the ice breaking up in the Pechora River. That's when the flooding started. It began with a slow seeping up through what was left of the lying snow, turning from white to a dirty boggy slush. It gradually oozed everywhere: a wet boggy soup during the day that froze hard overnight.

This messiness got worse and ever more miserable, until one day he was crowded into an open railway waggon and taken off a few miles to a slightly raised ridge cut in two by a tributary that narrowed through what hardly justified the term valley or gorge. It was barely some 10m deep and probably no more than 150m across, before it joined the slowly grinding, groaning and occasionally explosive white and grey plain of the ice-packed main river, where the jangled shards of ice and white pressure ridges stretched as far as the eye could see.

To his astonishment, where the tributary joined the Pechora, it reared up as a jumbled ice-packed dam that backed up the tributary into the low valley. He could see an ever-broadening lake behind this creaking mass of chaotic ice as the current bore ever more huge ice floes that carried on piling up behind. It was obvious that this was the source of the flooding in the camp.

Each man was handed a pickaxe and told to go out onto the ice and start smashing it up. There was no way they were going to make any impression on such a frozen and dangerously mobile mass, as it plainly grew before their eyes. Some of the men objected. The guards answered by shooting into the air.

Tomek was very worried, but one of the Russian prisoners – a more cultured man than the *Dzhuliki* – just laughed, saying that they dare not shoot any of them as he knew the guards would have to make up the numbers of any missing prisoners.

The whole scene became a game of staring each other down, the guards drawn up in a line, about ten of them, facing probably as many as thirty prisoners, now all armed with pickaxes. Finally one tall Russian stepped forward. Tomek had not seen him before but the man next to him whispered he was a former general. The guards lowered their weapons as he approached.

Whatever was said, the guards gradually nodded in assent until all the tension eased. The party then walked back slowly to the railway siding, where they handed back the pickaxes without any comment, before they were shunted back the way they came. The rumour went round that either the guards would have to call on sappers to use explosives or the air force would bomb the ice build-up. They had done it before.

The flooding was by now both insidious and pervasive. It percolated up through the reappearing moss and mud, permeating everything with a miserable damp chill. Felt boots were now useless, but nothing resembling waterproof footwear was issued. On one of his forced marches to the donkey engine, Tomek sank up to his knees in a mixture of mud, moss and icy water. Two other men pulled him out but he couldn't retrieve his boots. If anything, once he got used to the cold, his feet felt slightly better.

Conditions around the donkey engine could not have been any worse. The bottom half of the flywheel was under water and any attempts to start it were doomed to failure. Now both the engine and the saw were tilted at different angles as the frozen soil underneath them melted.

If Tomek thought that meant he had been spared extra work, he was soon to be disappointed. He was taken to one of the mine galleries and put in charge of another wheezing machine that ran on coal, belching clouds of brown tarry smoke that caught at his lungs. He had only seen steam engines from a distance before and had no idea how they worked. Two Russians were shovelling coal into a large firebox as steam built up.

When Tomek walked round, he worked out that it was driving a large wheel that operated a pump that, once the machine was running, would suck water out of the mine and deliver it along a trough that ran slightly downhill.

He was under no illusions that if he failed to operate this steaming beast he would be down in the mine, probably working up to his waist in inky, black, freezing water. He had to work out what to do before the steam was up to pressure.

Fortunately he had both a practical and a logical mind. A pressure gauge showed a red line, which was obviously well above the working pressure. He tapped it and the needle barely moved up the scale. The writing was in English not Cyrillic and he was able to guess at what the working pressure should read. From the look of the machine, he reckoned it was probably more than fifty years old and represented the pinnacle of Victorian engineering. He felt reassured that, unlike the Russian machinery he had seen so far, this imported steam pump would behave as long as it was oiled and maintained.

This was Tomek's first attempt at using logic when it came to engineering – a talent that would serve him well years later.

He came to appreciate this steam pump and even came to regard it as a reliable friend, as long as the Russians fed it with coal and water.

Each morning that spring was the same. He would be the first to arrive, along with his two burly Russian stokers. Tomek would polish the brasswork and oil the various sliders and bearings while the Russians lit the firebox. Then it would take almost two hours to get the beast up to a working pressure. Once all was ready, he had to open a valve and the beast would hiss into action. The first few gobs and gouts of black tarry liquid would sputter and gurgle before a mass of dirty water would shoot out of the pump outlet, before gurgling away down the trough.

Even without boots, Tomek felt that he had the better option compared to his compatriots who disappeared into the mine. He couldn't really rest, but felt warm without being as sweaty and hot as the stokers, who never gave him any trouble.

Slowly, Tomek was sinking into a state of unquestioning acceptance, where each day merged into the next. Now he could even heat up his meagre ration of fish soup and black bread. His horizons and prospects were narrowing.

One afternoon there was a rumble and a thump, which Tomek could feel through the soggy mush that passed for his workspace. The two stokers had paused; one shrugged and pointed at the firebox. They both carried on stoking. For some reason the jet of black water had stopped, although the pump seemed to be working normally. Tomek pulled the shut-off valve and went to the gallery entrance to see what was going on. He could not hear anything at first, then the water started, small ripples at first, relentless in their progress, almost like the tide coming in. Soon the ripples grew into wavelets and Tomek could hear shouting.

A guard appeared at the lip of one of the long coal tips that until recently had been frozen into long black barrows, looking like Gothic, industrial versions of the Neolithic graves he had seen once in the fields of Moravia. The guard was gesturing and shouting. Tomek couldn't hear what he was saying but he was pointing at the steam pump. His two stokers were also beckoning and shouting.

Suddenly he realised that he had to restart the engine. He splashed back to the regulator and opened the valve. With a juddering slurp it gasped back into life and an almost continuous writhing stream hosed forth, quickly overwhelming the drainage trough. He opened it up to what he thought was the maximum speed, as the stokers shovelled away with renewed urgency. To his horror, the pressure looked as if it was falling. He ran over to the water cistern and climbed the short ladder to look inside. It was full, but the outlet to the steam pump was seized in a half-open position. He picked up a small boulder and hit the short lever, trying to open the outlet even more. Eventually it gave about quarter of a turn.

The pressure gauge looked steady now.

Something was happening at the mouth of the gallery as three men emerged, soaking wet and black from head to toe. A pause then two others, dragging a body between them. Something about it, even at this distance, told Tomek that whoever it was would be sleeping in the communal grave that evening. One of the men bent down and removed the dead man's boots and threw them over to Tomek, it was both a callous and kindly action. There was no point in wasting good boots.

Out of respect, Tomek cleaned them up as best he could and placed them by the foot of his bunk to try on in the morning. Then he thought better of it, instead curling up with them as he slept so they wouldn't be stolen.

He later learned that there'd been a collapse and a flood in the mine. Some men were trapped; nobody knew if they were alive or dead. Any rescue effort was half-hearted and uncoordinated.

There were rumours that two men had dug their way out entirely by their own efforts a day later. The other bodies were never recovered. As one Pole said with a dismissive shrug, 'What was the point?' They were all going to die there sooner or later.

As the floods receded, the insects began. At first it was large black crawling things that looked like winged ants. They invaded every corner and crevice, scurried across the floor and bedding but didn't bite. Tomek would wake up being tickled as they crawled over his face. He soon followed the advice of some of the older prisoners who somehow had got hold of pieces of light cloth, like muslin, which they either laid over their faces when sleeping, or the more fortunate ones had enough to tie over their heads as a sort of beekeeper's veil. Tomek had neither and his first attempt at pulling his blanket up over his face nearly suffocated him. He next tried the woollen lining poking out of his torn *kufeika*. It looked like cotton wool, and after a lot of experimentation he found that a little pushed loosely up his nose and into his ears prevented the insects taking refuge in those orifices.

One prisoner managed to steal a bottle, which he filled with paraffin, wiping the legs of his bunk as a deterrent that worked for a while. The sickly smell was overwhelming, causing headaches, but Tomek soon got used to it, having blackmailed the thief into stealing more for the rest of the hut. He was helped in this by one of the *Dzhuliki*, who stood almost head and shoulders above everyone else.

This relief didn't last long as the thief disappeared within a week and the best guess was that the guards had caught him red-handed.

That's when the mosquitoes began. They seemed to arrive quite suddenly one evening. Then, as the days lengthened, they never went away. Tomek had seen mosquitoes before and had even been bitten quite severely one summer holiday on the Black Sea coast in Rumania, but these were enormous, to Tomek's eyes, almost the size of dragonflies, and they were relentless. Some of the prisoners covered their faces with oil or soot as a deterrent, while others smoked evil-smelling mixtures of tobacco and other weeds that gave off clouds of acrid smoke. Usually the effect was paroxysmal coughing among everyone in close proximity to the smoker.

Break-up!

Tomek was one of the lucky ones; after a few initial assaults, the mosquitoes gave up on him, inflicting on him less than half a dozen token bites each evening, then leaving him alone. The situation was not helped as the spring advanced into summer and the twilights lengthened, giving the insects even more crepuscular opportunities to feast on any available source of blood.

Lice were a permanent fixture despite the shaved heads and body hair. Paraffin was now in short supply as even the guards ceased smelling of the stuff. Occasionally the internees were allowed to bathe in one of the several freezing ponds, where fish would dart away as they jumped in. One of the men succeeded in chasing an Arctic char into the shallows and caught it. His joy was very short-lived as a guard poked him in the ribs with what looked like a Tommy gun and confiscated it.

The routine of standing naked while passing clothes over a brazier, hearing the occasional spit and fizz as the lice exploded, became a gamble as the mosquitoes immediately zoomed in on the acres of exposed flesh. It was only the fear of typhus fever that kept the faith as far as this routine was concerned.

It had just got to the point when night never really fell. Soon the sun wouldn't set at all, and that was when the rumour mill really began to churn. Thousands of Polish officers had disappeared from a number of prison camps. The NKVD were now touring the gulag, identifying Poles and pulling out anyone of fighting age who wasn't Russian. The fear was tangible.

Tomek was in the latrine when he heard a voice behind him speaking in accented Polish: 'Just a friendly warning, get out tomorrow and don't come back, or you'll be next.' Then with a brief tap on the shoulder the man left, leaving Tomek with no clue as to who it was.

The next day Tomek supposed he would be working on the donkey engine again. Instead he was nudged along by four guards, who seemed very slack. Tomek had mustered with a handful of Poles, Tartars and what may have been Finns.

As they passed the shed with the donkey engine Tomek peeled off and went directly to it. There were a few shouts and one of the guards came over and tried to push him back into the group. Tomek simply pointed at the silent engine, nodded repeatedly saying '*Da*' and smiling like an idiot. In the end the guard shrugged and wandered off after the rest of the party.

Whoever was supposed to be manning the circular saw had not arrived yet. He could see that the floor had dried out sufficiently for more planks to be pushed under the machinery to level it up and probably allow sawing to begin once more.

Everything seemed silent and neglected. There was no paraffin in the blowlamps and the fire under the bowl of diesel oil was out. So, having waited in the shadow of the shed while nothing happened, apart from a few other groups being marched past without pausing, Tomek decided that he had better look busy. He had little doubt that somebody would report him for not working.

He left the shed and aimed in the direction of the steam engine and his old mine gallery, expecting to be challenged at any moment. It was then he noticed another party of men carrying shovels. They were being monitored by a single guard who stopped, lit a cigarette, and wandered away to urinate against a dwarf willow tree. Tomek simply tagged along then gradually mingled with the party, all of whom seemed to be Ukrainian or Belarusian. He had sufficient Ukrainian to blend in and eventually found himself looking down into a large opencast mine pit. There were railway waggons at one end and a human chain was passing over shovels full of coal from one to another from a large pile of coal that obviously had just been hacked from the coal face. It looked very inefficient. Tomek registered that a large grey lorry was at one end of the pit with an open bonnet and two men were poking around inside.

Taking a risk, Tomek walked purposefully over to the lorry and crawled underneath. He tried to give the impression that he knew what he was doing and was supposed to be doing it. The ruse worked as nobody came over to question him. He didn't even emerge when someone clanged what sounded like a piece of iron and all work stopped. Tomek guessed that it was mealtime. He had no idea of the time.

Nobody returned, so feeling very unsure, Tomek emerged, smeared oil over his face in the hopes of not being recognised, and set off, trying to put as much distance as he could between him and his old compound. There were three groups in the distance and Tomek joined the last one. He didn't recognise the language they were speaking, but was surprised when someone whispered to him in Polish, not to say anything but just smile and nod. The man was old and emaciated and had on a stained jacket that looked as if it might have been part of an old Polish Army uniform. Tomek guessed that the man was a PoW taken in the war of 1919–21. It was not safe to ask questions.

When they reached the compound, Tomek was alarmed to see that they were being counted in by two guards, who looked puzzled. One looked at the other then said to the working party that they had one too many. The old Pole moved forward and said in beautifully clear Russian: 'You must have the wrong number on your board. Who would want to break into a gulag?' Both guards burst out laughing and simply waved them on.

Once inside the old man took Tomek to one side and told him he did not want to know any details, but Tomek was to wait until everyone turned in, then try to find a hut with a spare bunk. He was to avoid speaking Polish as his accent gave away that he came from Lwów and that was bad news. Anyone from that part of Poland who had been sent to a gulag had to be a political prisoner and probably was scheduled for liquidation. The old man was from the far northeast of Poland and had been in the camp for so long that nobody was bothered any more. Tomek had to keep smiling and pretend to be an idiot. That way he could survive.

It has to be borne in mind that by the spring of 1940, the Katyn massacres had begun. Stalin was determined to remove every chance of any Polish leaders emerging. All well-educated Poles were at risk and the NKVD chief, Lavrentiy Beria, was equally determined to concentrate all its efforts in purging all hints of ethnic nationalism. The Poles had long been regarded as a threat to Russian interests and naturally had come in for special attention.

By now the mosquitoes had been joined by midges and, whatever the hardships and privations of extreme cold had been, summer was a torment.

Tomek, though, was to face a new threat. The commissar in charge had disappeared now the NKVD had arrived to make sure that the gulag was running properly.

It began with an interrogation in which the NKVD officer was purple with rage. He could not account for Tomek being there and had no idea as to his true identity.

This was a very dangerous situation. Tomek knew full well that the NKVD were expert in divining if their victim was hiding something they wanted to know. He had to appear gormless, harmless and of no possible interest.

What followed came out only after years of marriage to his wife Angela, who was in turn reluctant to pass on anything until she was long widowed and well into her nineties, by which time social mores were very different from her earlier married life.

5

Rape and Abuse

During Tomek's conservative Catholic upbringing, homosexuality was never mentioned. Certainly he had read stories about Ancient Greek warriors, knew that Leonardo da Vinci preferred men and had often overhead his father joking with other Polish officers about what we would now call the camp and homoerotic uniforms and antics of the Nazis in 1930s Germany.

In all other respects sex was barely discussed and the nearest he had come to any experience was when his father took him round to a military VD clinic as a cautionary lesson in how not to behave.

He was now 18, with no beard growth at all, and appeared to be what the *Dzhuliki* had described as 'meat'. The significance of what that meant escaped him.

It changed after one of the many interrogations by the NKVD where, to their irritation and frustration, Tomek had just nodded and smiled inanely. Somehow he had even managed a silly grin when his tormentor cocked a pistol and held it to his head. He didn't even blink; he turned round to a young guard who was covering him with his rifle and stuck his finger in the muzzle. The guard looked shocked and close to tears, but Tomek was knocked from behind, unable to protect his head.[1]

He was only vaguely aware of being pulled to his feet, his trousers torn off, then he felt the cold steel of a rifle barrel being rammed into his rectum. He passed out with the pain.

He had no recollection of being thrown outside and was eventually picked up then dragged into a hut.

He was bleeding and unable to walk for two days. He dared not eat and made no attempt to go to the latrine beyond very painful attempts to relieve his bladder. This time there was no Polish doctor to attend him.

Just over a week later there were more interrogations with the same result, only this time they raped him with rubber truncheons. Soon he was in a continual grey fog of pain, but still he said nothing and pretended to be a grinning idiot.

He lost count of how many times it happened. Occasionally, while in a semi-conscious state, he would be thrown outside and guards would urinate on him. Then they would invite other prisoners to do the same. There was no shortage of volunteers.

One afternoon he came to in the latrine with his face covered in faeces. When he staggered outside and tried to find something to wash it off, he was held down while other prisoners jeered and washed it off by urinating on him repeatedly.

The interrogations stopped for a while and he was left to wander disconsolately around the compound and even outside, where he attempted to clean himself in one of the many creeks and streams that meandered across the tundra. Nobody attempted to give him any work. It was as if he was the gulag's idiot. He had no illusions though. He knew that as unproductive *Katurga* he would not survive the next winter as his rations were cut.

The NKVD made one more serious attempt to break him.

He had been left alone for a few weeks – he wasn't at all sure how long but it seemed that midsummer had just past. Something about his smell had changed and even fewer mosquitoes or midges bothered him, the wheals on his face and back were almost gone and he had just cleaned himself up when two guards grabbed him just inside

Rape and Abuse

the gate. He was stripped bare and thrown into a small wooden cell with no daylight beyond the tiny hints of greyness that infiltrated between the warped and shrinking planks.

After a few hours he was pulled out into blinding brightness and frogmarched before another NKVD officer, who bawled at him in broken Polish: 'We know who you are, you're Gubert Kazimir Kazimirovich.' Tomek just grinned inanely.

The same phrase was shouted at him again and again. He was hit around his kidneys with a rubber truncheon and still the screaming.

Finally the interrogator paused, smiled evilly, and said something Tomek couldn't catch. He then noticed two tattooed *Dzhuliki*, both of whom were stripped to the waist. One threw him across a bench and started whipping him with a belt, its large buckle biting into his skin, while the other raped him with evident satisfaction. Once he was done they reversed roles, with the NKVD guard jeering all the while. He produced a camera – it looked small, possibly a Leica – and started to take photographs. It was then Tomek notice the half-empty bottle of vodka. They were all drunk and this was turning into something like a sadistic orgy.

Somebody else entered the room and Tomek could hear shouting, then two shots and a groan. He was pulled upright by his hair and turned around. An older NKVD officer with thinning grey hair spoke softly as he pointed to one of the *Dzhuliki* sitting propped against a wall holding his shoulder. 'Get out! You've done your work.'

There was blood everywhere. There was no sign of the other, or the earlier interrogator. The officer turned to Tomek, his expression unreadable.

'You will be sentenced. It's no good playing the fool any more.' With that Tomek was untied and prodded outside, bruised, bleeding and naked.

Sadly, nothing much has changed, with an even greater degree of brutality being employed on the modern front line. There are even reports of brutalised Ukrainian prisoners being castrated by drunken Russian soldiers during the war in Ukraine.

Just like the situation in 1941, today the use of violent prisoners to do the state's dirty work persists in this technological conflict of drones and hypersonic missiles. The Wagner Group is made up of criminals released from prisons to add a level of brutality beyond that of the average Russian squaddie.

This is the ongoing reality of 'unofficial' Russia.

Being held without formal charge is still the norm today in Russia for any who are deemed to have 'slandered the state' or are suspected of espionage. In theory, it is possible for defence lawyers to intercede, and modern communications have complicated the issue for the Russian authorities, as maybe seen in the recent cases of Sergei Magnitsky and Boris Nemtsov, among others. In Stalin's Russia there were no such options and anyone contradicting any official line or Stalin edict was likely, if they were lucky, to be sent to Siberia.

Tomek's case was heard in absentia nearly eighteen months after his arrest in Lwów on 1 March 1941, not long before Operation Barbarossa, the German invasion of the Soviet Union, began on 22 June 1941.

Trials in absentia are not uncommon today and the Russian government under Putin has even tried to use the same tactic against US and British citizens, such as the human rights campaigner and money laundering investigator Bill Browder in 2016, who would have been facing up to eighteen years imprisonment for displeasing Putin.

It is hardly surprising that under an even harsher regime some seventy-five years earlier, Tomek knew nothing of the case against him or the sentencing until sometime later.

6

The Criminals Take Over

Like their Nazi contemporaries, the Russians under Stalin did keep records, though frequently buried them under layers of obfuscation or denial, especially when it came to summary executions and exile to the gulags.

Unlike surviving Nazi files, or indeed the much later Stasi files of East Germany, there has been no large-scale opening of archives for historical researchers beyond a very brief window during Mikhail Gorbachev's tenure. Yeltsin's subsequent chaos meant that later permissions were held up or lost and Vladimir Putin has no wish to admit Russia's past sins.

Much of what follows has been assembled and edited based on years of talking with Tomek, when he was of a mood to open up about it, other conversations with his wife Angela (my mother), and occasionally odd snippets of validation and verification from other Poles who had endured similar.

In the period of Martial Law in Poland under Jaruzelski, 1981–83, the author and his late wife Maria founded and ran Wales Aid to Poland, which brought them into contact with many older expatriate Poles through the good offices of the late Witold Kuczys, a travel agent arranging trips to Poland, who enabled many such conversations.

By then a number Poles had come out of the woodwork and wanted to get involved in food and medical aid to Poland. In some cases it was the first time they had talked about their own experiences. Some had come to Wales via Tashkent and Palestine. Often they wanted to know why non-Polish speakers such as ourselves were involved in such charitable efforts. Once they heard my father's story, they began to offer fragmentary accounts that tallied with what he told me.

What follows is based on what he said, with some modification, in the light of a variety of other much shorter verbal accounts.

The abuse and interrogations subsided in the developing summer of 1940. The coal mining effort in and around Vorkuta intensified and some more machinery appeared.

The earlier drift mining galleries were, to a large extent, excavated further, forming large opencast mines. The machinery operators were kept away from the Poles and *Dzhuliki* but Tomek had the impression that most were in fact exiled to Vorkuta for minor crimes.

It was not uncommon for such senior aircraft designers as Andrei Tupolev and Vladimir Petlyakov, along with hosts of other engineers and scientists, to be interned under slightly better conditions and ordered to continue working. So the exile of mining engineers and machinery operators to a slightly easier regime in Vorkuta would seem to fit with Tomek's memory.

However, the workload did not end there for Tomek. Each hut was marched out to shovel, saw wood that had been shipped in from the treeline further south and often bury bodies. There was ongoing abuse but more often from other prisoners. Tomek heard occasional screams and may have heard women but never saw them.

The few Poles he had encountered were usually spirited away or died through hunger, neglect or disease. Occasionally he had been approached in the darkness by someone who spoke Polish about organising a revolt, but nothing came of it. He later learned that in some camps a very effective underground movement had developed, but being the only Pole in a hut full of Russians, Ukrainians, Belarusians and a few other nationalities he never identified, he was effectively isolated from what later became known as 'the Secret State'[1] that, through a complex network of secret communication, managed to get information about the Poles held in the gulags back to the Polish Government in Exile under General Sikorski, based in London.

The Criminals Take Over

This ignorance was to cause Tomek problems as his internment marched inexorably towards another Russian winter.

The number of guards and the regular roll calls had dwindled away, with the routine becoming slacker and more disorganised. Food was often delivered late, in short supply or even not at all. Some of the Ukrainians talked about *Holodomor*, the great man-made famine of the early 1930s– a catastrophe Tomek had heard about when he was much younger. The Ukrainians were claiming that the harvest was going to fail again and they would all be starved.

Like most rumours, it gained weight as the food rations did not improve and it was inevitable that there would be a confrontation, led by the *Dzhuliki*, who had no particular fear of the guards.

At first they simply stole other prisoners' meagre rations. Tomek was in no position to argue; he was weak, malnourished and fearful of being isolated as non-productive labour and simply left to starve. Other prisoners started muttering about cannibalism, although at first Tomek ignored such talk, figuring that, as he and the weaker prisoners were so emaciated, they would hardly be worth slaughtering, butchering and cooking.

Fortunately the *Dzhuliki* started confronting the guards before matters got to the point of butchery.

The first protests were noisy, banging whatever they could find and causing uproar. The guards seemed unwilling to muster at first, and when they finally did put in an appearance, many of them looked as if they were in as bad a condition as the prisoners. Others appeared drunk and incapable. There were no NKVD officers to be seen.

One of the *Dzhuliki* shouted that the guards had no bullets and about a dozen ran at them. One shot was fired, then the guards turned and ran. This was greeted with cheers and jeering. Some of the bolder prisoners went into the guardroom and started looting.

Tomek was desperate for food, but hung back with the others, all looking fearful. They expected the guards to reassemble at any moment and begin shooting ... only they didn't.

Slowly those left behind began to drift away. Tomek went back to his hut, bewildered and not knowing what to do. There was talk of a mass escape and suggestions were made about using the Samoyeds, who caught salmon and char in the river, to feed them.

The only Samoyed Tomek had seen recently was the man who had a boat. There was no point in trying to stow away: that would never work, besides it floated downriver towards the Barents Sea and the ice floes of the Arctic beyond. He would find nothing more than isolated villages downstream before the bitterly cold blue sea with its white ice floes, even in the height of what passed for summer.

Archangelsk, the nearest open seaport, lay an impossible distance overland to the west. Getting there in the Samoyed's boat was very unlikely and to the north there was no other possible way out.

The only alternative from Vorkuta was the railway running south. That would mean hanging under the waggons for hundreds of miles in the faint hope of not falling off or being discovered.

The situation looked hopeless.

News had travelled slowly. The defeats at Finnish hands in the Winter War of 1940 had been expunged from all news reports and there was still a fear among the Russian prisoners that they would be rounded up and sent to perish at the front. Many had no idea that the war was over. The Finns had conducted a brutal campaign and were referred to as White Ghosts, materialising silently on skis to slaughter ill-prepared Russian troops before disappearing back into the forests.

Certainly something was happening, but they didn't realise it was because of a massive reorganisation in the Red Army that began in April 1940. The only radio bulletins comprised rousing speeches by Molotov that bore no relation to reality. The guards would have filled in the gaps for themselves, as experience had taught them the hard way that any good news coming in the form of long speeches did not seem to apply to them.

Morale was very low and many of the militia were fearful of change as old military ranks were in the process of being reinstated. The power of local and frequently corrupt commissars was brought under military control in many places. Political 'purity' and 're-education' was now the remit of a rapidly expanding and motivated NKVD. Unsurprisingly, given the vast distance and number of gulags involved, this took time with local administration unsure which way the wind was blowing.

It was not unusual for erring commissars and militia to find themselves summarily condemned to join the inmates they used to govern, with predictable consequences as old scores were settled.

It was during this hiatus that desertions became common, with militia and commissars alike attempting to disappear.

What little order there had been collapsed and it was against this chaotic background that Tomek was now forced to survive.

There was a rumour that the commissar in charge of the Vorkuta camps had disappeared. If it was true, nobody knew if he had deserted, died, been replaced or been liquidated by the NKVD. The *Dzhuliki* seemed to be running the place for now and the best advice Tomek was given was not to cross them in any way, but it was impossible to avoid their bullying and unpredictable violence. The only good thing, in Tomek's eyes, was that he could get out of the compound, forage and occasionally share rations with others better skilled than he in trapping animals and birds, netting fish, or stealing from the camp stores.

Slowly his strength returned and with it his morale was improving beyond the miserable acceptance that nothing would change.

It was getting towards the first frosts of autumn, with the sun now setting for longer, when some of the *Dzhuliki* started disappearing. Tomek had taken the risk of getting into yet another compound a few kilometres away and taking over an empty bunk. There were a few Poles, most of them older than Tomek, who had been reservists or orderlies, with no rank above corporal and therefore not deemed to be potential leaders or a risk to the Soviet state. They were just keeping their heads down and serving out their time. None of them showed any inclination to escape.

That all changed when one night they were all roused out of their bunks and marched several kilometres to join others at the railhead. Whoever was marshalling them was better organised and the guards were not the usual militia.

There was no roll call and they were pushed into open waggons, then shunted south for a few hours before being switched to a line that ran west. Tomek wondered if he was being taken to Moscow to face trial, but other Poles said it was more likely they were being taken off to be shot.[2]

Almost a day later, they were left unattended in a siding alongside several other empty waggons on adjoining lines. Tomek had no idea where he was. Nobody was guarding them. They were now free to leave the waggons, relieve themselves and drink from standpipes next to a water tower that serviced the locomotives' boilers.

One Pole had looked around suspiciously, then wandered over to a train facing in the opposite direction. He crawled under an empty waggon and disappeared. A couple of others followed him and Tomek, who thought he had nothing to lose, went over to find his own waggon. There was a sort of truss that held the axles in place, with just enough space to wriggle in. It was cold and very uncomfortable.

Once the train started it jolted and hurt his back but Tomek considered this was better than the probability of being shot in a forest somewhere.[3]

The noise was deafening. Several times Tomek feared he would be discovered when the train stopped, was shunted then set off again. After several hours the train juddered to a halt and showed no signs of moving on. He thought he could hear Polish voices among the shouted Russian orders.

A head peered under the waggon and hissed at him urgently in Polish that he had better get out if he didn't want to go back to where he had just come from. Reluctantly he eased himself out racked with pain. There were several groups of Poles, a few of them in ragged uniforms. One or two nodded at Tomek knowingly but said nothing.

After a few hours of milling around, as it was getting really dark, they started climbing back into some other covered waggons in a siding. Tomek was unsure what to do. Finally he joined a mixed group of Poles and Ukrainians for another long jolting journey, this time with no stops.

Just before dawn the train slowed, with a lot of clanking as it went over points before, accompanied by a lot of puffing, hissing and being thrown around, the doors slid open. A few shouts in Russian, then they all climbed out wearily. The guards were wearing the same unfamiliar uniforms he had seen at the last stop, but at least, as far as Tomek could see, they were not NKVD.

As his eyes adjusted to the cold grey half-light, he recognised some of the surrounding landscape and buildings. He was back in Vorkuta!

7

Another Year of Misery

The news of the Battle of Britain in August to October 1940 and the considerable actions of the Polish squadrons, initially flying Hurricanes,[1] were unreported in Russia. Tomek and all the other Poles interned in Russia were completely unaware of how their compatriots had moved on from Rumania, formed fighting units in France for a few brief weeks, then mustered in England to become an exiled Polish Air Force fighting alongside the RAF.[2]

The arrangements for screening, acceptance and training to RAF standards had already been agreed by August 1940 and these would become crucial to Tomek's future.

In the meantime, life in the gulags was becoming more organised but no easier as production targets were introduced, whether or not they were achievable.

For the first time Tomek and his companions were assessed, then assigned to compounds. Anyone wearing the slightest hint of a Polish military uniform was marched off. Polish civilians were divided up, brought in for interrogation, then given a job to do and told what hut they would be sleeping in. The previous slack arrangements had ended almost overnight. The whole operation had become alarmingly efficient.

Tomek's paperwork was already there and any attempt at assuming another identity was pointless. He was moved to a special compound where security had been tightened. He was told he would be staying there until he had been sentenced, but was not told when that would be. Exactly what his sentence would be also remained a secret from him. As for charges, he was simply told that he was an enemy of the state.

By the time the first snows came, the wire around the compound had been reinforced and for the first time searchlights swept the area at night. There was a curfew and anyone deviating from the direct route to and from the latrines would be shot. Nobody thought to try their luck.

There was now no escaping the old donkey engine with its cold weather intransigence. Since his last sojourn in its company, a raised wooden floor had been laid, with a few upright timbers to reinforce the sagging and warped walls, but still open to the elements. The large circular saw was already mounted with stacks of cut tree trunks lying alongside. He and several other prisoners were tasked with moving it and making everything weatherproof.

Every miserable and ever colder morning merged into the next. There was no variation in routine. Tomek and the others worked like automatons, chopping and sawing wood by hand. It was work, eat, sleep, then a weekly roll call with the latest propaganda shouted at them.

More than once their efforts were kicked down and they had to start again, with the guards shouting to build better and stronger, which was an almost impossible undertaking with a few poor-quality tools, a shortage nails and above all very few hammers, for fear that they could be used as weapons against their captors.

Every morning, the tools were counted out and assigned to the least troublesome-looking prisoner to share out, then checked back in and locked away every evening. Nobody dared secrete so much as a nail for fear of being called a saboteur and shot summarily.

Interrogations would happen, without any warning, if the camp officials thought that production targets had not been met. This was a constant fear, as the food ration depended on how well an individual had achieved their target. If for any reason somebody exceeded their target, then everybody else's target was increased. Failure to meet these new benchmarks meant another cut in rations based on the camp commandant's assessment. Frequently this cut meant further failures as hunger and weakness took their toll, until that dreaded label of 'unproductive labour' meant isolation, starvation and a lingering death in the freezing cold.

Clothing would be awarded on a similar basis. High output meant a less-torn *kufeika*, woollen socks and a pair of felt boots that fitted after a fashion. If this was being run as a meritocracy, then it was a particularly ruthless one.

Tomek didn't even know what month it was. He was tired, hungry and in pain.

Finally the machinery, which had been left outside while a new plank floor was laid and the walls and roof were strengthened, was retrieved from under a few centimetres of fresh snow. Once a new fuel storage tank, connecting belt and larger saw table had been installed, the donkey engine was loaded onto a makeshift sled that refused to budge at first. The snow had melted then refrozen the runners to layers of old ice and snow. The first day they barely made any progress at all. They had to abandon it until the next grey morning, taking most of the following day to get it into the now completed shed.

Tomek felt very worried, when having checked everything and spooned the still liquid oil into the hopper and given the cylinder head a long roasting from a pair of blowlamps, the wretched donkey engine would not start. He heated it again, kicked it, swore at it, but it still refused to turn over.

The guards were called and they in turn swore, hit out and kicked the prisoners, threatening them with even worse treatment if they didn't start it, but still it wouldn't work. Their own fear was tangible as any production failures, whatever the reason, could result in the NKVD stripping what they regarded as ineffective guards of their uniforms and being interned themselves.

Ruling by threat and terror was always the underlying template for how every gulag was run. Stalin worked by divide and conquer and had by 1940 killed an unknown number, possibly more than a million, of his own people in the purges since 1937. Officially recorded judicial executions in 1937–38 alone numbered 681,692.[3] Extrajudicial summary executions were common and reported locally. It is difficult to exaggerate how cheap and brief life could be under Stalin's repressive rule outside the gulags. The situation inside was inevitably so much worse.

Instead of a firing squad being assembled, an engineer was brought over from another compound. With Tomek's help and a couple of large spanners, closely watched by two guards who covered them with pistols, they wrestled off the bolts securing the cylinder head and between them they lifted it off after heating it again, then hitting it between back-breaking attempts that slowly shifted it as they blistered their hands. The engineer peered into the cylinder and swore. The bore was scored and corroded with a few drops of water on top of the piston. The crankcase was even worse. Melted snow had obviously got in somehow. Tomek was worried in case he was blamed, but for once he was not the centre of attention.

He shouted across to the guards: 'The engine's wrecked!' One of the guards came over and looked inside, then shouted, 'Sabotage!' At this the engineer looked very worried and tried to explain it probably wasn't sabotage but most likely a cracked cylinder head that let condensation in. Expanding ice would have done the rest, but the guard just shouted again, threatening him with his pistol.

The engineer just shrugged then was marched off between two guards. Tomek was left alone wondering what he should do next.

It has to be borne in mind that by the autumn of 1940 most of the Katyn massacres had already happened. Stalin and Beria had, as far as they were aware, destroyed or at least torn the heart out of the Polish governing and officer class. Large numbers of lesser civilian leaders had all but disappeared into the gulag system, many without the mental or physical resources to survive, being categorised as unproductive labour and facing ultimate starvation.

They still had a significant interned population of Polish lesser ranks, many of whom were drawn from the peasantry and not considered to be a threat.

Germany was still an ally of some sort and there was a series of transfers to allow those Polish PoWs from Western Poland, which was now under German domination, to be swapped for those German-held PoWs who could go back to their homes in Eastern Poland and be subject to Soviet rules.

Stalin was still pursuing the collectivisation of peasant holdings in the hope of having a more productive agricultural sector to feed the Russian millions, many of whom had suffered recent famine.

According to *Story of a Secret State*, published in 1944 and based on reports smuggled to the UK and USA earlier in the war, many officers, fearing retribution, had removed all insignia or swapped uniforms to appear as rank-and-file soldiers. This was in addition to the few senior officers and thousands of other PoWs that were kept alive as a possible bargaining chip as the fortunes of war changed.

The Polish underground in the gulags was not as well organised or effective as that which was developing in German-occupied Poland – the vast distances and poor communication saw to that – but it was not non-existent. Gradually information was beginning to be filtered back via transferred Polish internees and new arrivals who had not been resettled in Soviet-occupied Poland.

Ethnic cleansing had started from areas such as Lwów with sequestration of property, which was given to Ukrainians and Russians.[4]

Tomek's family home was already in Russian hands, and his mother and sisters deported, although it would still be many months before Tomek knew any of this.

Tomek understood full well that indolence would not pay; the question was what to do.

He did not have to wait long. After another roll call he was singled out and herded into a compound with several other Poles. No explanation was given. When Tomek asked what was going on, he was shushed immediately. One of the Poles told him that he must keep his mouth shut as the Russians might work out that he was either from a well-connected family or, worse still, a well-connected family from Lwów, which was being almost completely depopulated of Poles. That was the first Tomek had heard of it. Worse was to come. Within a few days they were moved further north to another camp and told they were to dig a new mine.

The only problem was they had no tools and the camp had not been completed. For a few nights they had huddled together, untroubled by guards, and inevitably some of them froze to death.

Being the youngest, Tomek was pulled out and lined up with a handful of other young men and marched off to yet another compound, this time comprising almost exclusively Russians and a large number of the ever-present bullying *Dzhuliki*.

This time they were given tools, checked out every morning and checked back in every evening. Their task was to build new huts, watchtowers and latrines. The *Dzhuliki* decided who was going to work and threatened the weaker internees that they would be denounced and shot.

There were guards but not so many as at the other compounds. Sawn planks would be delivered by horse-drawn sleds at first until the weather became too extreme. More huts were built and some Russian internees were taken off to build sleds and make skis, although Tomek never saw any of the results.

That winter seemed to Tomek to be particularly vicious. Cold took its toll and the few Poles that were left died, leaving just a couple who were brought in as the days started to lengthen. The interrogations were far less common and there were no suicides by hanging. The bitter Arctic weather made sure that death was easily achieved simply by going outside.

The moment any friendships were made, the *Dzhuliki* made sure that they were ended either by denouncing to the guards or by beating up anyone seen to be whispering, then throwing them out into the snow.

Once in a while they were moved on to make new huts in yet another compound. The food was as bad as ever and fights broke out among the prisoners when the fear of death by hunger broke down any sense of civilised behaviour.

Tomek was by now thoroughly institutionalised. His whole horizon was dominated by the gulag. He had lost all sense of time and place, followed orders numbly and gave the impression that his spirit was broken. That satisfied both the guards and the *Dzhuliki*.

The days were lengthening and the weather noticeably milder, when Tomek was called out and marched over to the commandant's office.

The man smiled, and Tomek feared that there was going to be another rape or some other form of torture.

'Gubert Kazimir Kazimirovich, you have been tried, found guilty and sentenced to five years' hard labour. Once that is over, you can go home or stay here. We will have no more interest in you.'[5]

Tomek did not regard this as a concession but refrained from objecting or asking what he had been sentenced for. His only thought was surviving long enough to get out and find his mother and sisters. He had learned from others that all information was withheld and nobody knew what had happened to their families. Sometimes the guards might jeer and say that all their families were dead, shot by the Germans, but few took that seriously.

Russian disinformation was now taken as the norm and nobody believed anything beyond what they saw for themselves.

It was around the time of the first thaw that more persistent rumours began. The numbers of internees had swollen, added to by disgraced Russian soldiers who had been deported for spreading negative propaganda about the Germans.

They had been on the border with German-occupied Poland and had received occasional reports of a German military build-up. One former corporal said that some Poles had shouted across a river to him that the Germans would invade with the better weather. He had reported it to his captain but was promptly arrested for passing slanderous rumours against the Russian state.

It was significant that some of the guards started asking for news from any new arrivals. As one Russian said in a hoarse whisper, whatever comrade Stalin thought, it would not alter the facts.

Tomek doubted if any of it was true, even though he wished it was. Anything had to be better than Stalin and Beria, but as an old Polish proverb had it: if wishes were horses then beggars could ride!

The winter had dragged into spring with more floods and the endless routine of misery. This time Tomek was assigned to work in one of the opencast pits, up to his waist in freezing water. There was no opportunity to dry off overnight before starting again the next morning.

Even the body lice had had enough; they had migrated from his groin and formed a tide line from his abdomen up. Presumably those lower down had drowned after eight hours or more under water. Those that remained were more determined than ever to make Tomek's life a misery.

Once a week one of the other prisoners would scrape away at his head to make sure that not a single hair gave refuge for any louse, but it made little difference. Once the sun had risen in March then the standard gulag-issued cap was worn. Bare heads would get burned even this far north and the sunlight dazzled the eyes without a peak to shield them.

That suited the lice, who simply took up residence in the cap while others scurried around from the collar downwards to the high-water mark of the latest miserable soaking shift in the black, dirty waters of the pit.

As spring gave way to the brief Arctic summer, and the waist-deep water migrated down to thigh then knee, the lice took up residence in these pastures new. No amount of standing naked holding infested clothes over smoking fires made any difference. The lice had adapted and now the mosquitoes assailed any naked flesh, so many of the inmates preferred to put up with the lice.

It was inevitable that sooner or later there would be an outbreak of typhus. Tomek was now past caring. Whatever happened was of no concern to him in his utterly demoralised and browbeaten state. He had become a barely functioning Rabotnik: the ideal gulag slave – miserable, uncomplaining, docile, broken in spirit and expendable.

If there was a future, then Tomek could not see it.

PART TWO
ESCAPE!

8

Saved by an Ancestor?

According to many sources, Russian intelligence had identified Hitler's intention to invade Russia and the existence of reconnaissance flights. This was backed up by messages from German-occupied Poland together with warnings from Churchill, as a result of radio intercepts and decoding by Bletchley Park (where Tomek's future wife Angela Oakeshott would later work). All of these were all dismissed by Stalin.[1]

Many suggestions have since been advanced for Stalin's lack of preparedness. Given his track record of using propaganda and disinformation as a tool, it is possible to infer that he regarded any reports from Churchill as designed to drag Russia into the war and open up a second front. Stalin trusted no one. In his estimation, opening up an Eastern Front would take pressure off the United Kingdom after the Battle of Britain and the unfolding U-boat war in the Atlantic.

Stalin had few illusions about Hitler, but could see little evidence of the Germans stockpiling the necessary supplies and equipment for prosecuting any war in the depths of the Russian winter. The Russians were looking for evidence of extra sheep being grazed that would supply fleeces for winter uniforms, and until that happened they felt confident that any attack by Germany was at least two years away. For all their own paranoia, Russian staff officers knew that a considerable logistical effort had to be built up to support any attack against their country and that would have been almost impossible to keep secret.

What they had not factored in was Hitler's self-delusion as to the technical superiority of his own forces. The success of Blitzkrieg in the West had bred overconfidence among German forces, leading to an overestimation of their abilities and the assumed inferiority of Russian training, motivation and weaponry.

It is equally possible that US Ambassador Joseph Kennedy, who was no enthusiast for Britain, may have been briefing his opposite number in London's Russian Embassy. He had reported several times that he thought that Britain could not support a long, drawn-out war.

Kennedy was dead against Churchill receiving any support from the then neutral United States and this would have reinforced any scepticism that Stalin had as to reports of Hitler's future intentions.

The Germans launched Operation Barbarossa on 22 June 1941, making extraordinary and unexpected early gains deep into Soviet territory. Before long they would stretch their supply lines to breaking point as they were unprepared for the sheer distances and emptiness of Russia.

Stalin, after initial dithering, started throwing ill-equipped young men into the front line (much like Putin is doing in Ukraine). In order to make sure that there were no desertions or retreat, front-line units were backed by NKVD squads with orders to shoot anyone turning their backs on the enemy regardless of cause.

In Ukraine the Wagner Group has adopted the same tactics. Nothing really changes with Russia.

Gradually the number of guards in the gulags were whittled down and NKVD units were also gradually pulled in to fight Hitler.

In Vorkuta the situation was easing slightly. The irony was that Hitler's code word for the invasion, Barbarossa, referred to the twelfth-century Holy Roman Emperor Friedrich I. He was of the Staufer family, a name shared by Tomek's mother, born as Stefania Staufer. Curiously, it was this use of a family name by Hitler that unwittingly set up the chain of events that would allow Tomek to escape.

That spring and early summer of 1941 was a time of slow change in the Vorkuta gulag. The work and brutality was much the same as before, but more of the Russian inmates were appointed as gang bosses. The guards were increasingly reluctant to venture far from the compound. Reports were passed back to the guards from the more literate Russians who kept records, and if any of the few Poles stepped out of line, or were perceived to be slacking, they would be denounced and their food ration cut.

With less supervision from the NKVD, the guards became more slovenly in appearance and less concerned about appearing drunk in front of the internees. The rumour that they had a still concealed somewhere had persisted, but Tomek thought that didn't explain this increased inebriation.

There had been reports of fuel and industrial alcohol being stolen and mixed in the illegal stills with herbs and antifreeze in the hopes of making some sort of vodka. Certainly, the *Dzhuliki* were up for anything on offer, though they had few bargaining chips other than doing the guards' dirty work for them. Some undoubtedly went blind and died of alcoholic poisoning.

In 2021 the *Moscow Times* reported that twenty-six Russian men died in one incident involving bootlegged alcohol stolen from tankers and mixed with other distillates. Nothing changes!

Alcohol had always been regarded (incorrectly) as a treatment and preventative against cold. Tomek's father used to drink prodigious amounts of *Wódka*, the Polish equivalent. It had been used as a disinfectant for wounds and as a substitute for anaesthetic. It was probably his father's occasional inebriated outbursts that put Tomek off drinking in any great amount for the rest of his life. Certainly, beyond the stinging sensation of having wheals from whippings, beatings and inflicted cigarette burns treated with alcohol, Tomek wasn't in the least tempted to deaden the pains of Vorkuta by drinking the stuff.

By the middle of July most of the younger guards had been rounded up by the NKVD and taken away, leaving only the older reservists in charge. These delegated even more to their favoured bullies in the hope of maintaining some semblance of order.

There were persistent rumours of fighting and qualified engineers being released to work on aircraft and weapon designs. Nobody really knew, and if their guards did they were not telling. Tomek took little notice. If it was the Finns again, they would lose eventually, and if it was the Germans, then what did they hope to achieve? Russia was enormous. The only thing really worth having was oil and that meant aiming for the Caucasus, thousands of miles to the south. Tomek had heard all these scenarios before from his father's contemporaries. Poland and Ukraine had grain, Rumania and Azerbaijan had oil. The Germans would ignore the Arctic with its gulags. Tomek had often heard the old saying 'What does it matter to the grass if it is eaten by the sheep or goat?' Tomek, like all the other internees, saw himself as little more than grass. If he wasn't going to be eaten then there was always the prospect of being mown.

Whatever was happening on some distant battlefront was of very little concern. He thought he was most likely going to die in the gulag.

What Tomek and all the other Polish inmates in the gulag system were unaware of was that Stalin had finally woken up to the fact that Germany was not just attacking, but making huge inroads into Russian territory. Most Soviet forces were ill trained and ill equipped. He needed allies. Churchill was prepared to offer help with conditions. The first of these was a demand that Polish PoWs were released, initially with the promise that they would fight with the Russians against the Germans.[2]

This meant that Stalin had no choice other than to negotiate directly with the Polish Government in Exile in London under General Sikorski through the Russian ambassador Ivan Mayski.

Sikorski knew that in total there were some 2 million Polish internees held in the gulags, most of whom were capable of military service, with 250,000 who had been trained as front-line servicemen prior to the fall of Poland. These were numbers Stalin could not afford to ignore.

With strong prompting from Churchill and the good offices of his foreign secretary Anthony Eden, diplomatic relations were restored between Poland and Russia following negotiations that began on 5 July 1941 with an agreement signed on 30 July, by which time the German thrust into Russia was looking unstoppable.[3]

Saved by an Ancestor?

What was called an amnesty was granted to many Polish citizens on 12 August 1941, followed by the signing of a military alliance two days later.

That was the theory. In practice the NKVD were reluctant to release anyone they perceived to be a threat, or anyone who could later accuse the Russians of torture. In one respect the NKVD were right. They feared that the situation would get out of their control as the numbers released converged on the headquarters of the nominated head of the Polish forces in Russia, General Anders, initially at Totskoye before being moved on several times as the situation changed.

Tomek heard nothing at all about any of these developments. Beyond rumours, there had been no briefings at all about the German attack nor had there been any talk of release.

If anything, the regime at his part of the Vorkuta complex had been tightened up, with a few more NKVD officers being seen. Nothing was said about his sentence, and beyond the usual cruelties of increased work targets and diminishing food, the number of beatings and violations had pretty well ceased. The *Dzhuliki*, however, seemed to be in charge of any discipline, as they saw it, among the internees.

Summer was drifting towards autumn as the sun dipped ever lower towards the horizon. They had experienced the first frosts and by the second week in September Tomek was allowed to walk outside the compound. There was no explanation. He met other Poles, who found this new freedom of movement inexplicable. One had demanded to speak with the NKVD officer in charge, but had been kept waiting for hours with no explanation. After two more days of this, he told Tomek that something was up, but he had no idea what it could be.

They were now worried that they would be left outside to die when the snows came. All the old miserable certainties had evaporated, to be replaced by a fear of the unknown.

This all came to a head when, in the middle of the night, having missed his evening cold fish soup and black bread, Tomek was tipped out of his bunk by a handful of *Dzhuliki* accompanied by a couple of terrified-looking Poles, one of whom told him to do whatever he was told.

Outside the frost was hard and the stars twinkled with that particular fierceness that only Arctic cold seems to provide. There was no moon, nor were there any searchlights sweeping the compound. It seemed deserted.

He was hurried over to the stores, where others were already handing out sacks of potatoes and black bread.

'They need us to carry the stores. They want us away before the moon rises,' was the only explanation Tomek understood. He felt both excited and weak. He had no real idea what was going on.

Nothing stopped them. They walked out of the gate and away from the compound. Tomek could barely manage the sack he had been given. Fortunately the frost was thick enough for them to see a rough track leading up a small rise. There was no cover and he half expected to be picked off from one of the watchtowers. He had heard stories of prisoners being allowed to escape and getting a few hundred metres outside the wire before the searchlights went on and the shooting began. It was an effective way of clearing up administrative irregularities by shooting those attempting to escape.

The moon rose with its last quarter's searing silver light throwing shadows behind them onto the frost, but still no shouts or shots. They must have been all of a kilometre away by now, plainly silhouetted against the glittering silver tundra. There were no trees to give the comfort of dark cover.

Tomek carried on, staggering with tiredness and hunger until the sun rose low on the pink-flushed horizon, while the by now pale moon sank towards the western sky and some gathering grey clouds. It might snow later. Tomek had no idea how they would survive.

They stopped in a low depression with a half-frozen pond, which provided some relief from thirst. Another Pole shared a black loaf with Tomek, while the *Dzhuliki* made a small fire from a few dwarf willow and heather twigs. It barely flared, just giving off some weak wisps of grey smoke, which Tomek was certain would betray their position. To his surprise, one of the *Dzhuliki* tipped half a sack of potatoes into the fire. From his Boy Scout camping experience, Tomek knew this was a useless exercise. They would never cook; the fire had no heat to it.

Saved by an Ancestor?

Instinctively he grabbed another black loaf and hid it inside his *kufeika*. He nodded at the other Pole, who surreptitiously did the same. A third Pole whom Tomek had not met before slithered down the frosty slope to squat beside them.

'The potatoes are useless, just extra weight. There's no way of cooking them.'

As Tomek took another bite of his black bread, his companion answered the newcomer: 'The bread won't last long, there are more of them than us and they'll just take all the bread and leave us to starve.' The other Pole nodded. 'They think I can't understand them. They're talking about eating us when the food gives out.'

Tomek's companion simply nodded. Tomek was now very worried. Perhaps he would be better off making a break for it and running back to the compound. Guessing what he was thinking, the other two Poles both shook their heads. The bread would last another three days. They had to form a plan before then.

Tomek was dead on his feet, but after a lot of arguing, during which he dozed, the *Dzhuliki* decided to set off, leaving the fire and potatoes behind. It looked as if Tomek's worst fears were going to be realised. It was then he noticed that one of the Poles had picked up a single sack of potatoes. The man wandered nonchalantly over to them.

'They might not be able to cook them before we get to a forest, but that doesn't mean we can't trade them.' The other Poles nodded sagely, while a second picked up another sack and joined them. Now they were five. Tomek felt a little more comforted by the increased number. They still had about eight *Dzhuliki* to deal with should it come to a fight.

Based upon the low sun at midday, Tomek reckoned they were heading south-east. If the *Dzhuliki* had a plan they were not telling the Poles, none of whom had any idea where they were headed. Fortunately the day was a little milder with a damp mist that Tomek hoped would help to conceal them from any pursuers.

The ground was becoming less flat and they frequently lost sight of the others as they disappeared down a slight dip or around the few rocky outcrops. That night they found a small corral and an abandoned hut, which one of the Poles reckoned must have been used by the Samoyeds for their annual reindeer round-up, marking and slaughter. Being crowded together in such a small space was uncomfortable but gave an impression of warmth. One of the *Dzhuliki* had found a bottle of vodka, which he passed round his mates. None of the Poles was the remotest bit tempted as there was no guarantee that the bottle held anything of the sort. Later that night two *Dzhuliki* went outside to be horribly sick. They were not in much better condition by the morning and the rest of the party had little inclination to be held up by the two victims, who were left groaning in the hut.

Now the odds were improving. It was five Poles to six *Dzhuliki*. Tomek felt less apprehensive. One of the slightly less intimidating *Dzhuliki* struck up a conversation in Russian with the oldest of the Poles. To Tomek's surprise, the Pole burst out laughing. As he later explained, that man had been a bosun on a whaler but had been arrested after picking up a Norwegian crew whose own fishing boat was adrift with no engine. The NKVD was suspicious of anyone who had had contact with Westerners. He had acquired the tattoos in order to blend in better.

It was he who was the party's navigator. He had said they were heading for a forest that lay some 60km to the south on the slopes of the northern Urals. There was a lot of lumber work there and the locals were rumoured to be left alone by the NKVD.

Later the Pole said he believed there was little loyalty among the leaders of their party. He expected that fighting would break out if things did not go according to plan.

Fortunately they came across a Samoyed family who were out foraging. They were led to an encampment of Kotta, which looked a bit like wigwams, where in exchange for the potatoes they were given cured reindeer meat and dried fish. These took some time to chew but were savoury and salty.

The Samoyeds said there was another camp some 15km away that did not have a lot of security around it. They called it a *kolkhoz*, which the older Pole said was some sort of village collective farm. He was not at all sure they should go anywhere near it as there was no agriculture this far north and they had almost certainly run into the NKVD. There was, however, a railway running some 10km south of it where the trains ran slowly enough to jump on. One of the Samoyeds said he had often used it to visit relatives further down the line. If nothing else, the Poles thought that would be their best chance of putting some distance between them and their captors.

On the fourth day, they had been walking since well before daybreak when they saw figures in the distance. The *Dzhuliki* stopped and started arguing among themselves. The bosun broke off and walked over to the Russian-speaking Pole, who turned to Tomek.

'The *Dzhuliki* think it's a trap as they don't recognise the uniforms. He thinks they're wrong and I think we should take a look.'

Tomek and the other Poles nodded. They eased their way back from the arguing *Dzhuliki*, who were now looking very angry. Lying on their stomachs, the five Poles crawled up over a slight rise whose moss and heather were broken by a few light grey boulders. Anxiously they peered out.

Tomek could not be sure but they looked like Polish Army uniforms in the distance with their green greatcoats and the distinctive *Rogatywka*, the Polish asymmetrical, peaked, four-pointed cap. They looked at each other in astonishment. Tomek whispered, 'They're ours! What are they doing out here?'

Behind them the shouting had increased and the bosun appeared, waving them away. It sounded ugly with the noises of fighting and groans. The Poles needed no second bidding, they just took off running as fast as their tired legs would take them towards the distant figures, shouting as loudly as they could in Polish.

The distance felt like the longest half kilometre Tomek had ever run. He was cramped and retching by the time he reached the astonished Polish soldiers. They looked in better shape than Tomek and his companions. The oldest Pole managed to gasp out: 'What are you doing here?'

'There's been an amnesty all PoWs are being released.'

Tomek could not believe his ears. He almost fainted with relief.

As they walked back with the company of Polish soldiers they learned they had been out foraging while awaiting their release documents. They were all due to leave soon and find General Anders, who had permission to form an army corps. The problem was that Tomek and his companions were obviously outside of the system. The question was what to do about it. They would stand out in their *kufeikas* with nothing to show that they had been in the army, all except for the oldest Pole, who still had the remnants of his greatcoat.

After some hurried discussion and a great deal of swapping, Tomek was now wearing a borrowed *Rogatywka* and greatcoat from a young corporal, who still had his tunic and boots, while other compromises allowed his mates to look as if they belonged, provided they stayed in the middle of the company sheltered from outside view.

It took nearly three-quarters of an hour before they arrived at their camp gate, where a solitary guard was relieving foraging parties of their mushrooms, lingonberries, crowberries and a few trapped birds.

The Samoyeds had been right: this was more like a *kolkhoz*[4] than a gulag. There was a moment's awkwardness when the guard said he was sure that more were coming back than went out. The company leader, a young lieutenant, made a joke in Russian that only madmen broke into a gulag.

The guard laughed and urged them all in.

For the first time since he had been arrested, Tomek felt that he had a future.

9

Where Are Your Papers?

If Tomek thought his troubles were over having got into the new camp, he had an almost immediate and very rude awakening.

The lieutenant took the greatcoat and *Rogatywka* off him and restored them to their original owners. He looked very serious.

'We were very lucky getting back in with you. I took a serious risk. The guard on duty is not one of the difficult ones. Had it been anyone else you would have been left outside.'

This shocked Tomek; he couldn't understand why.

Within a few minutes he was left outside a hut while his erstwhile companions were ushered in together. He could hear raised voices speaking Polish and it was some time before he managed to talk to the older Pole as he left the hut.

'We're OK but I'm afraid your problems remain. We can prove we are PoWs and none of us are from Lwów. If you can impress the major in there with any family connections, you must use them.' With that he shook hands and walked off to join the others.

Tomek was overwhelmed with disappointment, exhaustion and cold.

Tomek would never have guessed he was in the presence of a major. A man of about 60 years old, thin, grave with an expression of bitterness, he looked more like a functionary from a local council education department. He had had examiners who looked happier with their lives. He was well spoken and evidently dismissive of Tomek with his slight twang that immediately gave away that he was from Lwów.

'You say you're Polish. We've had Ukrainians, Ruthenes and Belarusians all claiming to be Polish. They all want the benefit of amnesty.'[1]

Tomek was furious. He had not endured torture, abuse and the threat of being eaten just to be dismissed by this man in a greatcoat with no rank or insignia badges. He had only had the young lieutenant's word that this man was indeed a major. What Tomek had not known was that most officers had torn off their decorations, rank badges, epaulettes and all the other insignia that would make them a target for special treatment and possible execution by the NKVD.

The major looked at him coolly. He had seen it all before: 'The NKVD are bastards. As you and I know, there's no guarantee they'll honour this agreement. They hold all the cards. I've had serious difficulties getting this far. My first batch is due to leave this afternoon and that's if I get all the documents through. You haven't been photographed, matched against the NKVD lists and given the right papers. I have no idea who you are or if you belong here. You expect me to risk several hundred trained soldiers for one boy, with nothing to prove who he is?'

'My father was a pallbearer at Piłsudski's funeral. He served in the legions with him!'

The major laughed without any humour. 'Everyone claims to have been in the legions and if I believed all the pallbearers' stories, the Marshal's coffin would be almost a kilometre long!'

Tomek was almost screaming with frustration now. He could see the opportunity slipping away. He gave his father's rank, appointment, how his grandfather Henryk had been active in the 1863 winter uprising, when the major interrupted him.[2]

'Henryk Hubert? That's a strong claim, can you prove it?'

It took almost an hour before the major, who was from Kraków, believed his story. He had heard of Tomek's two aunts – schoolteachers who had a good reputation locally. Tomek never thought that the names of Auntie Maria and Auntie Eugenia Staufer would have held his fate in their hands.

Where Are Your Papers?

Like many who had been interned in Vorkuta, Tomek was a special case who had no idea at all about how the amnesty process would work. The NKVD came up with a document written entirely in Cyrillic that many Poles couldn't understand.

The intention was for the Polish PoWs to find their way to General Anders and form a corps[3] that would fight alongside Russian troops against the Germans. The numbers released soon swelled to the extent that the NKVD were losing control of the situation. Anders, together with his hastily arranged staff, were moved further away from the front line several times, ostensibly allowing released PoWs to be trained and rearmed.

This was now becoming a serious worry to many Russians in the upper echelons of the Red Army, as they had doubts about the loyalty of what was rapidly becoming a brigade made up of soldiers who had little affection for their captors or Stalin.

Anders was then based for a while in Tashkent, before being moved to Tehran on the understanding that they were to attack the Germans through the Caucasus or Balkans. This would relieve the pressure on Russian forces who were trying to hold back the Germans at Stalingrad in the winter of 1941–42.

In the event, Anders' considerable forces were consolidated in Palestine to fight later in North Africa and Italy.

This constant movement made connecting with those capable of making decisions about undocumented refugees such as Tomek problematical. The Polish Army knew that the NKVD would be looking for escaped political prisoners masquerading as PoWs. This was going to cause problems as the major priority was to form an effective army brigade as soon as possible. The Russians never regarded Lwów as Polish territory, so it was vital that anyone from that area was not too obvious. There was the real fear of risking an entire operation involving tens of thousands of released PoWs, just for the sake of a few civilians. Tomek was vulnerable and probably expendable.

It was a very worried Tomek who was once again concealed among a large contingent of released PoWs as they marched to the nearest railhead. The major had relented and was probably as relieved to wash his hands of Tomek as he was to be on the move once more, wearing yet another borrowed greatcoat to conceal his *kufeika*.

There was no food and only a brief opportunity for relieving themselves and having some water before being loaded onto cattle trucks for the journey south. A fine freezing rain had started, which made the first few hours a misery.

They were unloaded in the middle of a forest with no instructions or idea of what to do next. An interpreter arrived in a motorcycle combination with a Russian colonel, who handed the senior Polish officer a map before driving off again. The Polish officer, a barely trained lieutenant who had been rushed from the academy to the front line and subsequent capture, had no experience of handling such a large number of other ranks. He simply pointed down a track and started walking. Not everyone followed at once, some of the soldiers breaking up into small groups. Tomek felt excluded once more, especially when he had to hand back his loaned greatcoat. Again he was pretty well on his own.

He followed the others miserably. He had no idea why the train had stopped where it was. He had heard that the railway ran all the way from Vorkuta to Pechora, where sizeable boats navigated the river from the south. He wasn't too sure of the geography, but had seen rafts on the Usa, which he learned flowed into the Pechora. The distances were huge. He had absolutely no idea that the Pechora already lay behind him.

He wanted to go south, as far away from the nightmare of Vorkuta as possible, but the majority of the soldiers on the train had been talking of going west along the Pechora River before it looped north. Tomek saw no sense in this suggestion. Based on what he overheard, he would head for Tashkent. There was speculation that the Polish Army would set up headquarters there.

The problem was that nobody had any maps to be sure where they were. He had the very uncomfortable feeling that he would not be able to bluff his way past any NKVD guard lying in wait to trap him.

Where Are Your Papers?

What Tomek did not know was that local commissars were already getting worried about the sudden influx of Poles released from the gulags wanting food and shelter. In theory the Poles should have been taken to towns along railway lines or embarkation ports on those several large rivers that lace their way through the Taiga forests and tundra to the north.

In practice many of the Poles were dumped in the middle of nowhere and left to find their own way, brandishing their release papers as an insurance against re-arrest. What all the released internees needed, more than anything, was money, jewellery, or goods to offer as bribes. Communism may have been the legislated way of doing business, but at local level 'unofficial' Russia ruled through a complex black economy.

Tomek was by now desperately hungry. It was noticeably milder here in the forest than it had been at Vorkuta. He could see mushrooms growing at the base of several pine trees, but wasn't tempted as he had noticed some soldiers looking at them, shaking their heads then carrying on. He had little idea of what was edible or poisonous.

It was then a movement deeper into the forest caught his eye. As he paused to look again, he was sure it was moving. It looked a sort of navy blue. Plainly it wasn't a soldier or NKVD officer, so having nothing to lose, he left the track and walked stealthily over to where he last saw it. A slight breeze wafted the smell of smoke over to him, so he attempted to follow the scent trail. It must have taken between twenty minutes and half an hour before he found himself in a clearing with a small fire in the middle. An old woman in a typically full *Baboushka* dress and headscarf was poking at it. There were some skewered mushrooms in the smoke and a small skinned creature – he wasn't sure if it was squirrel or rabbit – dangling much lower over the fire.

She smiled at him and beckoned him over. She spoke clear and almost unaccented Russian, which Tomek did not find too difficult to understand. He answered her questions as best he could. Her name was Irina, she had come from a wealthy family before the revolution and now lived on her own in the forest. She didn't like all the Polish soldiers she had seen, but had taken pity on this half-starved boy, who reminded her of a brother lost fighting the Germans in 1915.

Tomek could not understand why Irina was in the forest cooking over a fire. He guessed she must have a cottage not too far away but she never mentioned it. She did not look as if she lived rough. Without asking him, she shared some of the mushrooms and gave him both rear legs of whatever animal she had been cooking. 'Don't eat too much or you'll be very ill. Try to eat slowly and get your stomach used to food again. It will take days.'

She seemed to know what she was talking about. Tomek tried to engage her in conversation but she either could not or did not want to understand him. She talked about those things she thought important. All questions remained unanswered. Eventually it dawned on Tomek that this was probably a form of self-defence. If she controlled the amount of information she gave out then nobody could betray her, inadvertently or otherwise. She liked things the way they were and had no intention of risking anything. It had obviously served her well.

He was very surprised at what she said next. He had no idea if she was right, but was disinclined to ignore her. 'The other Poles will try to go to Kotlas on the Dvina. That is a big mistake; Stalin will make them fight against the Germans who are aiming for Rostov. Russian soldiers will only fight with the NKVD at their back. Go east! Don't follow their mistakes.'

Tomek was not inclined to disagree. There was something about this lady. Tomek realised that she wasn't as old as she looked. Perhaps this *Baboushka* appearance was an act. He felt so tired and he was getting some warmth from the fire.

He had no idea when he fell asleep or indeed for how long. He woke up as snowflakes landed on his face. He was stiff and cold. The fire was nearly out and there was no sign of Irina. He decided that his best bet was to find his way back to the track, which was easier said than done. The forest was gloomy and silent. In end it was the sound of distant voices that led him back to it. More Polish Army veterans were walking along, occasionally singing aloud to keep up their spirits. He now realised that the weather had really broken and night was not far away.

Tomek felt there was safety in numbers but at the same time realised that there was a certain reserve from the other Poles. He was past caring. He needed the security of company and still had no idea where he was headed.

That night he walked for as long as he could before almost falling asleep on his feet. He had been all for getting to a town or village and taking his chances on finding shelter, but had been surprised when he met a large contingent of Poles, who had stopped in a huddle discussing options.

A handful had gone ahead to a small town only to find chaos. Nobody knew what was going on. Some had commandeered rafts in the hope of getting to the main river, while others had stories of overloaded boats going up the River Dvina to Kotlas, in return for massive bribes. The rumour was that Kotlas was full of families released from working the *kolkhoz* collectives and no arrangements for the genuine PoWs from the gulags who had no money or goods to bargain with.

One thing was clear, there had been no arrangements for the Polish servicemen. There was considerable argument about where General Anders had set up base. Some had said they had been told it was in Tatishschevo near Saratov, others that it was definitely at Totskoye about 300km further away to the east of Saratov. Either way, wherever they should be headed, it was well to the south and possibly a week or two away on the train, if they could find one going there.

One gloomy individual muttered, 'If we can get on and the Russians let us,' which did nothing to lighten the mood.

Tomek was once more pushed into his almost default state of gloom at this, and the slight easing of hunger pangs he felt courtesy of Irina had passed. He was thirsty and had resorted to scooping snow off the scant cover on the low bushes and few dangling boughs that had acquired a slight mantle of fast-melting flakes. The ground had been churned up into a slippery, muddy mess that clung to boots and made any thought of sleeping in the open a non-starter.

He attached himself to a small party of older soldiers who seemed to know what they were doing. They left the main track and followed a narrower one that led, after half an hour or so, to what must have been some sort of fisherman's hut by a slow-flowing river that sounded as if it fed a pool. It was now so dark that Tomek could not be sure. One soldier had a small torch that worked off a dynamo as he squeezed a lever underneath. It gave a very dim and variable light accompanied by irregular whirring. As each man's hand became numb with squeezing the lever, it was passed on to another, who then led the way. They had paused before it was Tomek's turn with the torch.

Inside the hut smelled damp and chill, with a rough wooden board floor, a solitary bench against the wall and no fireplace. Nobody was inclined to go outside and look for wood for what appeared to be a rusted brazier lying on its side. It was obviously designed to be used in the summer and not in the hut. Besides, any wood they did find was likely to be soaking.

After a very uncomfortable night, they found some rotten nets lying at the bottom of a dugout boat that was half full of freezing water. Two men who claimed to have had some fishing experience had, with considerable help from the others, tipped the boat upside down to empty it and had cobbled together about 3m of almost serviceable net. They were going to try to get some fish, allowing Tomek and the others to forage for firewood and mushrooms or anything else that could pass as edible.

From his Boy Scout experience, Tomek was able to get sufficient dry bracken and pine branches that would flare enough to act as kindling at the base of the brazier. Judging by the encouraging smiles from the other men, Tomek felt he could justify his presence.

The fishermen returned after a couple of hours with three small perch and one reasonably sized burbot. Even so, it was a bit like the feeding of the five thousand as barely a dozen edible mushrooms had been found.

One man whom the others had referred to as Sergeant looked very worried: 'We can't survive like this and have any hope of finding the general. He's probably a thousand or more kilometres from here. If the Russians won't feed us we'll have to take what we need. We'll carry on downstream. This river will join the Dvina, then we'll need to come up with a plan before we starve or die of cold.'

The full impact of what lay in store finally hit Tomek. Any thoughts of going it alone evaporated.

He couldn't understand why, having got to the main river, they turned south, then away to the east. To him it felt like they were going back on their tracks. Nobody was saying anything. Others had joined them two days after setting out from the fisherman's hut. There had been a quiet conference with much head shaking. Nobody wanted to query what was going on.

They kept to what passed as a loose gravel highway heading east, occasionally hitching a lift on empty lorries driven by worried-looking drivers. More and more lorries caught up with them, as they paused at the side of the road to let other lorries pass, some of them laden with Russian soldiers who jeered at the Poles and whistled derisively, making unfamiliar gestures that Tomek guessed were obscene.

Finally one lorry driver broke the silence as Tomek was sitting next to him.

'Poor sods, they haven't a clue. The Germans have come much further than Comrade Stalin ever guessed. They'll either be blown up by the Germans or shot by the NKVD for retreating.' With that he spat out of the window.

Now Tomek understood why the Sergeant was leading them east. He wasn't going to have Polish lives squandered in a hopeless cause defending their recent captors.

There wasn't much snow, but it was getting much colder as they approached the city of Molotov, although their latest driver still called it Perm. He had given them a lift in return for them providing a human chain carrying cans of fuel from a dump to fill the lorry's seemingly bottomless tank.

He didn't look Russian, more Asian, and plainly didn't have much time for communist officialdom.

'Don't go into Perm. The NKVD are rounding up anyone of fighting age. Their families are upset, mothers crying, starving kids running everywhere. It's not a nice place, nothing good there. I'll drop you at a crossroads where you can go north to Berezniki. You might find a Polish camp there.'

The Sergeant didn't look too happy. He reckoned it would take two days to walk there. So far they had been lucky with the food. The release papers were supposed to have guaranteed some sort of payment in return for signing up, but that varied depending on which camp did the releasing and how corrupt the guards had been.

The few who did have any money had spent most of it on bribes to get them this far. Their party had dwindled a bit, down to about eight of them apart from Tomek. Others had decided they knew best and had set off elsewhere and a couple had developed fevers and were unfit to move. Tomek was appalled at first when the Sergeant decided to leave them with a small logging camp. He remembered all too well the fate of the wounded in the field hospital tents when the Russian tanks first came.

It took a while for him to realise that the Sergeant had a duty to all of them and, given the resources he had, his options boiled down to acceptable losses. It was a very hard lesson to learn.

The Sergeant insisted that when they halted, every evening, despite the cold, they all stripped off and destroyed as many lice as they could over whatever fire was available. There had been a few mutterings at first, which ended once the fevers started. Nobody wanted to risk typhus.

Tomek never got to Bereznik and was not sure if the others did. He described two incidents that were to repeat themselves several times during his escape.

It was halfway through the second day on the road north that they were overtaken by three black saloon cars driven by what looked like the NKVD, although at the speed they were going Tomek could not be too sure.

The day was cold and bright with a little snow remaining at the side of the road. It wasn't cold enough to freeze the spit as the men coughed and hacked, but he had little doubt it would soon go that way. In Vorkuta it wasn't unusual to hear a click and watch the spittle bounce on the frozen ground. Despite the Sergeant's precautions, it was obvious that a couple of the men had been infected and were looking ill. Tomek wondered how long it would be before these two were abandoned like the previous victims. He was still in good shape, but had little doubt that if he stayed with this group, it would only be a matter of time before he succumbed.

One of the older men had told Tomek a story he had heard before from his mother. In 1937–38, the NKVD had rounded up anyone with a Polish-sounding name, executed the men, forced the women out of their homes and forcibly deported the children to be adopted and brought up as Russians with no knowledge of their antecedents.

This had been done under NKVD secret order No. 00485,[4] signed by Nikolai Ivanovich Yezov, who preceded Beria as head of the NKVD only to be executed himself in 1940 as an enemy of the state. Sadly we now know that Putin's government have resurrected this policy with the forced adoptions of Ukrainian children captured during the invasion. The Russian Children's Commissioner Maria Lvova Belova is the subject of an arrest warrant,[5] at the time of writing, by the ICC as a war criminal as a result of her actions, but is unlikely to face the same fate as Yezov as her boss Putin is subject to the same arrest warrant.

At the time that Tomek saw the NKVD saloon cars, Stalin, finally facing the reality of the German invasion, ordered the dismantling of all weapons production to be transported east of the Urals, well beyond the range of German bombers.

The NKVD were charged with making sure that critical workers were also summarily deported to work under forced labour conditions designing and producing new aircraft, tanks and weapons. Tomek could not possibly have known this but this movement was about to have a profound effect on his progress.

Tomek was very worried. The Sergeant didn't look too happy, reasoning that if the NKVD were setting up a checkpoint, at worst it would be an inconvenience to have all their release papers checked and no doubt rubber stamped once more.

Tomek had no papers at all and so far had not told the Sergeant, whom he now suspected of being a commissioned officer masquerading as an NCO. He wasn't the only one with something to hide. The situation twisted itself into a tangle of confusion when half a dozen ragged men came running down the road towards them. Among them were two Polish civilians.

'Scatter! The NKVD are arresting everyone!'

When asked if there was a Polish camp further up the road, they all shook their heads and ran off. Nobody knew what to do.

They were still arguing among themselves when Tomek thought he heard a train whistle far off to his right. Because they were all talking at once, none of the others heard it and nobody showed any inclination to take him seriously.

Feeling that actions spoke louder than words, Tomek walked away into the forest, believing that once he went off, others would follow his example. It wasn't long before he realised that he was completely on his own.

It was very hard going through the forest. He never found a trail and at times was left floundering through knee-deep snowdrifts blown to the edges of the few clearings he came across.

At one point, after pausing to catch his breath, he thought he heard a few shots far away to his left. He waited for about quarter of an hour and heard nothing more, so risked carrying on.

Being brought up a Catholic, Tomek believed in God but never really thought deeply about it. His faith had been tested in Vorkuta but it was the belief in good eventually triumphing over bad that had kept him going. At this time he was feeling very hungry, and years later he described the one occasion when Divine Providence seemed to have worked in his favour.

He almost tripped over the single-track railway line before he saw it. The pine trees had grown almost up to the stone ballast on either side of the line. There was a slight curve off to his left, then the line ran absolutely straight to the east, where it got lost in the haze of the far distance. It was the first completely unobstructed view he had seen in days.

He wasn't sure, but there might have been a distant smudge of smoke against the green of the trees and white of the snow to the east, but it looked as if it was pulling away from him. The ground was absolutely flat with not so much as a gentle rise or dip to be seen in either direction. He guessed that if a train came, he would have plenty of warning.

He set off east and caught the faint whiff of wood smoke. With memories of Irina still in his head, he almost ran along the line until the impact of second thoughts hit him. Being this close to a railway line might mean guards. He slowed, but couldn't hear any conversation, so he decided to risk it and carry on.

By now the smell had got stronger and he had almost trodden in a small pile of human excrement with torn sheets of the Communist newspaper *Pravda* which had outlived its usefulness as a source of news.

He almost stepped into the fire a few metres further on. It was still smouldering and a tin cup lay half buried in the ashes. Gingerly, using his cuff as an oven glove, Tomek eased it out. To his delight it was a quarter full of *Kasha*, the buckwheat cereal that was pretty much a staple across Russia.

There was no spoon, so Tomek used a Y-shaped pine twig as a rudimentary fork. It lined his stomach at least. Feeling his luck was in, Tomek poked around the ashes and found two half-baked potatoes, which he reburied further towards the still glowing embers. That was something to look forward to.

Next he gathered up a mugful of clean snow and melted it to drink. From the stickiness and caramel smell on one twig he guessed that whoever it was had a sugar ration. He tried licking the sugar off the twig but the ash stuck to it defeated him.

Finding some more dead pine branches, he threw them on the remains of the fire, and after a lot of blowing managed to coax some flame that seared its way up and along the pine needles, leaving the branches only blackened. It would have to do. He arranged a few springy branches as close to the fire as he dared, to act as a sort of bivouac bed, without the risk of barbecuing himself as he slept. He had decided to wait for a train to pass in the hopes of stowing away.

Fortunately, although the sky was dull, it did not look as if it was going to snow. The other thing he didn't want was a clear sky, which would mean a plummeting temperature after dark.

As so often happened, he had no memory at all of falling asleep, but he was awoken by a loud screaming whistle that repeated as it came closer. Flustered, he scrabbled around the ashes and found his two precious potatoes; they were still warm. Stuffing them into the *kufeika*, he grabbed the tin mug and drained the water inside, oblivious to any ashes that stuck to his teeth.

The train was long and slow, being pulled by two steam locomotives. Waiting hidden by the trees, he was surprised to see two deer jumping across the line picked out by the solitary headlight. They were the first he had seen since being sent to Siberia. So far all he had encountered were droppings.

Almost painfully, the train staggered past. Tomek couldn't see any passenger carriages or cattle trucks, just flatbeds with strange shapes under tarpaulins. He couldn't see the end of the train as it stretched back into the darkness. There were a few winking yellow lights on the corners of some of the waggons, but no sign of any guards.

He jogged alongside after about a dozen waggons had passed, until he saw, half illuminated by one of the dim lights, about three rungs at the corner of a waggon with a loose rope hanging down. He grabbed it and jumped up, banging his shins on the ironwork as he climbed on.

One end of the tarpaulin was flapping open, so Tomek squeezed in alongside a smooth shape he could not identify and tried to make himself comfortable. It was cold but out of the wind chill at least. Progress was painful and there was a sort of chemical smell a bit like the dope he had smelled on the glider wings back in Poland.

For the next three days, Tomek survived the banging, thumping, jerking and occasional stops, he guessed for water and coal. He waited until night to relieve himself, standing up and watering the

Where Are Your Papers?

waggon behind. His potatoes were long gone and snow provided him with the only chance of slaking his thirst.

He existed in a sort of fugue-like state, barely aware of his surroundings. He didn't even hear voices when the train stopped. His whole world was this waggon with its mysterious contents and the odd glimpse of the waggon behind.

That all changed around the early morning of what he guessed to be the fourth day. The train had stopped and showed no sign of moving. He crouched in the gloom of the tarpaulin, still unsure of what the train was carrying. He had not been able to crawl around, squashed into a tiny corner of the waggon, and had only been aware of a smooth wooden surface behind his back.

It was then he heard the unmistakeable sounds of waggons being uncoupled. With some difficulty, he squeezed round and poked just his head out. He was horrified at what he saw. The train had stopped at a large marshalling yard and ranged neatly beside it were rows of aircraft fuselages. A crane appeared in the distance with the tail and fuselage of a brown aeroplane[6] swaying below before it disappeared behind another train.

Tomek had to get away as quickly as possible. He now had little doubt that if he was caught he would be summarily shot as a spy or saboteur.

What Tomek did not know is that, with Stalin's agreement, Polish liaison officers had been sent out to many railheads and likely crossroads to give food vouchers and money to those released. This was not widely known and the Russians did little to publicise it. Sadly, for many who had come from gulags in the north, this information came too late to save them from death caused by hunger, malnutrition and disease. It is probable, but by no means certain, that Tomek had unwittingly bypassed opportunities for food and help in Kazan and Chelyabinsk in stowing away. He was lucky to survive as it is now reckoned that, of the 20,000 deported to the Vorkuta complex, something like just 120 actually survived long enough to reach safety in the West.[7]

It is tempting, with the wisdom of hindsight, to query why Tomek and others from Vorkuta, once they had learned of the amnesty, did not seek help. The truth is that Vorkuta was very much a rule unto itself, remote from many of the other gulags, critical to Stalin for the production of coal that was needed to fuel his war production machine and the preferred destination for those who were regarded as irredeemable enemies of the state. From the Russian perspective, at least they got some necessary work out of what was effectively a slave labour force before they succumbed.

The Nazis had a similar philosophy, working on the principle that a slave labour force could be pushed to impossibly high production figures without any welfare or pay considerations.

In those circumstances, Tomek had absolutely no reason to believe any rumours or feel confident that the NKVD intended to abide by any agreements. Among most Poles in the autumn and winter of 1941–42, distrust was endemic. In Tomek's case it was an incontrovertible article of faith.

This distrust of arrangements, particularly those that had a political, managerial or pragmatic dimension, would endure for the rest of his life.

Tomek was stuck under a tarpaulin, squeezed next to an aircraft fuselage; given its wooden construction, it was probably a LaGG-3,[8] at that point of the war the most modern fighter in the Russian Air Force.

He had little doubt that the Russians would not take kindly to any unauthorised person being so close to a critical element of the Soviet war machine. He was weak, dizzy, in pain and desperately hungry.

His salvation came when he noticed a work party dressed in rags being marshalled to uncouple waggons on an adjacent line. Someone blew a whistle and they stopped work. Most appeared to shamble off, probably for food, while about half a dozen went behind the waggons to relieve themselves. Nobody was paying much attention to anyone else and Tomek did not see any guards.

Taking a massive risk, he eased himself out from under the tarpaulin and dropped down between the waggons. He then straightened up and pretended to hitch up his trousers as if he had just relieved himself, scratched his crotch and tagged on to a group that was coalescing on the far side of the next line of rolling stock. A very young militiaman in a blue uniform was handing out vouchers.

The line of men waiting were grumbling in a variety of languages. No Polish, but Tomek heard Ukrainian and reckoned he could get away with that.

The militiaman gave Tomek a voucher without any comment or second glance. It was bleak and cold standing in a long line of what may have been as many as a hundred waiting outside a hut on the far side of the marshalling yard. He guessed it served as a canteen.

After about half an hour he was able to squeeze inside and sit on a long bench that ran down the length of a table that must have been all of 20m from end to end. There were about three or four similar benches and tables with a constant ebb and flow of workers as they arrived or left, pushing their way, without ceremony, into any vacated space, however small. The background babble was almost as deafening as it was unintelligible.

At the far end, an old man and a couple of young women were serving from cauldrons of soup and handing out small loaves of coarse black bread in return for the vouchers. Everyone got one ladle of soup and one loaf. Perched uncomfortably on the end of one bench, Tomek couldn't tell what flavour it was. It tasted like potato with some fishy undertone and a few bones, but he didn't care. It was warming.

From what he could understand, he guessed this was Omsk, a major stop on the Trans-Siberian Railway. The workers looked to have been recruited from nearby *kolkhoz* collectives. There was very little supervision.

After eating this uninspiring but very welcome meal, the men left the canteen in small groups who seemed to assemble themselves into different work parties. Hanging back at first, Tomek then wandered over to join an unsupervised party of about two dozen equally ragged and undernourished men, who were shunting empty flatbed waggons by hand and coupling them up to a locomotive that was getting up steam. It was pointing east.

Tomek simply helped, grunting as if he were putting his back into it and occasionally nodding if anyone made a comment. He was going to carry on until dark then see if he could hitch another lift going further east. He had no real plan.

He did not have to wait long. It was getting gloomy and had started to snow quite heavily. Ducking out of sight, he scrambled up and under a flatbed and tucked himself between the bogies. He would hang there until he was safely away from Omsk.

It was bitter hanging under the waggon, and once the train had started moving, Tomek realised that with the chill of the train's albeit modest speed, he was going to suffer from severe frostbite in a very short time. He was caught between freezing to death or possibly being shot if he emerged at the wrong place and the wrong time, even assuming the train would stop before he died or dropped onto the track when he lost all feeling in his hands and legs.

To his relief, the train did stop after about half an hour. It was already dark and it was still snowing, reducing visibility and giving him the chance of being unobserved.

The train was waiting parallel to what looked like a main line. Within possibly as little as ten minutes another train pulled alongside, slowing to barely a walking pace. This time it comprised covered waggons and, to his surprise, Tomek thought he could hear Polish voices singing.

With no second thought, he trotted alongside and pulled himself up into the first cattle truck with an open door. The sight and noise that greeted him was overwhelming in its surprise. About two dozen men in Polish uniforms were braced against the sides of the truck pulling at loaves of black bread while a small stove in the middle lifted the temperature, its open door revealing a slight red glow as a small shovelful of coal was added. A solitary lantern swung from the roof and one soldier in a corner was playing an accordion. The soldier with the shovel raised it as if he were about to defend himself.

The music stopped as Tomek pulled himself in and there were a few shouts of disapproval.

'It's all right I'm Polish!' This was greeted with silence before someone shouted, 'Are you sure? What were you doing in Sverdlovsk? It's dangerous!' Tomek was nonplussed; he had no idea where he had been or where he was going.

'I'd no idea. I've been lost for days. I'm really Polish. My dad was a colonel in Lwów! He was in the legions!' Tomek was afraid he would be thrown out, until the mood changed quite suddenly into roars of laughter and backslapping.

'Where are you from? What are you doing here?' A tin mug of sweet mock tea, made of unidentifiable leaves and sweetened with sugar, was pushed into his hand. 'Come on this'll warm you up. Which camp are you from?'

When he answered 'Vorkuta' there was absolute shocked silence, then someone made a low whistle, followed by quite a lot of murmuring. Finally one voice called from the back, 'You must be very special. We heard the Russians say there were no Poles left in Vorkuta.'

'They're lying bastards!' Nobody disagreed with him.

Over the next few hours Tomek related his whole story, with many interruptions. He was surprised to hear that this waggonload of PoWs had come from several camps around Kazan. They had been trying to catch up with General Anders at Buzuluk, but had missed him and were now heading east in the hopes of meeting up with some Polish liaison officers now rumoured to be in Novosibirsk.

The pressures of war changed any hope Stalin may have had when it came to controlling the number of liberated PoWs. Territorial losses to the German advance were so severe that Stalin needed every fighting man he could get. He knew that Polish loyalty to him was, at best, a compromise. At this stage of the war it was beginning to look as if the Germans could reach Moscow. Now it was critical for their strength to be diluted by a counterattack in the south.

The original agreement was for 30,000 Polish troops to serve with the Red Army. That was quickly superseded as such a small number of Polish troops would not be enough to swing the balance in Stalin's favour. Now it looked as if quarter of a million would be needed and that was a number Stalin could not hope to control operating within the Red Army. There were additional problems that had to be addressed in terms of training, rearming and deploying men who were not in good condition. Under a great deal of pressure from his own generals and strong urging from Churchill, via the Polish Government in Exile under General Sikorski in London, he had to face the reality of not only letting all Polish PoWs go but also allowing civilians to be released, who could be trained sufficiently to act in second-line and supporting roles.

Already questions were being asked about the lack of Polish Army officers and Stalin needed to distract from awkward questions that might expose the Katyn massacres. The released PoW floodgates had to be opened. America was not yet in the war (the Japanese attack on Pearl Harbor was still a few weeks away). Stalin needed to use the Poles but in the absence of any organised recruiting, training and deployment structure, thousands of released PoWs were wandering almost aimlessly across the Russian steppes and forests. Tomek had just encountered one such contingent.

Once he had settled in with his companions, the next three days passed in a blur for Tomek. The routine was the same. The train stopped twice for coal and water, the trucks emptied as the Poles stretched their legs, relieved themselves and queued for soup or potatoes and black bread, then it was off again. Tomek felt pretty conspicuous as only a handful were dressed like him. Most had remnants of Polish Army uniform and one pilot who had a flying jacket stuck out like a sore thumb.

The pilot (Tomek never got his name) was very much in a world of his own, taciturn and disinclined to talk with the former soldiers. He brightened up slightly when Tomek mentioned gliding and parachuting. His only advice was to make sure that Tomek passed the stringent physical exam, which was very demanding. Only then would he start on the ground-based courses, which had a very high pass mark. He was not very encouraging.

'Don't even put your name forward for pilot training until you know you are really fit. They will filter out anyone who doesn't meet the highest of standards.'

Tomek never saw the pilot again after they arrived at Novosibirsk.

Any thoughts of asking about flying training were promptly dashed when he finally met the liaison officer. All he was empowered to do was to hand out travel warrants and ration cards. The situation had changed yet again and he was not at all sure where they should be headed next. They were not to go any further east as the NKVD were arresting anyone they accused of running from the prospect of fighting the Germans.

The liaison officer said: 'We had one officer who was pretty generous with the vouchers, but he's disappeared. If that's not bad enough, nobody knows where Anders is headed, but it might be Kazakhstan. We've got nothing out of the NKVD.'

Tomek was getting demoralised. Russia was much bigger than he had ever imagined, he had no idea of what was happening in the war, or what had happened to his mother and sisters, and the final straw came when the Polish officer told him to act as if he had been in the army and not give any clue that he was born in Lwów. Above all, any mention of his father being a colonel or pallbearer at Piłsudski's funeral could mean instant rearrest.

Worse was to follow: 'Don't trust anyone! We've had Jews, Ukrainians, even Volga Germans claiming to be Polish. Some of them may be spies. They sent you to Vorkuta for a reason. You don't want to go back there. Get to Ufa, then go south for Tashkent.'

Suddenly Tomek wasn't sure if he should rejoin the group he had arrived with. He had been completely open with them and that could have been a mistake. His only compensation was the ration card and a spare discharge certificate in Russian. The name was illegible as the ink had smudged, but it could have read 'Hubert'.

The Polish officer smiled and shrugged. 'Sorry, it's the best I can do.'

10

Disappointment in Tashkent

Tomek needed to head south before the Siberian winter finished him off. He fell in with another group of Poles, this time a mix of a few much older First World War veterans and some Polish civilians who hoped to meet their families in Tashkent. This group were better organised, had been in Siberia before, understood how Russia worked and, having been interned in a *kolkhoz*, had been allowed to earn money and still held on to a few personal possessions.

Tomek felt awkward after a couple of days as they had pooled their resources, while he had nothing at all to add into their modest kitty. He was very alarmed when one of them suggested that the best they could hope for was better employment feeding the Polish Army by working the land.

As one man in his fifties said: 'None of us has any military experience and we won't be enlisted. The Russians told me that General Anders will be fighting as part of the Red Army defending Russian soil. If we're lucky we might get back to Poland when it's all over.'

Another younger and more studious man looked directly at Tomek, whose appearance was ragged and so much worse. He appraised Tomek as some sort of peasant, before chipping in with an almost reproachful look: 'I trained as a doctor and I expect that my services will be required, but that all depends on where they send us.'

Their condescending attitude made him feel very uncomfortable, as if he were some inferior being who was only looking for an easy way out with no fighting. Tomek vowed that he would move on from this group once they got to Karaganda in Kazakhstan, which he hoped would be a lot milder than the bitter weather he had experienced so far. Once again he felt like the outsider.

The journey was unremarkable and boring. This group found a carriage, almost certainly assisted by a substantial bribe. The atmosphere was so awkward that he sat in the corridor for more than fourteen hours before they had to change trains in the hopes of going west once they reached Barnaul. The weather wasn't any warmer, but at least he was inside a train.

The station at Barnaul was chaotic and he was soon separated from his companions, whom he thought wouldn't be too upset by finding him missing. He had no idea of where to go next, or indeed how to go about it. He met other Poles, mostly civilians, a few of whom were plainly very ill. To his surprise there were whole families who existed in a state of panic, as they spent almost every minute running from one end of the station to another with children in tow. The saddest aspect was that the children were hollow eyed, plainly tired and past crying. Years later, when seeing refugee children on TV during the Biafra war, Tomek had to get up and turn off the set as it brought back too many bad memories of that railway station where hope had evaporated.

Occasionally there would be a rumour that grew into an insistent murmur. Then, like flocks of starlings, the whole crowd would surge off towards the platforms only to be met by armed guards trying to push them back. This made matters worse as inevitably the guards were overwhelmed as the melee flooded onto the platform, causing those at the front to be nudged off onto the tracks. It was only the non-arrival of the long-hoped-for train that prevented carnage.

Tomek was deeply unhappy about pushing his way in, especially where pregnant women, babies and small children were in desperate need of an escape route from that hell of cacophony and frustrated hope.

What finally decided him on a course of action was seeing a ragged Polish military doctor and another woman delivering a baby on the station steps, while he and a few others held up coats and a blanket in the vain hope of providing some privacy. Judging by the squalling, the baby seemed healthy enough, though Tomek did not feel he should intrude to ask if it was a boy or girl. He was deeply upset, wondering what kind of a world awaited this poor little mite bundled up in a *kufeika* against the cold. He looked around to see if anyone was now shivering in the biting wind, but had no idea who the donor was. He was pretty sure there was no way that the baby would be spared by the inevitable lice that inhabited every item of clothing.

He joined a group of freezing, shuffling men, who looked as if they were headed west through the gathering gloom. There was not a single smile of acknowledgement as they moved like grey ghosts though the falling snow. Tomek stayed at the back, feeling he didn't belong. Nobody spoke, and the only sound was the occasional bout of paroxysmal coughing that stopped the victim in his tracks until it passed. Sometimes the victim was left far behind, lost in the swirling white to be joined by another and another as the coughing worked its way through the weakest.

Tomek was distressed and confused. This indifference bothered him. There was no camaraderie, not even a spark of compassion.

Finally he tapped the man in front of him on his shoulder.

'Where are we going?'

'Away from here; we heard an official say we could sign up for the army at Karaganda. The others reckon it's true. So we're better off taking our chances. I just want to get away from those crowds at the station. I've had three days with no food and nothing happening.'

Tomek had very little idea of where Karaganda was, or indeed how long it would take to get there. In in the absence of any further information, he pulled down his cap and braced himself against the snow, following the others.

After about an hour, he noticed a shadow playing about in front of him that seemed to be intensifying as a whining sound crept up behind him. This went on for about ten minutes before the first lorry in a very slow-moving convoy made painful progress overtaking him.

Having nothing to lose, he scrambled up and over the tailgate to find himself sitting behind a pile of frozen snow-covered coal. At least he was out of the wind. As far as he could tell, nobody else felt inclined to join him. It was only marginally better than trudging onwards with the others.

It didn't last long as the wind picked up and the snow swirled round as the lorry sped up running downhill before slithering to a barely controlled stop.

It was with a mixture of disappointment at the brevity of the journey and relief to get out of the cold that he jumped down once the lorry had stopped. They were in a marshalling yard among large bunkers of coal.

He was wondering what to do next when a Russian voice told him to come in out of the cold. He followed it to a small office building, where about a dozen men and women were warming themselves around a stove. They looked not at all hostile or surprised, but mildly curious.

It did not take long for Tomek to learn that the trains were avoiding the main station as the situation was chaotic. The railway workers knew all about the amnesty for Polish PoWs and had been told to assist, but given no orders as to how. Whatever system was supposed to be in place was plainly not working at all.

Some trains had extra cattle waggons for the Poles, others didn't. Some of the Poles had been given warrants to wherever they asked to go in the USSR, while others, like Tomek, had nothing of the sort. They had all heard stories of the NKVD helping the exodus, only to be contradicted by others who forced the Poles into waggons, then left them for days in a siding. Little or nothing had been said officially as far as they knew.

They had all heard rumours and the best guess that any of them had was for Tomek to leave on a train that was supposed to be headed for Akmolinsk, then transfer to another headed south for Karaganda. There were no passenger carriages but there should be cattle waggons with stoves inside or, failing that, one of the workers was scheduled to be a guard and would sort something out.

They were as good as their word. There were cattle waggons and they were not full.

This time Tomek found himself with a mixed party of Jews and Ukrainians, who accepted him without much comment. He couldn't understand why they were there, but a Jewish lawyer who had worked in Lwów explained that they were taking advantage of the amnesty by saying they had signed up for the Polish Army.

Tomek asked if they were serious and the lawyer explained gravely that the only thing that made any sense was for the Polish Army to be assembled in Palestine and mount an attack from the south against the Germans. He seemed to be convinced this would happen, although this was the first Tomek had heard of such a plan.

The lawyer made one comment that gave Tomek a moment to pause, then nod in agreement. 'There's no way that a Polish army of any size could be controlled by the Russians. It makes much more sense for them to open up another front and take the pressure off Stalin. The British are tied up in North Africa, they could have lost Iraq, which would have been a catastrophe. No, a Polish assault from the south preventing the Germans getting oil is the only military option.'

Years later Tomek often wondered if the 'lawyer' was really a British spy.

The situation, which was almost always chaotic, was not helped by the NKVD issuing a *kompostirovka*, an endorsement, that only allowed the released Poles to go on the first leg of this journey. Some gulag and *kolkhoz* commandants ignored this and wrote out warrants taking them to as a far as the Chinese border! This was probably motivated more from a desire to get the troublesome Poles as far away as possible than any overt sense of philanthropy.

This only added to the confusion as nobody was sure what was legitimate and what wasn't. To this must be added some very convincing forgeries, which only helped to muddy the waters further.

Anders and what few staff he had tried to speed up the logistics of managing large numbers of former PoWs, deported families and the few officials who had escaped Poland with their lives, by getting as many designated 'Persons of Trust' (Mężowie Zaufania)[1] out to as many railheads and major junctions as possible to act as enablers, giving money, food and directions to where the PoWs could enlist in the army.

In common with many, Tomek was unaware of these arrangements, and even if he had found himself at the right place at the right time, given the sheer numbers of displaced persons milling around, it was by no means easy to connect with them.

It was about to get so much worse. Tomek could not possibly have known that the Russians, fearing a fifth column among the Volga Germans, had begun the summary deportation of tens of thousands to camps around Karaganda. This flow of displaced families, often at a moment's notice, was only adding to the confusion. There are accounts of Polish refugees coming across what had been German-speaking villages where a tractor had been left running and food was still warm on the table.

Unsurprisingly, some of the menfolk tried to join in with German-speaking Poles going in the opposite direction and some Poles with German-sounding names could find themselves rounded up once more by the NKVD. Karaganda was the nexus of confusion.

Few in the West have any understanding of the sheer brutality and speed of ethnic cleansing and forced deportation. Stalin had what would normally have been a well-oiled machine when it came to the violation of human rights. The exigencies and rolling tide of war put that machine under strain, in much the same way that Putin's forces have found with the fighting and confusion around Kherson in Ukraine. This is especially true of the situation following the mining and destruction of the Kakhovka Dam on the Dnieper River on 6 June 2023. Decisions made under the stress of war, when winning at all costs becomes the prime consideration, create more problems than they solve.

Tomek was completely unaware that Japan had just changed the balance of power by attacking Pearl Harbor. Now the USA was in the war and the compromises about to be made would affect his future in ways he could not possibly imagine.

Karaganda in Kazakhstan may well have been Tomek's introduction to another culture where Islam was still holding out against Russian cultural domination, but it was still hellishly cold in the winter of 1941–42. Russia and its weather was still calling the shots.

He needed to find Polish recruitment officers who, he was assured, were actively signing up anyone who wanted to join General Anders' fledgling army and possibly get away from Russia. What he could not possibly have known is that the numbers already signed up had far exceeded the numbers originally envisioned.

Many of the recruiting officers were working in the dark, making decisions on eligibility without any hard and fast rules or templates to follow. This resulted in raised eyebrows from one officer, who said he could not deal with Tomek and he would have to carry on under his own steam. Tomek had seen prejudice against Jews before in pre-war Poland and had wondered how some like the Jewish lawyer had fared. Even so, it was quite obvious that many Ukrainian Jews were being signed up, especially if they had much-needed skills such as being trained as a doctor.

He had also seen others in old Polish uniforms that could not have possibly been in the army of 1939 as some had barely a few words of anything resembling Polish! This made the officer's rather dismissive tone all the more surprising. Tomek made matters worse by referring to his father's service record, raising his voice and giving every impression he would hit the recruiting officer when someone grabbed him from behind, pulled him away and told him, 'Don't be a fool! That officer's scared out of his wits. He knows who you are, your accent alone is enough, but any mention of Lwów is poison. Keep your mouth shut. The NKVD has eyes and ears everywhere. As far as they're concerned, Lwów was never Polish. Your father being the senior colonel only makes matters worse.'

Tomek had remembered earlier advice about Lwów but had ignored it. He thanked the man who pulled him away. It turned out he was from the same neighbourhood, knew of Tomek's father by reputation and had been far wiser in what he said in public. It was a lesson that Tomek was to learn the hard way.

Disappointment in Tashkent

The key to the many attempts to silence Tomek on the subject of Lwów lay in the complex whirlpool of competing nationalist interests after the fall of both the Russian and Austro-Hungarian Empires in 1918–19. Lwów (known as Lemberg to the Austrians) was the capital for the Austro-Hungarian province of Galicia. Poles made up the majority in the cities, while Ukrainians and Jews were the majority in the countryside. This boiled over into a local conflict that began in December 1918 when Polish children and teenagers known as the Orliki (Eaglets) withstood a siege, before victorious Polish forces forced out Ukrainian and Jewish interests. Inevitably scores were settled, businesses taken over and synagogues and Orthodox churches closed once the resident Poles became the de facto governors of the whole province.

An attempted invasion of Lwów by the Red Army in 1920 resulted in an alliance with Ukrainian forces that ultimately repulsed the Bolsheviks. Inevitably this increased the sense of Polish triumphalism and military overconfidence that ultimately would spell disaster in 1939.

As a result, Colonel Kazimierz Hubert (Tomek's father) became the effective arm of the Piłsudski autocracy in Galicia following the eventual defeat of Bolshevik forces in 1921. That all ended for good with a functioning parliamentary democracy when Marshal Piłsudski died in 1935.

Tomek's whole upbringing was rooted in the story of how Polish nationalism triumphed at the expense of both social and political inclusion. Elsewhere in Poland, a nascent political pragmatism was taking over even before Piłsudski's death and Tomek had not yet woken up to the reality of being almost a decade out of step with the majority of Poles he had encountered.

Even so, despite attempts at integration, like Northern Ireland, memories were long and old wounds still festered. Russia under Stalin would play up any hint of ethnic divisions in the hopes of weakening Polish resolve. Although he was barely 20, Tomek's attitudes had not moved with the times. He was very lucky not to have been picked up by the NKVD. As he said many years later, that Polish recruiting officer in Karaganda must have been wetting himself as the town was crawling with their agents and informers.

Tomek had begun to withdraw into himself. The effects of confinement, torture and abuse in Vorkuta had been lying in the wings waiting to pounce. Now, although he was far from safe, he felt he had the opportunity of being borne along on the tide of assembly and recruitment that would end in the relative security of being part of General Anders' army. There was one proviso: he had to abandon the importance of his previous history, upbringing and belief in his home town being the bastion of *Polishness* against hordes from the East.

Basically he had to swallow his pride and keep his mouth shut. That is when the resentment began, which would endure for the rest of his life. As he often said, he felt a nagging sense of betrayal that started to take root during this last chapter in his sojourn across Stalin's Soviet Empire.

Having little real idea of the geography or distances involved, he decided to tag along in the general direction of Kazalinsk and maybe stow away across the Aral Sea. Several ex-PoWs were convinced that once they got to the shores of that inland sea they would be taken care of by being steamed across and up the Amu Darya River to Kiva or even Bukhara, where some Polish Army camps were being set up.

Tomek was doubtful as to whether this was indeed the case, but guessed that going with the crowd would at least give safety in numbers and mean it would be less likely he would be picked up by the NKVD.

The first hitch in the arrangements came with the realisation that there was no train there and they would be reliant on lorries. Nobody knew where to find them, so they split up into disconsolate parties intending to forage along the way. Tomek was at the back of about a dozen all wearing old Polish Army uniforms. Nobody queried if he belonged there and he resisted the temptation to strike up any conversation.

The weather was cold and spiteful with some snow lying across the steppe, but not enough to cause many problems. Progress was slow. The few villages they came to were fearful and most either barred their doors or even fled, leaving the Poles effectively to loot food and camp out where they could. Tomek was distressed as he recognised that most of these villagers were barely living a sustainable existence and what the Poles took to eat could well have led to starvation as the winter advanced.

In one abandoned village some of the Poles found a stray dog, which they killed and butchered, cooking its tough, scraggy flesh over an open fire. The village looked as if it had been abandoned for some weeks and there was speculation that this was one of several where all the inhabitants had been deported.

Tomek felt even more isolated noticing that the Poles' humanity broke down as hunger, cold and the increasing threat of disease began to take its toll. The first casualties started swaying dizzily and mumbling to themselves, then they collapsed. Someone negotiated for a donkey cart, or *arba*, as they were known locally, but soon the number of sick men exceeded its capacity.

They left the *arba* and three very ill men at one *kolkhoz*. The local commissar looked very worried and announced that the best he could do was allow them to be left in a barn. He promised that soup would be left at the doorway for them to help themselves until they got better, but he wasn't prepared to let disease rampage though his little community.

It was soon obvious that the commissar had good reason to be afraid. Within a few kilometres along what passed for a road, they found a number of small mounds covered in grass and snow. Tomek had the sinking feeling they were graves, but nobody really wanted to know. That all changed when they saw chewed remains in ragged Polish uniforms. Tomek's first thought was that these were men executed by the NKVD. That was dismissed as unlikely as they were not mass graves. From the state of what was left of the corpses, he was told that they had died at different times, probably from disease. Guessing that either wolves or dogs were responsible for digging up the bodies, it did not take much imagination to realise that there would be many other PoWs who were not going to be joining any army.

Every evening Tomek redoubled his efforts to kill off all the lice in his clothing by stripping off and searing them over whichever fire had been lit. Others, equally scared by the threat of typhus, soon imitated him. It was a bitter choice between freezing naked or dying of fever.

Tomek soon drifted back into his earlier fugue state. He had no idea how long he was on the road, he lost count of the places they stopped, and he was past caring if they stole food from unguarded stores or terrorised villagers. They had merged with other groups who had stalled in their progress either through weakness or disease. Everyone was demoralised. All talking had stopped. Some exhausted Poles just sat down in the snow and refused to go on. Occasionally their comrades urged them to get up and stagger on, but most of the time they were left beside what was little better than a rough stony track that meandered aimlessly across the dreary landscape.

One incident stuck in Tomek's mind. They found the frozen bodies of a mother and two children in an irrigation ditch. A toddler was just sitting next to the body of her mother. Surprisingly she didn't look starved. He guessed that the rest of the family had favoured this little tot with food they could ill afford.

One of the Polish NCOs picked her up and wrapped her inside his greatcoat. There was nothing they could do about the bodies. There was a small abandoned farm nearby that offered little shelter and no food. Now they had a problem.

The best thing they could do was to struggle on and hope to find someone, anyone, who could take care of the child. One of the ex-PoWs suggested that the only thing left was prayers. He then intoned at great length the whole litany of the saints and all the others answered with 'pray for her' instead of the usual 'pray for us'.

This form of spiritual exercise re-energised the party and they picked up the pace. The little girl was barely able to speak and probably was not yet 3. Everyone took it in turns to cuddle and carry their latest recruit; in some way she had given them all purpose.

That's when they came across a roadblock. No, they couldn't go any further as the town of Kazalinsk was closed to everyone without special permits. There were no ferries across the Aral Sea, they must go north to Totskoye as General Anders had moved there from Buzuluk, away from the German advance.

The NKVD officer's mood changed when he saw the child. Tomek couldn't believe his eyes. The man was crying. He waved the Poles

Disappointment in Tashkent

on, saying he would take personal charge of the child. His wife had lost their own daughter to German bombing. That was the first and only time Tomek witnessed real humanity from anyone in the NKVD.

The route north was leading back into forests. Tomek had a brief glimpse of the Aral looking grey in the far distance. It did not much look the way to salvation.

A few Poles did indeed cross the Aral Sea in 1942. As a result of disastrous irrigation projects begun in the 1960s to increase cotton yields, the sea began to dry up as the two major rivers feeding it, the Amu Darya and Syr Darya, were dammed. Now it is largely a salt desert[2] and any crossing would be an unpleasant trek rather than a ferry ride. This has been described as one of the biggest single environmental disasters on the planet, testament to the failures of communist central planning and an unwillingness by those in charge to entertain dissenting views – a lesson that Putin today is reluctant to learn.

Tomek's party soon encountered a railway siding with empty cattle trucks that would soon be going north. He felt very uncomfortable about this, worrying that in all probability their likely fate was to be given a rifle and sent to the front line. The last thing he wanted was to be fighting the Germans with the NKVD at his back to shoot him should he show any reluctance.

Progress was surprisingly rapid until they stopped alongside another train going in the opposite direction filled with Polish troops and some senior officers. After a brief explanation that they were all going to Tashkent, Tomek's group was ordered out to join the rail trip south. His initial frustration was tempered by a feeling of relief and the thought that at last they had come across a well-organised group who knew what they were doing.

It wasn't quite that straightforward. The staff officers and their entourage were in better shape, had better uniforms and had been deloused. They were not in any hurry to share a carriage in close proximity to Tomek's group and risk being reinfested. They didn't have any means of treating severe infestations until they got to Tashkent, and that was over a week away.

So Tomek spent more than two weeks in a closed cattle truck with food left outside at interminable stops en route when they could stretch their legs. They hardly saw any senior officers, who were keeping their distance, avoiding all contact. Christmas passed without anyone doing anything other than wish each other a better year.

There was a rumour that all senior officers had been put on a faster train, together with a chaplain who had expressed a wish to say Mass for them but had been spirited away a few days before that could happen. Disillusion had set in. The only plus points were that the weather was getting noticeably warmer and dried fruit was now appearing in their diet, washed down with sweet mint tea.

Having heard stories about the old silk route, Tashkent was a major disappointment. The part of town Tomek saw was just like any other dreary grey Soviet estate of unremarkable apartment blocks. He had barely registered them before he was assigned to the back of an open lorry and driven out of town along a bumpy dusty road for about an hour before being dumped in front of a massive tented camp.

He joined a long line of dirty unkempt men to be interviewed and photographed, then given a ration book. Tomek thought at last he could be honest about who he was and where he came from. The corporal who was noting down his details looked up sharply.

'If your identity can be verified, you might be assigned to the 6th Infantry Division, which will be made up from others like you. They want to be called the Children of Lwów but that's not going to happen. The Russians won't like it.'

When Tomek objected, saying he wanted to fly, the corporal just shrugged, saying, 'That's not up to me.'

Now Tomek realised that his battles were far from over. His misgivings were not helped when he was told he would be deloused and given a British Army uniform. There was one problem. Tomek had not been signed up to anything yet.

Tomek's father, Colonel Kazimierz Hubert.

Tomek's mother, Stefania Staufer.

First Communion, Tomek and Basia.

Stefania, Tomasz, Madzia, Baska, Aunt Jozefa, Uncle Ludwik and Fr Jan Dudziak in 1934.

```
M-58

Hubert Kazimierz Tomasz
s. Kazimierza, ur. 1921
areszt. 27.10.1939 przez UNKWD OL,
więz. Lwów, Czernihów, art. 54-2-11, wyrok
OSO 01.03.1941 – 5 l. ITŁ, Workutłag
do 11.09.1941, skier. do AP
M-248; L-758
```

Arrest record, published in 1987.

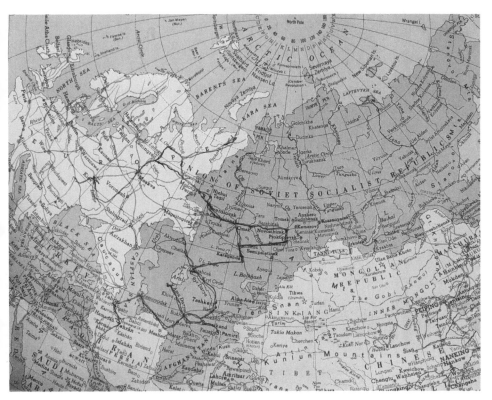

Tomek's route.

Tomek's Aunt Maria, whose reputation corroborated Tomek's claim to be Polish.

Arrival in Tashkent.

Ground school. Tomek is third from left, front row.

First solo.

Preparing to fly a Miles Master 2.

A logbook entry for the Master 2.

Posing with (left) and training on (above) a Master 2.

Angela.

Tomek and Angela's wedding.

Sint-Denijs-Westrem, 1 January 1945, when Tomek downed one Fw 190 and damaged another. (Polish Institute & Sikorski Museum)

Tomek's first logbook entry with 317 Squadron.

No. 317 Squadron, early 1945. Tomek is on the left.

Fw 190 wreck.

Armourers on 317 Squadron.

Official operations record, February 1945.

Tomek's entry into Angela's autograph book.

Ruined Antwerp.

The effects of war (possibly Antwerp or Brussels).

Cycling pose, 1945.

Squadron Mass.

An adopted dog,
Germany, spring 1945.

The war is over. Cloppenburg, June 1945.

The crashed Auster: Tomek didn't know where the brakes were!

Idleness with nothing to do, summer 1945.

Tomek, more summer idleness, Germany, 1945.

Tomek's 317 Squadron activity record.

Discharge record.

Angela and Tomek Hubert, c.1950.

131 Wing Memorial, Ghent.

11

Frustration and Fever

By the time Tomek arrived in Tashkent, the situation was already getting out of hand with new uniforms and weapons being held up by the Russians and many more Poles wanting to sign up than anyone had envisaged. The original PoW cohort was being swamped by civilians, many of them women and children desperate to get out of Russia before Stalin or the NKVD changed their minds.

There had been a tradition of women working in a supporting role in the Polish Army, but many of the applicants were older or plainly had other demands from small children. General Anders and his staff were sympathetic, having few qualms about enlisting those women who had previous military or nursing experience. The real problem came down to resources. Supplies coming from Britain on the Murmansk convoys had a long overland route to reach Tashkent, corruption was rife and, understandably, many Russian commanders were desperate for resources to hold back German advances.

President Roosevelt had little understanding of how bad the situation really was on the Eastern Front. This was not helped by him sending relatively inexperienced 'ambassadors at large' such as Averell Harriman to talk to Stalin, who was a past master at misdirection. In order to keep the Americans on side, he organised lavish receptions in the Kremlin, despite food riots in Moscow. His strategy was to appear friendly, get his visitors drunk and keep them away from any controversies or the front line.

In this he would appear to have been successful, as on one occasion Harriman displayed displeasure when he learned that a percentage of US and British aid was destined for Anders and the Polish Army. Back at home the president had problems of his own getting US production onto a war footing and bringing US weaponry and training up to a similar level as that of the British, who had sharpened their skills and technology on the grinding wheel of more than two years of war.

General Sikorski in London understood that he was walking a tightrope when it came to having overall control of all Polish forces as long as Anders and his army were confined in the USSR. Already promised finance was being held up and other promises remained unfulfilled. He had met Anders and Stalin in Moscow shortly before America's entry into the war and was already contemplating options.

This was made easier once the USA was fully committed to the war effort as an ally and had decided that supplying the Polish Army through Iran and up into Kazakhstan and Uzbekistan was an easier option. From that point onwards the notion of moving the entire army south made a lot more sense and ultimately encouraged the eventual evacuation to Iran.

There was one issue Stalin would not budge on, namely the arming and inclusion of ethnic Germans who had served in the Polish Army before the war. Many were hostile to the Nazis, but that was not an argument that Anders (himself of German extraction) could win. Tomek was not to know this but Hubert was a name with origins in Austria and southern Germany. That alone would be enough to cause a second glance, adding to the initial sense of alienation he already felt.

Stalin, though, was to cause even more strain as he had already wished on Anders a number of potential moles who believed in communism or had given up resisting under torture in the gulags. The lack of more than 20,000 officers whom Stalin had suggested 'escaped to Manchuria' when he already knew they lay in mass graves in the Katyn Forest pushed Anders into a corner when it came to capable staff officers. It was not only Tomek who had to be careful; not everyone wanted the Polish forces in Russia to have a free hand, and that would impact how quickly Tomek could get away from any threat of being a future guest of the NKVD.

Frustration and Fever

Tomek was about to be sorely disappointed. He was ushered behind a row of canvas screens and told to strip off. He expected his clothes to be burned and that he would then be issued a new uniform. Instead his head was shaved once more, along with any body hair. Fortunately for him, having no beard or chest hair, that just involved shaving his legs and pubic area, then being given an evil black chemical-smelling ointment that was lathered on and usually left for about twenty minutes.

His clothes were taken off and fumigated, then returned to him smelling of chemicals. He was about to argue when the orderly, a tired-looking man who looked as if he had seen it all before, simply shook his head: 'There are no more uniforms, or boots. Keep that smelly stuff on, it'll kill any more lice that survived the fumigation.'[1]

Tomek had no idea what to do next, but once dressed joined a queue for some food, which turned out to be of only marginally better quality than he had suffered in the Vorkuta gulag.

He had barely finished when he was told to report for a roll call. Once his name was read out he joined a queue for a line of lorries and was eventually loaded onto the back of one along with eleven others and driven off with no clue as to where he was going. His companions were equally mystified. Tomek's initial puzzlement morphed into a sense of panic when he learned that none of them had been signed up for military service. One man suggested they were being taken north to work in the cotton fields for the Russians. At that point Tomek felt like jumping off. This was the ultimate betrayal. All hope died within him.

It took six hours before they were dropped off at Samarkand with no instructions what to do next. The town was disappointing. Any thoughts of sightseeing in a place that romantics over the generations had described as 'the golden road to Samarkand' could not have been further from any of their minds. The Soviets had barred access to the mosques and everywhere had an atmosphere of deliberate neglect.

It wasn't snowy, but it was windy and cold. They were disorientated, hungry and very apprehensive. They saw a few men in traditional robes and veiled women who scurried away. The few notices upon the walls were not written in Russian, but looked, to Tomek's eyes, Arabic. There was one torn poster with the heads of Stalin and Lenin in profile and the Russian wording had something else painted over it.

The place didn't feel Russian, but didn't feel hostile either, just indifferent. After wandering around looking for something to eat, they came across a large square that must have been a marketplace before communist ideology had shut down such capitalist enterprise.

In one corner an old man had a stall with a brazier and what looked like a large coffee pot. The aroma was too overwhelming. Tomek had been given a few roubles along with a single brown document stamped at the camp, so he attempted to negotiate in Russian. The old man smiled, shook his head and indicated for the Poles to sit down on the stony ground. He then proceeded to pour out tiny cups of very strong coffee.

As if by magic an old woman appeared bearing a tray of very sweet pastries, which she handed round. Again beyond the sole Russian word '*Nyet!*' she refused the offered money. Tomek was completely mystified. He later learned that money changing hands would be interpreted as capitalist enterprise and lead to arrest.

After about an hour a young Polish soldier, with the inevitable NKVD officer, found them. It was obvious that the Pole was under some severe scrutiny.

'I can't say too much, you're all going to be found work to do while headquarters decides on your cases. It's nothing to do with us, the Russians are being very specific about who we accept.'

The shrug of his shoulders spoke volumes. Obviously he was hoping that Tomek's group wouldn't cause trouble.

The tactic was clever. By isolating this group and probably many others like it, the Russians were hoping to keep numbers under control before General Anders and his staff had set up an effective system of dealing with everyone who turned up in Tashkent. He might have been assembling an army and Stalin could have done with the military help, but this far from Moscow, and the NKVD was going to play things their way for fear of losing control.

That night they slept in an abandoned mosque. It was dusty with holes in the roof and stank of urine.

Halfway through the next day, another party of Poles were dumped on them, only this time there was a Russian officer with them who spoke reasonable Polish. He wasn't NKVD. His manner wasn't particularly hostile, more embarrassed than anything. He had a clipboard with several sheets of paper.

He read out names and assignments. Most were scheduled to work in nearby fields without any explanation as to what was being grown or how they would go about it.

To Tomek's surprise and initial pleasure, he was taken out of town to a large compound and introduced to a Russian-speaking Tajik tribesman, who ran a string of camels ferrying tobacco, salt and tea between Dushanbe and beyond Bukhara. Each return trip lasted from about ten days to a month depending on the load and distances involved. That's when Tomek became very anxious. There was no mention of joining the army.

It didn't take him long to become totally disillusioned with camels. These were the two-humped Bactrian variety and they had a mind of their own: happy to wander off unless they were tethered, bad tempered, and they would spit at anyone in range and bite or kick out when they were being loaded or harnessed.

Tomek wasn't allowed to ride on them at first as their entire capacity was taken up with large sacks that were hung over them like panniers. When Tomek asked what they were carrying, the camel master just smiled knowingly and laid one finger alongside his nose, which was understood, or so Tomek thought, to mean: 'Don't ask questions.'

Their first destination was not too far from Dushanbe. Having been told that Afghanistan and British India lay beyond the distant Pamir Mountains, Tomek thought that slipping away and walking there was an option. That idea soon faded as day after day they drew nearer and it became colder. These mountains in their icy white glory were higher than anything Tomek had imagined before. They were also much further away than at first appeared.

Occasionally they were blocked out by cloud and the camel master told him about the one time he approached the foothills. It took over a week, and three of his men got caught in an avalanche that swept down from high up and carried them away to certain death. Over camp fires of wood or camel dung, depending on what was available, he heard stories of parties of Russian mountaineers going off to plant flags on the highest peaks never to return.

Tomek asked about passes across to Afghanistan then India and the camel master roared with laughter.

'Forget it my friend, whichever way you go there are more mountain ranges you cannot see. All the passes are so high you cannot breathe and beyond that are tribesmen who hate strangers. If you think it was difficult coming from Siberia, this would be many times worse.'

Tomek would have to think again.

Another proposed trip would have taken them very close to the border with Persia (modern-day Iran). Noticing Tomek's sudden interest in their route, the camel master was quick to quell any question from Tomek before he could ask it. As he explained at great length, the border used to be wide open, but the few roads through the mountains were now patrolled by Russians who didn't let anyone out or in. There were rumours of mines on other tracks that led up to the higher passes. He reckoned that going that way, without permission, was a passport to Paradise or Siberia if you survived. In any event, their way was barred beyond the curiously named town of Mary surrounded by the Karakum Desert. There was a rumour that all camel trains headed that way were being stopped by the NKVD and searched.

Tomek was once again deeply depressed, disillusioned and beset by fleas, which he was sure had hopped from the camels. It was just another misery piled upon all the others he had endured. Some days he scratched himself raw, but the camel master just laughed, saying that he would get used to it.

There were days when nothing happened. The camels were hobbled with one leg bent double under them so they wouldn't wander off while waiting by a stream or pond for a rendezvous with tribesmen bringing sacks of dried poppy heads on their donkey-powered *arbas* or strange bundles that Tomek was told he must not open. Plainly there was a black market going on that the Russians knew nothing about, or were bribed to look the other way. Some of the tribesmen looked Asiatic, as if they had come from Mongolia. They would unpack the camels without a word then disappear as silently as they came.

Once Tomek caught sight of a gold coin, which the camel master covered up very quickly. He realised that something highly illegal was going on and years later wondered if it was part of the drugs trade. He knew about opium, but had no idea how it was harvested or transported. The camel master tried to convince him that they only dealt in poppy seeds for baking in return for tobacco or cotton, but Tomek knew better than to ask any searching questions.

It was the smell of baking that lured Tomek on one trip north and west almost to the southern end of the Aral Sea. The source turned out to be a clay oven outside a substantial wooden hut at the edge of a cultivated field where it ran up against a forest. He was greeted by a Pole from his home city of Lwów. It was bizarre. Like him, this Pole had been shunted around with no end in view. He had noticed that a lot of the area had been given over to wheat, but the Russians had not thought it a worthwhile candidate for collectivisation, reckoning it was simply subsistence farming.

The Pole, tired of the local flatbreads, had somehow managed to encourage a yeast culture and was baking bread, which was a total novelty for the locals. He could not supply them fast enough and said he had the beginnings of a lucrative business. Having enjoyed, for the first time in two years, the sheer glory of freshly baked bread, Tomek wondered how long it would be before word got back to the Russians and they shut down this small green shoot of capitalism.

There was one last incident before Tomek left the camels for good. The camel master, having studiously avoided every settlement of any size, insisted he go on alone to do some negotiations and told Tomek he would pick him up the next day. It was cold but not particularly frosty. He had been left a small tent and some water with a compressed block of Russian tea, but no food beyond some almost inedible dried meat that defied Tomek's teeth.

As he had a few roubles, Tomek went in search of a possible trade for something a little more palatable and came upon a fenced compound with what looked like a reasonably sized peasant's hut at one end. A sizeable almost black dog was sniffing around the door. It didn't look as if it had rabies. (He had been vaccinated twice in Poland after encounters with rabid dogs, enduring twenty-one injections in the abdomen each time, despite assuring the doctor he had not been bitten.)

Tomek approached the dog with an open hand but the animal backed away with teeth bared. It shot off out of the compound as a large man opened the door and shouted 'Wolf!' in Russian, then reappeared with an ancient rifle and loosed off two rounds in the direction of the wolf as it rounded a corner and disappeared. That caused a great deal of amusement, back-slapping and soup with black bread followed by *kvass*, a fermented drink that made Tomek quite ill.

It was on his way back through Bukhara that the Polish Army caught up with him. Tomek had been accepted and was to report to a camp where he would be deloused (again!) and issued with a uniform and papers. Having said goodbye to the camel master, he was taken off in the back of a lorry, which stopped and picked up some other Poles and deposited them after a gruelling and bumpy few hours at the Yangi-Yul camp, not far from Tashkent where General Anders would be headquartered.

It had started to snow and Tomek felt miserable. He was assigned to a tent with five others who had been on the same lorry. However, for the first time since he was deported, Tomek felt he was in a system that was on his side.

General Władysław Anders had decided that Tashkent was the safest place to base his headquarters. It wasn't free from the interference of the NKVD but he knew that anything untoward that upset them would take two days to get to the Kremlin, be decided upon, then instructions sent back. That would give him sufficient time to put things right on his own terms.

As noted before, he had justified suspicions of some of the staff officers who had been wished upon him by the Russians, especially in the absence of those who had been massacred at Katyn – a fate he knew nothing about until 1944. It was a case of keeping his potential enemies where he could keep an eye on them. He was deeply suspicious of Colonel Berlinger,[2] whom he would later court martial in absentia. It is possible, but not proven, that Berlinger and others who had been influenced by Stalin were deliberately frustrating efforts at recruiting those from areas such as Lwów, which Stalin was determined would be purged of all Polish influence.

It is also significant that the Russians, after an initial reluctance, let thousands of civilian refugees and orphaned children through, in order to tie up Polish military resources in dealing with a humanitarian disaster.

At the time of writing, following the breach of the Kakhovka dam,[3] it seems evident that Putin has held his own resources back from attempting any rescues of the many flooded towns, relying instead on Ukrainian forces and NGOs to frustrate the long-awaited Ukraine counteroffensive. This would appear to be another well-worn tactic from the Russian playbook.

Tomek, once again deloused, was finally wearing a new uniform. He hoped that his old *kufeika* would be burned and not offered to some freezing refugee. The uniform might have been free from lice, but it wasn't as warm.

He made enquiries about being sent for pilot training but was told that wouldn't happen yet. First he needed to be screened and tested. There was no way he could prove his academic qualifications and some sort of aptitude exam would need to be arranged, which was well beyond any of the facilities to be found in the camp.

All he could be told was that he was officially in the arm, and once they decided what he was best suited for then basic training would begin. In the meantime they needed him and many others to forage for food, as supplies were consistently being held up by the Russians.

Once again, Tomek was in an effective limbo.

On one foraging expedition he and a few mates came across what looked like an abandoned compound with tobacco leaves drying inside. He wasn't much of a smoker, but had discovered like many who took up the habit that it helped calm the pangs of hunger. What is more, it had great value in trading for food and simple indulgences such as soap or even cologne, which was highly prized as masking the pervasive smell of body odour and sweat.

Having knocked on the door and received no answer, they went to help themselves. Catching sight of something in the shadow of the outer wall, Tomek realised that the Muslim owner was at prayer on his mat. Shamefacedly they replaced the tobacco leaves and left as silently as they could.

That was the last thing Tomek would remember for several days as he woke feeling feverish. He was taken to the medical officer's tent, where he collapsed completely and lost consciousness. He did not know it but he had just come down with typhus fever.

In 1942 there were no antibiotics available and the unhygienic conditions of the gulags and camps were classic breeding grounds for the lice and flea-borne varieties of the disease. To quote from the Virginia Department of Health:

> Epidemic typhus fever occurs most commonly among people living in overcrowded unhygienic conditions, such as refugee camps or prisons. The disease also occurs in people living in the cool mountainous regions of Asia, Africa and Central and South America.
>
> Common symptoms include high fever, headache, chills, tiredness and muscle aches. About half of people who are infected develop a flat red rash that begins on the back, chest and stomach and then spreads to the rest of the body except for the face, palms and soles. Other symptoms may include vomiting, eye sensitivity to light, and confusion. In severe cases, complications of illness may include kidney failure and brain inflammation (encephalitis).[4]

Tomek was delirious for almost five days, with his fever breaking at a high point of 42°C. Years later, in 1969, following a severe accident, a scan revealed old scar tissue across part of his brain. The neurologist at the time suggested that it was consistent with the damage caused by an extreme high fever.

His first memory as the fever abated was of his mother bathing his head with cold water. For a while he thought he was either dreaming or hallucinating. It was some time before he realised that she was really there, having been deported, then released from a *kolkhoz* not too far from Tashkent. She was nominally working as a nurse. Just for once, Tomek's outspokenness and noticeability had paid off and some army clerk, having made the connection, had managed to tell Stefania that her son was gravely ill.

She had news of his sisters; they were both alive and working with the army but nowhere near Tashkent. Magdalena was nearer in Uzbekistan but she believed that Barbara was still north in Buzuluk. There was no way they could be reunited. She genuinely believed that seeing Tomek was a miracle. He was not inclined to disagree.

Sadly, needing to convalesce, he was moved to another camp up in the mountains about 80km from Tashkent. He was not to see his mother again, although he did get occasional letters from her.

After one medical examination the doctor shook his head, saying that it sounded as if Tomek had a slight heart murmur. If that was confirmed then he would never pass the medical for flying as a pilot. This was a major blow and for the next two weeks Tomek went for a run up the mountain slopes and back again, extending the distance every day. He would also do as many exercises as he could think of, hoping that the thinner mountain air would put him in good stead for another medical once he was back at sea level.

Someone somewhere had taken pity on him as he received a formal written message saying he would be evacuated from Russia to Iran. He was to be ready with whatever kit he had and report to headquarters to get an embarkation permit before carrying on to pick up a ship across the Caspian Sea to Pahlavi in Iran. Tomek could not believe his luck.

He was warned to be careful as it was now widely known who he was and the close relationship his father had with the old guard who had fought in the legions against the Bolsheviks. There were some who wanted to earn favour with the NKVD.

By the time he arrived back in Tashkent, he was told his mother had been moved on, but he did not know where. As one young officer suggested in a hoarse whisper, it would have been for her own and Tomek's safety. He was urged to take particular care, leave Tashkent immediately, keep his head down and merge into as many crowds as possible. Above all he was to keep far away from anyone on Colonel Berling's staff.

Tomek took that to mean that Berling was a puppet of the NKVD and Anders could not do much about it just yet. He was shown a photo of the colonel and told he was in charge of the 5th Division, who could be checking all embarkation orders at Krasnovodsk, which was nearly 2,000km away by rail.

If he was very lucky, he might get there in seventy-two hours; if he was walking and hitching lifts, probably seven to ten days. With that he was wished good luck and advised not to use his travel warrant if he could possibly help it.

He joined a party of soldiers who were mustered outside and fell into step behind them. As they marched out of the city, Tomek noticed that two Poles with military police armbands were arguing with an NKVD officer who was trying to set up a checkpoint. He wasn't getting out of Tashkent a moment too soon.

They made camp a few kilometres into the countryside. Tents had been set up and fires lit. It was cold with a few frozen snowdrifts at the side of the road. Tomek was not happy about staying so close to Tashkent overnight and decided to carry on walking on his own. He was lucky, as a convoy of lorries crawled past with what he could just make out to be Polish insignias painted on the side. He flagged one down and was relieved when it stopped and the door opened. He squeezed in beside the driver and his mate, flashing his travel warrant as he did. In the darkness neither man took much notice.

They were not going as far as the Caspian, stopping for an overnight stay, then refuelling and awaiting further instructions a little way into neighbouring Turkmenistan. They were not bound for Iran yet, but expected to go there having set up fuel dumps and facilities along the way. Both men were agreed that the number of women and children had surprised them, with many waiting patiently in rows alongside the road just hoping for something to happen.

They finally stopped some way out into the beginning of the desert. It didn't take long before it was viciously cold in the cab. There was a rolled-up tent in the back of the lorry that was packed in between large oil drums. The smell of petrol was oppressive and had infused the tent, so when they finally erected it, it didn't smell much better inside.

The rest of the lorries were strung out along the road. A sergeant walked back telling the men not to smoke anywhere near the lorries or the tents. A fire pit had been set up in the mix of pebbles and sand and something was cooking in a large pot. Despite feeling worried, Tomek was relieved that the sergeant didn't even give him a second glance, walking on to give similar instructions to the rest of the convoy. Someone had set up another fire pit and it was obvious the sergeant was making sure that all safety precautions had been taken.

Tomek wasn't too surprised, when he approached the nearest fire pit a little way back from the front of the convoy, to see that most of the men who had eaten their fill of what looked like beans or lentils were bringing out bedrolls and laying them out around the fire.

Not at all sure what to do next, he was surprised to be tapped on his shoulder, a voice whispering, 'Follow me.'

Within a few hundred yards they were out of sight and could not even see the twinkling flames from the fire pits.

At the bottom of a sandy depression, a torch flicked on but Tomek could not recognise the face at first. He looked so different from the Gabriel Michailowicz he had known in Lwów. Everyone called him 'Gigil'. Tomek was shocked.

'I saw your mother and she told me you were ill. We've been lighting candles for you and got the chaplain to say Mass. We had to cover up the reason for it as there's a rumour the NKVD would like to see you.'

Gigil had always been the cautious one and now it looked as if he was once again trying to keep Tomek out of trouble. He had been tipped off by a friendly major who had found Tomek's records and realised who he was. Somehow he had made the connection with Stefania, Tomek's mother, and as Gigil was one of the few from Lwów who had been able to get this far, he had been told to keep an eye on Tomek and see he got away to Iran.

Most of the internees from Lwów had been singled out for special attention. Anyone born there or with any links to the old guard from the Legions were not being allowed to leave Russia. Gigil was lucky; he had been born in Poznan and, being a little older, had been fighting the Germans, and was then picked up by the Russians with his unit after being ordered to make for Rumania.

He had been following Tomek at a distance, under orders only to intervene if Tomek got into trouble.

Tomek guessed that Gigil had his own connections and they ran pretty far up the Polish Army hierarchy. Gigil explained that Anders' staff wanted to make sure that someone from the so-called 'always Russian' towns such as Lwów in Galicia got to England and told the story of what it was like under Russian occupation. So many were now missing that they were afraid that Britain would do a deal with Russia once the war with Germany was over.

Tomek had to be very careful who he took into his confidence. There was one other Pole from Lwów called Stasek who was already waiting up ahead, and the idea was to get them both out, smuggled among the hundreds of others scheduled to leave by ship from Krasnovodsk. Nobody knew how many ships would be made available and how long they would have before the Russians found a pretext for stopping the evacuation. There were so many rumours flying around, ranging from one that women and children were not going to be allowed to leave, to a contradiction that only women and children would eventually leave because the Russians wanted all Polish soldiers to fight alongside them on the Eastern Front.

As he explained and Tomek believed, no matter what assurances Stalin gave Churchill and Roosevelt, the situation on the ground would be quite different.

Even in a situation of total war, which the Second World War certainly was, it is difficult from a twenty-first-century perspective to understand how allies could work against each other. The mythology of the struggle has been promoted as some sort of crusade where good was battling against evil.

In a broad sense, the Second World War was an imperial battle without emperors. Immediately post-war the phrase 'spheres of influence' was substituted for the word 'empire' but in practical terms there was not a great deal of difference.

The main battle, since the early 1920s, had been between capitalism and communism. Both forms of economic doctrine had changed significantly by 1940 but had come down to both a sprawling Soviet Union and a pan-American hegemony glaring at each other across the Atlantic and Pacific. The rise of Nazi Germany and the Empire of Japan were initially regarded as blips, with political pragmatism taking little notice of atrocities committed against lesser economic powers and minorities, right up to the time when their expansionism towards getting hold of strategic materials, with oil being the most important, became a reality.

The invasion of Poland in 1939 and its subsequent partition between Russia and Germany was not really regarded as a top priority despite treaties, and there was not a lot of appetite for outright war, even among the British, until Germany invaded the Low Countries then France. From that point onwards the political establishment in the UK sided with Churchill's view that Nazi Germany had to be stopped at all costs.

Churchill knew that Germany probably would not be utterly defeated without US support and an attack from the east. The USA was ambivalent, with domestic politics threatening to cut any suggestions of aid to the UK in the interest of saving money and building their own economy after the Great Depression.

There are similarities with today, where expressions of support for Ukraine are cheap but the direct supplies of modern weapons systems and strategic support are tempered with a fear of being drawn into another expensive war. Hitler knew this and was effectively crossing his fingers that the USA would stay detached from the fight in much the same way Putin has been hoping that NATO will remain as he nibbles away at Ukrainian territory.

By 1942, Poland was ultimately an irrelevance. Using its forces to boost military success in various areas such as the Battle of Britain and the eventual North African and Italian campaigns made sense, but in terms of any post-war balance of power it was not a player.

Ukraine's Zelensky knows that an eventual sell-out to Russia without regaining all of its lost territories, particularly Crimea, is always at the back of the USA and NATO's minds. Poland's historical precedent is there for all to see, and only Poland and a few other potential front-line states such as Finland and the Baltics understand this.

Tomek's ultimate fate, once he succeeded in leaving Russia, was to play out as a microcosm of what would happen to Poland and still have ramifications for the Eastern European situation today.

Tomek's immediate goal was to board a boat at Krasnovodsk at any cost and get as far away as possible. The idea of compromise and fighting the Germans on the Russian front never crossed his mind. Hitler's Germany was an enemy, but not in any personal sense. He had been arrested, tortured, interned, brutalised, starved, abused and harried by Russians every step of the way. His family had suffered at Russian hands over several generations. There was no way he was going to give in now. He had a deep hatred of Stalin and his brand of communism and he had seen that it had turned Russia into a dangerous, seething and cynical melting pot of corruption and competing interests.

Getting out, then fighting his way back to his home town in a free Poland, had become an item of faith. Ever since he was a small boy he had tended to see everything in black and white. Now he had become utterly intransigent in a belief that the world had to see things his way or he would die in the attempt.

He knew now that nothing would stop him getting on that boat and sailing to freedom in Iran.

This was just as well, because here he was stuck in the middle of a desert at night, having no means of transport, with two others whom he hoped shared his grim determination.

Staśek was waiting for them a couple of kilometres further on into the desert. He had not lit a fire and was huddled into a ball under his greatcoat. For some reason he and Tomek hit it off immediately. Once in the company of Gigil and Staśek, Tomek felt he was among friends – a feeling he had not experienced since the night of his arrest in Lwów.

They needed a plan and Gigil had one: 'There's a railway siding about ten kilometres from here. I've been told that it's mostly women who've signed up with the army who'll be loaded up there in the morning. There might be some civilians and children; I don't know how that's happened, but there'll be a few men, like us in these British uniforms, organising them. We'll simply be among the organisers.'

Tomek was worried in case the other soldiers realised they were not part of the team deployed to do the organising. Gigil simply said: 'They'll be too busy to bother and grateful for any help. It's going to be chaotic.'

It was.

12

Iran and the *Aviateur*

The journey to Krasnovodsk took three days of screaming children, crying mothers, stony-faced young women, many of who looked as if they were nursing some sort of deep resentment, and a handful of overwhelmed soldiers who had been given inadequate supplies of dried fruit, grain and powdered milk to feed their charges.

Fortunately, at either end of the cattle waggons, there were two bowsers of water, one for the steam engine and another allegedly full of drinking water with which they filled three enormous samovars in what must have been, at some time in its past, a restaurant car. They were able to make something that gave the appearance but not the taste of tea once the boiling water had been blasted through the mess of black leaves in the receptacle below. At least having been boiled, it wasn't too full of bacteria. There was also a *kipyatok* tap that dispensed constant hot water, which the mothers used to make up the powdered milk or melt some of the closely guarded sugar lumps for the many children on that train.

Nothing really made sense any more. This was supposed to be part of a military movement order. Tomek had no doubt that these women needed to get away, but could not see how or why they had been given any priority over potential fighting soldiers.

He was angry and bitter. Staśek and Gigil picked up his mood as Tomek sat cross-legged on the floor of the waggon looking disconsolately out of the open sliding door as the brown, unremarkable countryside ambled past. He had folded in on himself, uncommunicative, tending to snap when someone attempted a joke or light-hearted observation. The constant noise of the train, the querulous demands of the children, the low singing of mothers trying to calm crying babies, the odd explosions of grief from women recalling the loss of loved ones – it was all getting on his nerves.

For Tomek, memories of his Scout troop singing on their way to camp in the Tatra Mountains should have been answered by the robust singing of patriotic and morale-boosting songs from soldiers on their way to battle, not this cacophony of misery and frustrated hope.

He was descending into what his family would later call his 'deep Slavonic glooms'.

His father had told, in his strident voice, of selfless acts of courage among his highly motivated freedom fighters; now Tomek was beginning to doubt the devil-may-care swashbuckling stories he had been brought up on. So far, over the past two and a half years he had only seen fear, betrayal, mindless violence, confusion and cowardice. He was angry at his own lack of energy and knowledge of how to attack efficiently. The heroes of those films he had seen at the cinema led charmed lives, disarming a dozen armed guards with athletic ability and cheerful courage. He had been misled. Life under occupation, the gulag and war had drained every morsel of initiative out of him.

He knew that his old friend Gigil was basically his nursemaid and that only made Tomek even more resentful. Staśek was cheerful enough in accepting his lot but that contrasted with Tomek's mood as he knew that, being the son of a heroic much-decorated colonel, he should have been able to carry this burden of history and use it to make his mark. Instead here he was on a slowly chugging train with a load of women and children, having no real idea of where his future lay.

Matters got considerably worse when, a few kilometres short of their destination, Tomek and the other soldiers on the train were ordered out by a young Polish officer, who looked very uncomfortable standing on his own beside the line. When asked why they had stopped, the officer, who was plainly unhappy with his orders, told Tomek and his comrades that before any of the civilians were let out, he now had the sole responsibility for checking the validity of everyone else's permits. The instruction had come through a few hours ago and the officer was sure that the NKVD was behind it.

He also said that he had been told that the civilians had to abandon their personal possessions and any money, as the Russians said that nothing of value should leave Russia as that would count as theft from the Soviet proletariat. When asked what they should be looking for among the various paperwork and permits, the officer looked really uncomfortable: 'Anyone who's not *Prawdziwy Polak*' (real Poles), and that included German names, Ukrainians, Orthodox, Greek Catholics, Ruthenes, Belarusians, in fact anyone whom the Russians regarded as really being citizens of the greater USSR.

That made Tomek very angry, as he was probably the sort of candidate that the NKVD officers were looking for. Being in uniform, it looked as if he was now being called upon to check up on other unfortunates, who by dint of birth were about to be excluded from their chance of freedom. He felt like a hypocrite. Staśek didn't look too happy either but was probably doing a better job of concealing his true feelings.

Gigil went up to the officer and said something that Tomek could not hear. After a minute or two, with a lot of head shaking, he walked over to Tomek and Staśek. He said: 'I told him to forget it and asked if this order came from the NKVD through Colonel Berlinger. He doesn't know. So I suggested we do nothing until he's confirmed it in writing with General Anders in Yangi-Yul, that should buy us some time. Let's hope the ship's there already waiting for us.' This did little to lift Tomek's mood.

Once the young officer had left, there was a general rush to the docks, which took just under two hours. Gigil was all for barging ahead, but Staśek said that if they could get as many as possible onto the quay waiting to board then they could hide in the crowd should Berlinger or the NKVD arrive.

It wasn't easy. They managed to bribe some *arbas* and a Muslim lorry driver to run a sort of shuttle from the train to the docks. Word quickly got out and a variety of vehicles appeared out of nowhere, happy to take bribes in coin or kind from whoever could offer them. Others rooted around any abandoned luggage taking blankets, clothing, old clocks and even a dinner gong that someone had left by the train. Tomek had the thought that the train itself was now being looted as he saw a samovar carried aloft above the bobbing heads of the crowd. This was a good sign, as if the NKVD had been seen in town nobody would be taking the risk.

As Gigil pointed out, the young officer might find it a better idea to join them rather than risk Colonel Berlinger's wrath. It was obvious that nothing had been properly organised yet.

As he approached the docks, Tomek was feeling a lot less confident. There was no sign of any Russian officers but the faces of the several Polish soldiers present at the dock gates were not happy as they waved them through.

The ship was still unloading whatever cargo it had brought from Pahlavi in Iran. Hundreds of troops were sitting on the dockside in serried ranks, chatting or smoking, while their own consignment of women and children surged around offering papers and warrants to the few soldiers who were trying to organise them.

Tomek was now chafing with impatience. The unloading seemed to have stalled with nothing happening, with one load left dangling from a crane, swaying slightly, while the stevedores just looked up shouting in an unfamiliar language. This went on for some time with nothing useful happening.

A British officer appeared on deck shouting and waving to the assembled soldiers, who got to their feet in fairly good order, shouldered their kit bags and started marching up the gangplank. Neither Staśek nor Tomek had any kit beyond their issued backpacks and it was looking as if they would stand out against this troop of well-organised and obviously professional soldiers, many of whom looked like they may have been veterans from 1939. Tomek was worried that he looked too young and green.

A second gangplank was rolled up and lifted onto the ship while the first few civilians were beckoned forward. This time two soldiers were checking documents before they boarded. Now Tomek was getting very worried. This was going to take much longer than he had imagined. The rest of the crowd, mostly women, were pressing from behind, obviously afraid that they wouldn't be allowed on board. More soldiers appeared, trying to hold back the steadily growing throng of desperation.

Gigil was looking worried. He motioned Staśek and Tomek to stay where they were while he went over to talk to an officer. This time Tomek was sure he was a captain and probably had a better idea of what was and wasn't allowed. The tension was palpable. The captain looked across at them and shook his head.

If they were to get away with it, Tomek and Staśek had to join the tail end of the troops boarding by the other gangplank. They needed a distraction. Fortunately it came as an unexpected answer to prayer. The load that had been swinging was lowered quite suddenly with a lot of shouting, hitting the quayside quite hard and its mass obscuring the captain's view of them. Tomek tugged at Staśek's sleeve and they ran round to the other gangplank, picking up a couple of dumped kitbags from an abandoned pile. Holding them high on their shoulders to obscure their faces, they inserted themselves into the last party of soldiers boarding the ship.

At this there was a lot of shouting and wailing as a mass of humanity surged forward past the army captain just as the ship gave two large blasts on its siren. Tomek could hear the engine start with a rumble as the rear gangplank was detached and lowered to the quayside. More women had overwhelmed the two guards at the forward gangplank and it took another squad to restore order as that one was detached and lowered as well.

Tomek had lost sight of Gigil when he noticed a large black staff car pull up behind the crowd, and he was sure that it was Colonel Berlinger who was waving his arms and must have been shouting. Staśek could not resist a rude gesture as the ship began to pull away.

Tomek tried to stop him. He would not feel safe until they were out of sight of land and well on their way to Iran.

He could not be sure, but it looked as if Berlinger had pushed past the masses still left on the dockside and appeared to be shouting, though nothing could be heard above the noise of the ship's engine and the wails and cries coming from those left behind. Once well clear of the docks the ship turned to port and for one awful moment he was afraid that it would return to the dock, but it didn't and before long the crowds on the quay were lost to sight.

There was a slight swell and the wind picked up. It was cold on deck but Tomek didn't care. He was just relieved to be on his way to Iran. He lost sight of Gigil but gave up trying to find him among the crowds on deck.

From a mixture of exhaustion and relief, he found a small space behind the funnel and curled up, falling asleep.

Later, feeling very hungry, he went in search of something to eat. There was still no sign of either Gigil or any other familiar face. The ship was of no great size, not much bigger than the ferry that had once taken him across the Danube while on one of his summer holidays. He was hungry but couldn't see anywhere resembling a canteen and the few people who were eating seemed to have brought their own provisions.

It was crowded on deck and below, with the smells of urine and vomit, groans of the seasick and screams of hungry children, none of which bothered him as he hunched up in a corner, having lost his nook behind the funnel. He was well beyond discomfort, unresponsive to nudges, kicks, shouts and pangs of hunger, barely able to drag himself back into awareness and full consciousness some thirty hours later, as they neared the Iranian port of Pahlavi. Almost as soon as the gangplanks were positioned, both Staśek and Gigil seemed to appear as if by magic. Together they were jostled down the gangplank and onto Iranian soil.

New uniform or not (Staśek was already using the English word 'battledress') once disembarked, they were marched off a couple of kilometres to tents erected along the beach, where once again they had to strip off *en masse* to be deloused. Scores of naked young men were standing, sitting and lying down in the already strong sunshine. None of them cared any more. The overarching sense was one of relief. The few married men with families who had managed to be smuggled aboard were concerned, wondering when they would see their loved ones again. The few orderlies in attendance did not know anything beyond saying that a separate camp and shelter had been set up for women and children a few kilometres away.

For the first time since he had left Tashkent, Tomek wondered if his mother would be evacuated later or may even possibly be in Iran already. There was no way he could find out.

Once the indignities of delousing were over, Tomek was able to look at himself in a mirror. He looked clean shaven, youthful and reasonably dressed. He realised that he would need to start the process of volunteering for pilot training pretty soon if he wanted to avoid having a rifle put in his hand and being taught the noble art of square bashing. He had heard several veterans complain that they would have to learn not only the English way of doing things but the language as well. It was at that point when Tomek realised that his path to flying an aircraft in battle was going to be a lot more complicated than he had first thought.

He was then surprised to be told that he would be put on a train to Tehran with several others who had volunteered for flying training. Tomek was unaware that anyone had taken any particular notice of his wishes. This was a very welcome development. As it turned out, the whole process was rushed, overwhelming and utterly slick in its operation. He had no time for sightseeing and felt a little cheated, seeing groups of Poles sitting outside cafes or taking photos of the ornate blue-tiled mosques, so unlike the neglected specimens he had seen in Uzbekistan, as he was driven past.

It had been decided that General Anders was going to raise an army in the Middle East,[1] which meant that only specialists in the shape of aircrew would be sent to the UK for training. General Sikorski in London needed a substantial Polish presence on British soil if he were to maintain any political credibility.

Fortunately Polish squadrons had acquitted themselves admirably during the Battle of Britain[2] and those squadrons needed to make up numbers lost inevitably through attrition and promotion. Even so there was a case to be made for some transport squadrons to be based in North Africa in support of Anders as the war developed.[3]

There was also a developing need for experienced fighter pilots in the Mediterranean Theatre[4] to cut off supplies to Rommel's Afrika Korps,[5] alongside a need to expose experienced and battle-hardened fighter commanders to the developing role of tactical air warfare[6] in anticipation of an ultimate invasion of northern Europe. These would form a cadre of leaders and tactical warfare trainers for an expansion of the Polish fighter squadrons already based in Britain.

While Tomek and evacuees from Russia were being prepared for their journey to the UK and ultimately training, plans were being laid for their eventual leaders and instructors to go in the opposite direction as far as Algeria.

The need for well-trained extra aircrew was accelerating rapidly and Tomek was already being caught up in this process.[7]

Training infrastructure was being developed as the risk of Luftwaffe intrusion into British airspace slackened and the Empire Training Scheme had taken off, with multi-engine advanced training in Canada being followed rapidly by other training centres throughout Canada, the USA and South Africa.

Air superiority was recognised as being key to any successful invasion and that meant massive numbers of aircraft, pilots, armourers, riggers, engine fitters and all the ancillary staff that are required to keep a squadron at operational readiness.[8]

The Poles, having proved their worth, were now part of a massive war machine that would result in better-trained aircrew flying superior equipment against a German Air Force that was already losing its best pilots to attrition, faster than they could be replaced.

It is not just the quality of the front-line fighters who win wars but the whole logistics and training infrastructure that eventually led to what General Eisenhower would describe as being 'the Firstest with the Mostest'.

Tomek did not know it yet, but two and a half years of intense training lay ahead of him before he became part of the 'Mostest'.

His progress was rapid and confusing. The initial interviews were hurried and in Polish, before he was bundled out to stand in front of an RAF medical officer. He simply manipulated Tomek into various positions, listening to his chest, getting him to cough, checking muscle tone, peering into his ears and so on. The eye test was a bit more confusing as the optician pointed at various characters on a board and Tomek read them out using Polish pronunciations, which must have been sufficient as he was handed a slip of paper and ushered into another room where various documents were stamped.

He had just over twenty-four hours in Tehran, where he posed for a photograph with Staśek and did little else, before being bundled aboard a train for Khorramshahr.

Polish NCOs organised them into lines where documents were checked, then marched up gangplanks aboard the liner *Aviateur* for the long journey around the Cape of Good Hope, bound for Great Britain. That much was clear; little else was explained.

The overall feeling among the Poles was relief, tinged with confusion. The ship's crew spoke English, although some looked as if they may have been Indian or Arab. Very few of the Poles had any English at all and, for the first few days at least, all communication was by gesture.

Things improved slightly and shockingly for them at their first stop in Bombay (modern-day Mumbai). A Polish-speaking officer came on board with the pilot vessel and warned them of the likely risks during their brief spell ashore. Any money was fair game, the pickpockets were very skilled, they were to avoid certain areas and wherever they went they would be mobbed by children begging for money. On no account were they to engage with any prostitutes as disease was rife. Even so, as a precaution, they were all issued with quinine tablets that they had to take and each man was handed a packet of three condoms. This was a surprise to Tomek as he had never seen one before. Evidently nobody expected the Poles to stick to the rules.

As they tied up, a fleet of small boats surrounded the *Aviateur* and some of the crew started throwing coins overboard. Tomek and the other Poles were astonished to see men diving overboard from the small *bumboats*, as the crew called them, often catching the shiny coins before they disappeared for good into the murky depths.

This was a different sort of poverty from that seen by the Poles in Russia and Uzbekistan. The fetid, almost cloying smell everywhere was overpowering.

Tomek went for a walk with Staśek, often avoiding masses of vegetable and probably human waste in the streets. The sight of humped cows wandering around freely, some of them adorned with garlands, was a surprise. Tomek had heard of Indian sacred cows, but seeing them in reality was a very different experience.

The real shock came when he saw caged women who were scantily dressed, plainly being offered to service the Poles by entreaties and smiles from greasy and fat-looking men, whom Tomek guessed to be their pimps. Neither he nor Staśek found it in any way enticing.

Further down the road two crowds suddenly erupted in a vicious fight. Tomek could not work out what had caused it. Stones were being thrown and it completely blocked the road. Another crowd had appeared from nowhere and started chanting. Tomek and Staśek were cut off. The thought that they had survived this far only to be killed by a mob for something they didn't understand, after all they had gone through, seemed a very cruel irony.

A whistle blew several times and turbaned policemen appeared as if by magic, directed by a young English officer in khaki shirt, shorts and a solar topee. His questions were incomprehensible to the two Poles. In the end, smiling and beckoning, the officer assigned two uniformed and intimidating Sikhs to lead them back to their ship.

Tomek later learned that he had witnessed one of the several riots that were erupting between Hindus and Muslims. He couldn't wait for their ship to slip its mooring and get as far away as possible from the smell, heat, noise and threat of Bombay.

There were a few changes on board. Some crew had been paid off while others, mostly British, had taken over. Their numbers were small, but there was now an English teacher among them who had a very few words of Polish. Every morning, before it got too hot, he set up a blackboard on deck and began the thankless task of trying to impress upon his class the intricacies of the English language.

Those who already spoke German were the quickest on the uptake. This had a slight sting in the tail as the best students were taken off at Durban for training in South Africa, possibly to fly against Rommel in the Western Desert of Egypt and Libya once they had completed their training.

Tomek and his mates were not allowed off the ship this time as there was a fear that they might get involved in the local racial politics that very much favoured the white man.

The voyage was not as comfortable as Tomek would have wished. More aircrew embarked at Cape Town, not all of them Polish. In the way that such things happened in wartime, what the Poles thought they already knew turned out to be wrong and briefings were frequently updated.

There was now a new urgency, with a couple of naval officers appearing and some equipment, looking a bit like torpedoes, being installed up in the bow. The Poles were not allowed anywhere near.[9]

Before leaving Cape Town, there was a very serious briefing, translated into Polish, about the hazards they were now about to face. There was a very real risk in the Atlantic from U-boats and pocket battleships. The *Aviateur* was going to keep well to the west at high speed on a zigzag course to elude the U-boat threat. Occasionally they might have a screen of destroyers if intelligence suggested specific risks. In coastal waters they would deploy the equipment loaded at Cape Town, which comprised two paravanes that would each tow a steel line to cut any sea mine's mooring chains. A couple of heavy machine guns mounted at the stern would be used to shoot them as they bobbed to the surface. Any Poles who had experience of handling such weapons were welcome to train in addition to the ship's crew.

Tomek bluffed his way onto one such session but failed to score even a few hits on the yellow floating target buoy towed behind the ship once they were at sea. After that humiliation, his services were never called upon again.

Tomek was disappointed that a few familiar faces, not exactly friends, had departed. He learned that some of the new faces had already done some training, and even in a few cases had seen action flying against the Italians in Abyssinia and the Germans in North Africa. They did not mix with Tomek's new intake, despite the fact that all those embarked in Iran had some very tough experiences of their own. It was as if those who had faced the Germans had little in common with those who had been through the Russian mill.

This made him very uncomfortable. He often remarked that attempts to strike up conversations were met with anything from restraint to downright cold indifference. What he had not realised was most of those embarked in Cape Town were already serving commissioned officers and before long an almost unwritten segregation was agreed, with the officers keeping to one deck, the NCOs who had already done their advanced flying training on another, while the Iran contingent, who were not yet officially in the RAF and had no military rank, were kept to the stern.

The only time they did mix was when Mass was said by a Catholic padre, who did not seem to be attached to any particular group.

They were lectured frequently about lights out and even the dangers of smoking on deck at night. The fear of U-boats was tangible and the repeated lifeboat drills added urgency. There was no wireless allowed as it was believed that the German Navy could pick up even the faint radiation given off by a simple receiver. They were told that they were operating under conditions of strict radio silence.

They were also told that they would be keeping close to the South American shore and once past Brazil they would have a destroyer escort sweeping ahead of them clearing mines and deterring U-boats. By now the Poles were becoming more than a little blasé about the whole business until a grey shape appeared off their starboard side and a signalling light winked at them. He didn't know it at the time but it was an American destroyer warning the *Aviateur* of dangerous waters ahead.

Later research has shown that once the USA was in the war, Admiral Dönitz had encouraged his U-boats to patrol very close to the American coast, where there was no blackout. This provided an ideal backdrop, outlining ships and making easy targets for the U-boats lying in the darkness offshore.

By early 1942 the Germans were using magnetic mines and deploying them in coastal waters both from the air and U-boats, which could also lay them as far away as the eastern seaboard of America. These twin threats would have been uppermost in the minds of the *Aviateur*'s crew as they sailed north of the Equator and into Allied waters.

Tomek noticed that the ship was now sailing in a more pronounced zigzag and appeared to be forging ahead at higher speed. Several times he saw huge fountains of water sent up and felt a judder go through the hull, though whether this was caused by depth charges fired off the accompanying destroyers or the triggering of mines by the minesweepers ahead, unseen from the aft deck where he was confined, he had no real idea.

The effect was very noticeable. Many of the Poles took to wearing lifejackets all the time and it was not at all unusual for several pairs of anxious eyes to scan the sea for any sign of enemy activity from the guardrails. This was a very different and alien world from the plains of Eastern Poland and Russia. One of the Poles insisted he had seen a trail of bubbles from a torpedo as it passed astern. Nobody was inclined to disbelieve him and the number of lifejackets worn went up considerably.

The tension grew even more as they approached UK waters. Everyone was now on watch, reporting any aircraft seen, nighttime flashes in the sky and even distant searchlights as they passed Northern Ireland. Sleep was once again at a premium and it was understood by all the Poles that it would be a sad irony if, having survived war with Germany and the frigid horrors of Siberia, they perished in the grey waters of the North Atlantic in sight of their hoped-for destination.

There was one minor incident that made Tomek feel very insecure. They were well into the North Atlantic with the weather getting steadily cooler on deck. One of the off-duty crew had spread out a boat cover and was lying underneath it in the sunshine. He beckoned Tomek over, lifting up one corner of the cover by way on invitation. Thinking nothing more of it than a friendly gesture, he slipped underneath and was shocked when the sailor grabbed the inside of Tomek's thigh and tried to kiss him on the cheek.

A shocked Tomek lashed out, punching the man in the eye, and he fled shouting back at the sailor. Someone must have reported it as Tomek never saw that sailor again and no other crewman was seen sunbathing or resting anywhere near the Poles' recreation area on the aft deck again.

When they finally disembarked, Tomek was stressed, bewildered and very unsure as to what was supposed to happen next.

PART THREE
SPITFIRES!

13

Scotland to Brighton

For someone who had only the sketchiest understanding of simple English after six weeks of lectures, arrival in Glasgow was a culture shock. The locals were friendly, but completely incomprehensible.

If Tomek thought that he would instantly be in training for the RAF, he was to be disappointed. He was subjected to endless interviews in Polish and English, many of which needed extra explanation. The biggest shock was being told unequivocally that Russia was now an ally.

Tomek tended towards a sense of injustice, and was renowned for rising to the bait. Given his recent experiences in Siberia, and having little or no first-hand exposure to the German invasion, he regarded Russia as the biggest threat to Poland. He was allowed one initial outburst before being shut down unequivocally.

An English officer, accompanied by a rather supercilious Polish ex-cavalryman from Sikorski's staff in London, lectured all the Poles from Eastern Poland, which he dismissed as *Kresy*, a somewhat pejorative term, making them feel like second-class citizens. It was made absolutely plain that they would progress no further and spend the rest of the war in internment unless they individually signed an undertaking not to talk about their experiences in Siberia. This was a major shock and disappointment.

Tomek was seething, as were several others. Staśek was more pragmatic. He pointed out that most of the officers that now served with

Sikorski in London had been fighting the Germans, then got out via Rumania. To them, Germany was the real enemy with Russia a necessary and critical ally.

Tomek was to say many times that his whole life would have been so different had he stayed in Rumania and not gone back to Lwów for his mother.

The Siberia contingent had arrived later, bringing their own legacy of misery that was totally out of step with the aims and priorities of the Polish Government in Exile, based under Sikorski in London.

Sikorski had a cadre of senior officers who had been drawn from the old Prussian-occupied part of Poland. Not all of them had shared the late Marshal Piłsudski's mild socialism and desire to reinvent the Commonwealth of Poland and Lithuania. Since his death there had been a movement away from his ideals towards an industrialised, modern, Western-looking Poland.

None of this cut any ice with Tomek, whose sense of isolation grew into a major chip on his shoulder. Nevertheless, his desire to fly overruled any of his misgivings. Even so, it was not until 4 August 1942 that he was finally signed up to the RAF with the rank of AC2 (aircraftsman second class) and given the service number 703915[1] when he mustered at 'P' Depot near St Andrews in Fife for his basic training. This was a very long way from even beginning his flying training.

The lectures were a problem. Tomek, in common with many others, wrote his English notes phonetically, substituting w for v or ł for w. There had been a change as the Polish squadrons had now adopted British ranks and organisation in order to integrate with RAF strategy and tactics.

The routine was grinding and at times depressing. There was a lot to learn about organisation, ranks, duties, who to salute and when, and some of the Poles complained. However, Tomek realised that, compared to Vorkuta, this was a holiday camp.

What he was not prepared for were all the aptitude tests on co-ordination, spatial awareness and comprehension. Morse code was an essential and Tomek had the advantage as he had learned it in the amateur radio courses with his Scout troop. His familiarity with what the British still called wireless, both in practice and theory, put him ahead, as did the theory of flight and introduction to meteorology, all courtesy of his gliding experience.

For the first time, Tomek had opportunities for sport, which was encouraged. Volleyball was his favourite, with few of the Poles taking much interest in football or golf on the much-abbreviated courses that had survived requisition as training areas.

In common with many of these displaced and dispossessed Poles, Tomek had a certain fatalism about him. They had all seen how cheap life was in Russia, unlike those Poles who had only fought the Germans and got out via Rumania to fight again over the skies of south-east England in 1940.

All the Poles on his course were as highly motivated as he, but Tomek felt that his chances of survival were low. He became determined to find a wife and be sure that his progeny would carry on the family name and traditions.

This caused some misunderstandings among the local girls in Fife, many of whom found the Poles glamorous, different and more exotic than any local lads who had not been called up yet. It was an unfair competition as those remaining Scottish boys, approaching marriageable age, were in heavy industry or mining – distinctly less glamorous than Polish fighter pilots in training.

Proposals of marriage after a couple of dates tended to scare off many of those girls just seeking a good time and scoring off against their peer group. Most were very young, still in their teens – a source of worry to their parents, who were less enthusiastic about welcoming into their homes a handsome stranger whose command of English was not brilliant. What was even more worrying was that these Poles were unquestioningly Catholic, at odds to local Calvinism. Lying in wait behind it all was a belief that these young men were all old beyond their years, marked by the scars of suffering and torture. They were from a totally different and incomprehensible world without prospects and whose futures were in considerable doubt.

In those days, unmarried mothers were ostracised and often denounced, with many forced adoptions and girls 'disappearing' for months at a time under the guise of doing war work or recovering from injury. Occasionally a young woman would turn up with a baby and wedding ring claiming to be a war widow, but this general atmosphere of potential disapproval kept many young women on the straight and narrow, which, coupled with the Polish recruits' need to seek permission to marry from their commanding officers, dampened down any local baby boom.

Tomek admitted to two additional fears: that the war would be over before he finished training and that he would never see his family again.

He found elementary training frustrating at times, going over old stuff he knew already when it came to the theory of flight and meteorology. He was neither ill disciplined nor specifically insubordinate, but he was a loner and frequently complained about a general lack of progress towards flying with an operational squadron. Several times he was lectured about curbing his irritation at the long process of indoctrination, the need for better English and what was perceived to be his lack of team spirit. Unlike many of his cohort, he would spend hours alone writing to the Red Cross in the hopes of tracking down both his sisters and mother.

At other times he would walk for miles along the coast, his whole manner being one of gloom and suppressed tension.

Tomek was very religious and never missed Mass, although he shunned confession or the opportunity to bare his soul to the Polish chaplain who visited, usually once a month, with there being other opportunities to go to the local church in St Andrews, where he could follow the Mass in Latin but rarely understood the sermons.

What he did not know at the time was that his overall conduct was being noted.

He had completed a number of basic induction courses when interviews were set up and different groups of Poles were lectured on their options. Tomek was told that he would be offered the opportunity of going to Canada for further officer and possible multi-engine training, which would delay his eventual posting to an operational squadron by at least six months. There were no guarantees, as his flying training would be intense and most likely would result in him being posted to a bomber or transport squadron and not to one of the several Polish Spitfire squadrons that were already operational.

What finally persuaded him was the knowledge that he would not be in sole command of any bomber, needing to serve as a co-pilot or even flight engineer if he did not make the cut, as only the top 25 per cent would be considered for posting to a De Havilland Mosquito intruder or night fighter squadron. Already they knew that heavy bomber losses over Germany meant a low chance of survival. Even so, like most young men, they thought they were immortal.

Before he made any eventual decision, he was told that so far his grades were good but not that good. He would be facing further assessments before any final decision was made.

As Tomek would say in later life, he felt compelled to stay in Europe as his best chance of settling down, having children and finding his family.

If he thought that decision would speed up his transition to real flying training, he was to be sorely disappointed. What he did not know was that the training period was being extended considerably to give trainee pilots many more hours than their predecessors in 1940, in order to increase their effectiveness and chances of survival once they faced the enemy. It seemed to him that the prospect of flying was as far away as ever, as he was then posted away for yet another course to learn about ranks, organisation, hierarchies and how the Polish squadrons worked in the broader context of the RAF.

The misery of life in a transit camp didn't last long as Tomek, along with a couple of other recruits, found himself being sent to Brighton for further meteorology and navigational training. Christmas had been a very low-key affair apart from a Polish midnight Mass, but the prospect of somewhere new and the news that he would be billeted in the Hotel Metropole on Brighton's seafront cheered him considerably. He had little idea that this posting would change the course of his life.

Having been dropped off outside the hotel, they found the place empty with just a couple of orderlies wandering around, who were totally disinterested in the Poles and where they should stow their kit.

After checking each floor, they eventually found a large room with several camp beds in it, two of which had no kit arranged next to the neatly folded blankets. He and another man were both tired and had no idea where they were to report or what they should be doing next. Tomek once again felt that the world was against him.

Exhausted after his very long trip from Scotland, with its frequent interruptions caused by air raid warnings, he was relieved to find somewhere to lie down and was asleep instantly. Sometime later loud voices and laughter bounced him into a state of unwanted wakefulness. The lights were on and the room was filled with Poles throwing pillows, making derogatory remarks and pushing each other around. It was good natured, loud and probably inebriated.

Tomek could not make sense of what was going on, and any questions he asked resulted in more laughter and no intelligible reply. Then, like a flock of starlings, there was a mass of whirling activity followed by calm. It was as if they had all flown down and roosted in their beds. Blissful silence ensued, but the lights were still on. There were a few groans, then an argument about who should turn them off. This was cut short by one of the Poles producing a pistol and, after a few misses, he succeeded in shooting out all the lights. Tomek wondered what he had got himself into.

The next morning more chaos ensued. Sometime around 6 a.m. he heard a shout of 'Wakey wakey!' from a floor below, footsteps up the uncarpeted stairs, then a louder 'Wakey wakey!'

This was too much for some of the Poles, who got up and started banging their shoes on the wooden floor, accompanied by a loud concerted shout back: 'Shut up! Shut up! Shut up!'

They heard someone running upstairs, so with almost one accord there was a flurry of activity as the Poles dressed and started stripping their camp beds just as an English RAF corporal ran in. Looking puzzled, he paused when further banging and shouts of 'Shut up!' erupted simultaneously from the floors above and below.

This continued for the next twenty minutes or so with the harassed corporal getting worn out running from floor to floor, only to be confronted with scenes of ordered discipline as the men made their beds, shaved and dressed, while even more choruses of drumming shoes and cries of 'Shut up!' started up from every other floor.

As if by magic, silence fell when the corporal was spotted leaving the hotel. Ten minutes later he returned with a Polish group captain, who inspected each floor in turn. Every room was immaculately turned out with the airmen standing to attention beside their impeccably arranged camp bed, hair brushed, properly attired in shirt and battledress, shoes gleaming. He smiled and made a quick comment in Polish: 'You made your point, nice joke, but don't do it again!' before turning to the corporal and speaking in English.

'Corporal, these men are pilot trainees and not AC2s bound for menial duties. They are to be treated with respect. Each one will have superior rank to you in a few weeks' time!' His implication was clear: beware of whom you alienate!

Even in early 1943, after three and a half years of war, Brighton's Hotel Metropole still looked like an opulent building faced with red terracotta. Its interior, however, had lost all its lavish fittings, being equipped for the billeting of several hundred Polish airmen. It overlooked the West Pier, whose appearance was one of forlorn neglect, festooned with barbed wire and notices warning of mines.

To Tomek's surprise, he found that he enjoyed Brighton with its squalls, fresh air and sea breezes, totally unlike landlocked Lwów. It was different, refreshing, not so chill and prone to sea fog as St Andrews and somehow to his mind, despite the war, still felt connected to Europe only 80 miles away.

When he was free he used to take a stroll west to the large bronze angel on a stone plinth that the locals called the Peace Statue, which stood where the promenade of Brighton gave way to the open lawns of Hove, where tents, sandbags and gun emplacements had sprung up.

Most mornings, when summoned to muster beneath the arches of Medina Drive, he had set off along the promenade. Not too far to the east, he could see the distant white cliffs towards Ovingdean and

Rottingdean, past the nearby Palace Pier, abandoned, booby-trapped and as inaccessible as its western neighbour. From the Kings Road, below the endless parade of requisitioned hotels, the views seaward were interrupted by parked lorries, trailers and marching soldiers being drilled incessantly, above a beach denied to all by barbed wire and anti-invasion blocks known as dragons' teeth.

Most evenings, as he wandered towards Hove's lawns, all the anti-aircraft guns appeared tranquil, poised against the setting sun like some modernist sculptures, fashioned by the keening wind off the sea as canvas flapped and the sea roared, its spray drifting across the scene adding to its drama.

It was at times like this that Tomek pondered the point of it all. He knew he had to fight, knew that Hitler had territorial ambitions, that he had started this whole mess, that he had some sort of magic power over Germany, but at the same time felt in his bones that Russia, with all its corruption and indifference to human life, was his traditional, implacable and brutal enemy. He had little doubt that it would be the Russians who were the greatest risk to Lwów, his home and family.

Hitler's 'Final Solution' to what he regarded as the 'Jewish Problem', the bestialities committed by the Gestapo and Waffen-SS on entire populations, their extermination of villages as reprisal for resistance were not widely known in the Allied population at large. Stories had emerged about the harsh yoke of Nazism, and indeed by 1942 some very brave Poles had managed to infiltrate ghettoes and even death camps disguised as German soldiers.[2] Their reports were in the process of being smuggled out at great personal risk.

Many at the top did not want to believe stories of death camps, mass killings and the often-reported desire of the Nazis to destroy every vestige of Jewish and Romany life along with the mentally ill, severely disabled and homosexuals.

There were sound political reasons for this at first. Until they were certain that Germany could not bring the war to a resumed state of stalemate similar to that in the First World War, they needed to keep open the possibility of a negotiated peace. That meant keeping a lot of the worst information out of public hands. The situation was not too dissimilar to that which exists today, with the Ukraine government knowing full well what Putin's Russia is really like, and the Western Allies still hoping for a change of regime and a negotiated peace in order to stave off another full-scale ruinous war that would incur the inevitable rebuilding costs when hostilities were finally over.

What Tomek and his fellow countrymen did not know was that the Casablanca Conference[3] had already agreed a couple of weeks beforehand that, despite Churchill's reservations, Roosevelt had pushed for a total defeat of Germany with unconditional surrender as the only option.

This effectively began the process whereby the Tehran Conference,[4] held at the end of 1943, would push Poland's eastern border back to the much-disliked Curzon Line of 1920, leaving once and for all Tomek's home, where his father was buried and the city he knew and loved, well beyond Poland's borders and firmly under Stalin's control.

His future war would be entirely against the Germans with no recompense for what he had suffered in Siberia. Effectively, Tomek had lost his war even before he began fighting.

The courses were now more intense and covered instrumentation, aircraft systems, signalling, aircraft recognition and an introduction to R/T procedures. This was proper ground school work that brought him nearer to his desire to fly. To his joy, he was told that upon completing these courses satisfactorily he would be posted to No. 25 Elementary Flying Training School for Poles at Hucknall, near Nottingham.[5]

Between lectures and tests, the Polish airmen were positioned in groups below the arches along Madeira Drive to develop their marksmanship shooting at clay pigeons. They soon graduated from using shotguns to service rifles, which made hitting the target a far more difficult proposition. A couple of times Tomek was convinced that he had hit the clay pigeon, but as it failed to disintegrate the hit was not counted.

Once he heard machine-gun fire from the roof of the hotel. He later learned that there was a machine-gun nest there that had shot at a lone Focke-Wulf Fw 190, which had returned fire. Tomek was a bit disappointed that he had missed the action.

For the first time he saw German aircraft as occasional Fw 190s[6] zipped in from the Channel at very low altitude on tip-and-run nuisance raids. From the Brighton Aquarium, running east across the road from the arches, up as far as Black Rock, there were anti-aircraft gun emplacements set at about 400 yards from each other. The noise when they opened up was terrific and overwhelming.

Tomek never saw them hit anything until one unfortunate day when all the guns along the seafront opened up. A rumour went round that a German Ju 88[7] was reported crossing the English Channel. Ignoring the advice to stay undercover, all the Poles ran out from beneath the arches to watch. To their horror, they saw an RAF Mosquito[8] trailing smoke. They ran screaming at the gun battery commander to stop firing but he could not hear them over the noise. He looked at them, mouth open in blank incomprehension. 'It's a Mosquito! A Mosquito you bloody fools!'

The firing stopped and they all watched in distress as the trail of smoke thickened. Almost immediately the stricken plane began a slow descent to be lost behind the town. They later heard that it crashed on the South Downs and both pilot and navigator were killed. The lessons of poor aircraft recognition were rammed home. Tomek was very bitter at this waste of life. He knew there would be casualties but to lose one of your own through incompetence and poor recognition was, to his mind, unforgivable.

It was a very solemn crowd who shuffled in to the next lecture on aircraft recognition. Tomek was furious, shouting at all who would listen that they would never make that same mistake. That night, with one accord they assembled in the foyer as the Polish chaplain led them in prayers for the souls of the Mosquito's crew. Tomek was furious that none of the anti-aircraft gunners attended. He had yet to learn that this was just another sad statistic in the futility of war.

It was the first time that he had witnessed loss of life since arriving in the UK. It would not be the last.

14

Life-Changing Tea and Cake

It was recognised that the Poles needed to have good English if they were to be an effective fighting force capable of being co-ordinated in the air.

By 1943, the RAF had considerable experience of deploying Polish, Czech, Free French and Belgian squadrons who had all proved their worth in combat across the gamut of RAF operations. It was recognised that over and above innumerable lectures in English, socialising was an excellent way of getting the Poles to improve their English, especially when it came to meeting girls.

The Poles had a reputation of being 'dandies', wearing cologne (there was no aftershave around during the war), having their uniforms altered to appear less scruffy and shapeless, and taking care with their appearance. Pretty well all fighter pilots were regarded as heroes and called 'the Brylcreem Boys' with their pomaded hair and white silk scarves draped carelessly about their necks, and, of course, the reputation they had fostered during the Battle of Britain. Add to that the Poles' courtesy, natural charm and accent and they could not fail. There were few fathers around armed with shotguns to ward off 'fast' suitors – the war took care of that – so a handsome young Polish fighter pilot turning up with flowers for the mother (always a good move) ensured that many young women were putty in their hands with a parent whose caution had already been charmed away by the romance of it all.

The RAF were pretty enlightened in allowing time off for meeting and wooing during these training courses, as improving communication, howsoever learned, was highly desirable in the pursuit of operational efficiency.

The Women's Voluntary Service, various parish groups, chambers of commerce and local councils would organise opportunities for locally based servicemen to relax and get to know the locals, laying on concerts, dances, tea parties and even concessions at local cinemas as a means of improving morale. These were opportunities that the Poles, in particular, were swift to make use of.

Tomek was being drawn a little out of his self-imposed shell. Although he had no particularly close friends, he started going out on evenings off with a group of other young Poles. There were tea dances at various church and civic halls and evenings out at the Regent ballroom above the cinema in North Street and Sherry's, which was more of a club, in Middle Street. The Poles were frequent and popular visitors, having little trouble in attracting girls.

There was one event arranged by what was then known as the Women's Voluntary Service (now Women's Royal Voluntary Service) that gave rise to something of a local legend. Mrs Rose-Hoare was a very statuesque woman in her late fifties or early sixties, who was renowned as a great organiser and friend to what she called 'our heroic Polish allies'. She could look a little intimidating, but most certainly grand with her well-corseted hips and mantelpiece bosom somehow shoehorned into her uniform. She was without a doubt an imposing figure but with a curiously knowing and friendly smile.

Tomek, along with his old friend Gigil Michailowicz – who somehow appeared in Brighton, only to disappear again a few weeks later – was attending one of these get-togethers, where the Poles could improve their language skills by chatting up local girls. Gigil's English was slightly better than Tomek's and he was evidently impressed by Mrs Rose-Hoare. Looking slightly nonplussed, he plucked up enough courage to embark upon a brief conversation that deserves to be recorded.

'Excuse please beautiful lady, what means uniform?'

Mrs Rose-Hoare drew herself up to her full height and declaimed in a loud voice: 'This ... this is the uniform of the Women's Voluntary Service!'

Gigil looked a little taken aback at first before replying: 'Oh ... I see, in Poland we have to pay!'

To her credit the grand lady laughed uproariously, at which the Poles, still not quite getting the joke, joined in.

It was then that Tomek noticed an attractive girl who was deep in conversation with a rather dashing dark Australian Army captain who had a certain grandeur about him. Tomek's attempts to peel her away from the captain met with a gentle rebuttal. The girl, Angela Oakeshott, was totally taken in by this English public-school-educated captain who, as she said later, was unlike any other Australian she had ever met.

Angela's younger sister Anne (known as Maureen in her family), however, was very friendly and chatted quite openly to the Poles, who were unaware that she was not yet 16.

Tomek saw Anne several times at the Regent, using the excuse of dancing with her to get to know the two older sisters, Angela and Agnes, the latter of whom had not been at the WVS event.

He eventually managed to get a dance with Angela, who protested that the cigarette case in Tomek's uniform top right pocket was pushing into her breast as they danced the foxtrot. This was not a good start to any relationship and it took Anne to invite Tomek and a couple of his mates to visit them at their bungalow in Patcham, a short way out of Brighton, to set things in motion.

Fortunately for Tomek, his Australian rival had been posted away by the time he arrived at the Oakeshott home.

Angela's mother Arlene had been abandoned by her war correspondent husband Arthur. She was living in genteel poverty with her three daughters, who quickly became known as 'the Three Graces' by the succession of servicemen from all Allied forces who spent a quiet afternoon there with tea and scones (if they could get any butter), and real eggs from the chickens in the back garden.

Arlene had gone through an unfortunate episode of trying to use liquid paraffin and castor oil in cakes and puddings as butter was rationed. It was only after several visitors had complained of being confined to the lavatory and a doctor warning Arlene that she was depleting these young men's ability to fight through a combination of dehydration and mineral loss that she realised her mistake.

Sadly, it was becoming obvious to all that Arlene's health was beginning to decline. She had not yet had a cancer diagnosis; that and a double mastectomy still lay in the future. To their credit, a significant number of their visiting servicemen of all nationalities would roll up their sleeves and set to, maintaining the large garden, in appreciation of the home from home provided so distant from the horrors of war they would undoubtedly face.

Tomek, perhaps rashly, pursued Angela, inviting her to the cinema and even suggesting marriage after knowing her all of a week. Needless to say, she did not accept.

As his training intensified, Tomek would spend almost all his spare time with Arlene and her girls, trying to improve his English, swotting for his next test and spending hours writing letters to the Red Cross and Polish Government in Exile, hoping to find out news about his mother and sisters. Sadly, news was always going to be months late and gradually Angela began to appreciate that here was a man cast adrift, desperately in need of sympathy, family life and affection. As she was to say many times later in life, she felt sorry for him. Angela, her mother and sisters began referring to him as 'the Lonely Pole'. Inevitably these domestic interludes couldn't last.

At the end of April he sat a number of exams and passed even more assessment tests before being posted to 25 (P) EFTS at Hucknall near Nottingham to begin flying training in the De Havilland Tiger Moth biplane. The first few days were spent in safety briefings, learning the ground checks, how to put on a parachute, strap in, assess wind, understand the circuit and endless briefings on procedures.[1]

Meanwhile, Angela's life changed as she had been invited to the Foreign Office in London, then told she had to sign the Official Secrets Act before being posted to the Traffic Office at Bletchley Park. On no account was she allowed to mention to anyone where she was based or what her duties were. The one advantage was that she had sufficient time off and railway warrants to visit Tomek, by staying at a bed and breakfast in Nottingham she could only just afford.

This arrangement meant, at best, a few hours spent during odd days in each other's company. Slowly, this allowed them to get to know each other a little better. Circumstances, opportunity (or the lack of it), their shared Catholicism and Angela's convent upbringing ensured an intermittent yet chaste courtship that more often than not would be continued through letters. Tomek had learnt to bide his time but did confess to another Pole, on the same course, that he had found his future wife.

Tomek liked the Tiger Moth. He called it a 'paper plane' as it flew slowly, rarely killed its pilot, was easy to fly, yet was notoriously tricky to fly well. In many ways it was the perfect *ab initio* RAF trainer for its time.

Tomek had an inbuilt advantage, having had some pre-war gliding experience that gave him a natural feel for the aircraft and its primary controls. His first flight, on 21 May 1943, was more of an air experience, getting to know the local landmarks and circuit, and gain familiarity flying the Tiger Moth with his instructor, Flight Sergeant Gawłowski. It lasted all of thirty minutes.

The next few days were short endurance flights of less than an hour as his experience grew. The weather was often unreliable and the smoke from the many industrial plants and power stations in Nottinghamshire often caused a dull haze that made navigation difficult.

There then followed many of what were called circuits and bumps, perfecting take-off, approach and landing. After ten hours and fifty minutes, no more than twelve days of instruction, and having been signed off by Flying Officer Sobieski and Warrant Officer Widlarz, Tomek went solo on 2 June.[2] Then the flying intensity mounted up, with solo flights interspersed with advanced exercises, aerobatics, cross-country navigation, flight planning and all the other basic skills that any RAF pilot had to demonstrate to a high standard.

Perhaps unsurprisingly, Tomek became overconfident, having competitions with other student pilots at low flying and cutting vees in the meandering River Trent with their wingtip vortices. It was inevitable that the chief flying instructor had it reported to him and went up to catch the miscreants at it. Two others realised the game was up and returned immediately to face the music. Tomek, though, had other ideas. Determined that the CFI would not get close enough to read his aircraft's serial number, he embarked on a very low-flying tour, weaving among trees, chimney stacks and even over Nottingham Castle in the hope of not getting caught.

He reasoned that as the Tiger Moths had no radio, there was no way that the CFI could order him to land. Sure enough, the CFI broke off the chase and, after a suitable hiatus, Tomek landed with as much precision as he could muster, and reported to the control tower with an innocent smile on his face. It did not work. The CFI had simply looked at the log to see who had booked out for a solo flight, saw Tomek's name and grounded him for a couple of weeks with extra guard duty.

It is doubtful if Tomek really learned his lesson as he was itching to be operational and fight back as an aggressor and not a victim, though he had no idea how he would carry out his fight against the Russians. He was warned several times not to say anything about that ambition.

His sojourn of being grounded did bring about one incident that he often related, to the embarrassment of his later wife and family.

Part of his punishment was to be on duty throughout the night. Most of the trainee pilots either went back to their billets or girlfriends in the evening. A small mix of Polish and English aircraftsmen remained on duty handling maintenance, stores, signals and security throughout the night.

The conditions were strict blackout with the only permitted illumination being shielded torches. Most often the men would rely on night vision, unless it was a particularly cloudy or foggy night.

It was on such a blacked-out night that Tomek was sitting in the latrines when he heard two Englishmen enter, talking as they were presumably at the urinals. They had no possible way of knowing that there was anyone else in there. One told a joke in English that, for

Life-Changing Tea and Cake

the first time, Tomek understood. His laugh at the best of times was raucous; among the bland, sound-reflective bricks and concrete of the wartime latrine it was positively sepulchral. It echoed hideously followed by silence, a short strangled cry, then running feet.

A few days later one of the Poles told him that the British now thought the latrines were haunted.

The flying intensified with an introduction to night flying where the flare path comprised oil lamps that looked like watering cans with a single flame coming out of the spout. They went under the curious name of gooseneck flares. These were sometimes extinguished if there were reports of a German intruder such as a Ju 88 looking for easy pickings among the trainees. Then their orders were to stay aloft and look for any illuminated airfield.

Inevitably student pilots got lost and there were accidents. One student misjudged an approach, overshot, hit a farmhouse chimney and flopped nose first into a duck pond. Tomek and the hastily assembled rescue party found him sitting astride the rear fuselage, which was sticking up at a crazy angle, determined not to get his shoes wet.

The nearest Tomek came to having a serious crash was when he was tasked with a spinning exercise. Some of the Tiger Moths were equipped with slats that sprang out from the outer leading edge of the upper wing as the aircraft approached its stalling speed. These slats helped to smooth the airflow, allowing the plane to continue flying at a lower speed.

It was vital that the slats were locked before attempting a spin, as if not the outer wing would remain unstalled while the wing on the inside of the spin would still be stalled. The result was always a tightening spin with fatal consequences as recovery was almost impossible.

Tomek had locked the slats, but one opened and the spin tightened, pinning him into his seat. He released his harness but could not get out of the Tiger Moth, being forced into his seat by the G force. Nothing he could do worked.

Desperately he tried kicking in the side of his cockpit in the hope of being flung out in time to use his parachute. He barely made any impression and the blurred whirling landscape of farmland and airfield was getting ever nearer. He realised that if he didn't succeed soon he would be too low for his parachute to open. He was still kicking desperately when the other slat opened and the Tiger Moth stopped spinning. He was now pointing at the ground below 500ft with the speed building up. He hauled on the stick and felt he must have overstressed the plane as it levelled out below the height of the hangar rooftops.

He landed exhausted, trembling and bathed in sweat. One of the instructors came over and told him off for pulling such a dangerous stunt. Tomek pointed to the scuffs on the cockpit wall explaining what had happened. The instructor was having none of it and was keen on having him put on a charge. Fortunately, by the time they reached the CFI's office one of the riggers confirmed that the slat locking cable had snapped and that the Tiger Moth had been rigged incorrectly.

Tomek decided that he would make doubly sure that everything worked twice before taking off.

By 1943, the number of pilots passing through flying schools had accelerated to such a point that there was now a shortage of experienced instructors, aircraft and riggers to service the needs of the rapidly expanding RAF.

It is often overlooked that a significant number of fatalities during the Second World War were through the demands of intensive training. By modern standards, Tomek was thrown in at the deep end as aircraft instrumentation, safety and navigation equipment, particularly among the training fleet, were nowhere near what one would consider to be even the barest minimum today. Operational pilots' needs were sacrosanct and equipment was prioritised for them. Trainee pilots really were learning through the school of hard knocks.

RAF standards were set very high and the trainee pilot was expected meet an acceptable level through grim determination, a burning desire to learn and aptitude. There were no featherbedding, motivational talks or counselling. One was expected to push on regardless and there was little compunction in washing out any student who showed any signs of slowing down. By this stage of the war, industrial capacity was such that aeroplanes were easily replaced – good-quality pilots were not. There was no room at all for the mediocre and any fatalities were taken in their stride. There was little time for agonising, reflection and talking sessions. The war had to be won at any cost.

Having learned to fly on primary gliders in Poland, with no instruments or even a cockpit to shelter the pilot, who was strapped to a seat with only a skid beneath him, Tomek had a natural feel for flying. The Tiger Moth course held no horrors for him and he quickly achieved an acceptable standard prior to being posted off for advanced training.

There was a tendency for RAF instructors to try to put the brakes on natural risk-taking pilots, who had a tendency to cut corners and not fly by the book. Procedures were critical to operational success and that is probably why each CFI would only mark Tomek as 'satisfactory' or 'average' in his logbooks. A good service pilot had to be consistent, a team player and, most important of all, capable of bringing his plane and himself back in one piece. Tomek used to feel quite resentful at this, feeling that he was unappreciated.

He was rarely prepared to adopt any precautionary principle, preferring to fly with élan, often desperate to show off in the hope that his true worth would be recognised.

15

The Hazards of Fire

Tomek was posted to 16 (P) SFTS on 25 August 1943.[1] This was based at RAF Newton, not too far from his elementary flying school and still within easy reach of Nottingham. Here the intensity of training really stepped up to a new level. The Miles Master II[2] and III[3] he was due to fly were far more demanding, with a retractable undercarriage, constant-speed propeller, radio, more complex instrumentation, a far more powerful engine than the familiar Tiger Moth and much higher speeds in cruise and landing. It was a no-nonsense military trainer whose engine needed careful management and demanded skilful flying if it was not to bite the unwary or inexperienced pilot.

As the weather deteriorated through the autumn of 1943, a great deal of time was spent in navigation exercises, sometimes in the Link trainer,[4] which was an early forerunner of the flight simulator. The student sat in a stubby, small-scale plywood aeroplane mounted on a gimbal, allowing limited movement about all three axes. The pilot sat within a closed canopy with no view outside.

The intention was to simulate flying on instruments following instructions on headphones from an instructor seated at a desk outside. As the student progressed, the exercises became ever more complex with drift and turbulence being simulated.

Given a course to steer, his progress was followed by a remote motorised wheeled device with a pen that traced his journey across

The Hazards of Fire

a glass-fronted chart. The intention was to increase the number of hazards and workload, ensuring that the trainee pilot would not become disorientated and lost flying in cloud or at night. This was particularly difficult and even claustrophobic. Tomek, in common with many others, would emerge bathed in sweat after a particularly complex exercise relying on very basic instrumentation.

This would be followed up with the real thing, coping with engine management, navigation over a blacked-out countryside and even doing complex manoeuvres under a canvas hood while the instructor raised his seat and looked over the top of the canopy, occasionally cutting hydraulics to undercarriage, flaps, simulating engine failure, while making sure that the situation did not get too out of hand and result in the loss of aircraft, student and himself.

Even so, there were losses. Engine fires were not unknown, with the Bristol Mercury engine on the Miles Master II going through a spate of incidents. One of Tomek's new friends was lost flying solo one night. He could see the flames streaming back soon after take-off. Tomek and the other students looked on in horror as the aircraft continued in a straight line, losing height all the while.

They later learned that flying control was in touch by radio and that the flames were searing the student pilot's right leg. He could not climb to a safe height for bailing out and found manoeuvring almost impossible.

This poor lad's funeral was the first of many that Tomek would attend in the course of his advanced flying training. This only served to make him even more withdrawn and tense. Sometimes, on the few occasions that Angela was able to visit, she found herself wondering why she had made the effort at all.

There was little room for sentiment; the RAF could not afford to let standards slip. Training was intense and safety margins would not be at all acceptable today. In some ways the ferocious number of training accidents that occurred was part of the toughening process. Most of the instructors had flown operationally, shot at the enemy, lost friends and experienced the full horrors of war. They knew what lay in wait for these trainees once they were posted to a fighter or bomber squadron. They had to perform to an exceptionally high standard regardless of personal feelings.

Unlike Germany's Luftwaffe, who kept their *'experten'* at the front line building up impressive scores that were the subject of much publicity and pride and fodder for Goebbels' propaganda machine, the Allies regarded operational pilots as a critical resource in the wholesale improvement of standards. In reality, many operational pilots hated being posted away from their front-line squadrons, losing the camaraderie that had grown up among their peers. It could be argued that some may even have been bad instructors in the hopes of being posted back into the fray.

What is undeniably true is that there was little in the way of a bond between instructors and students. The training machine for the RAF and its Polish squadrons was designed to turn out motivated, capable and hardened pilots well able to take up their duties and survive those first few critical weeks fighting the enemy. Bitter experience had shown that earlier training regimes had ill equipped pilots for the realities of war, with many succumbing to the enemy's guns within fewer than half a dozen sorties.

Tomek was already being hardened even more than that bitter survivor of the Vorkuta gulag.

Procedures were tightened up after a number of accidents and it was drummed into Tomek and his contemporaries that over-priming the engine would lead to fires. Even so, the fatalities continued for a while longer and the Miles Master was to number among Tomek's least-favourite aircraft; that is, until he was taken aloft with four other students on cross-country navigation exercises in the Avro Anson.[5] This throwback to the 1930s with its hand-cranked retractable undercarriage was famous for its undulating progress after take-off as the pilot frantically wound away at the handle to retract the wheels.

This, coupled with the incessant noise, fabric-covered wings that seemed to shiver and bend in the breeze, and the wide gap between the wing's trailing edge and the fuselage made Tomek airsick. He could barely take in what the instructor was saying and, as he often said, he felt he had to develop telepathic powers in order to understand what was expected of him once he was in the air.

These exercises invariably happened when the weather was too bad for routine training in the Master. As the Anson stooged around at low level, the air was anything but smooth, frequently when returning from a training sortie in poor visibility. Then the Anson's pilot would drop lower in the hope of picking up any landmark to help him navigate back to Newton. Tomek's confidence in the pilot's abilities would drop to an all-time low as he feared that his flying career and probably his life would end wrapped around some miserable, smoking chimney stack in the smog and drizzle.

On the very few occasions he was allowed to act as a co-pilot it helped persuade him that single-engine fighters, and the Spitfire in particular, were the only aircraft he should fly. He reasoned that the way things were going, he would be unlikely to complete all his twin-engine training in time to fight in the war and win an opportunity of going back to Poland. He, Tomek, was going to lead a victorious band back to his homeland and expunge all the legacy of torture, humiliation and defeat that he and Poland had suffered.

It was that burning desire, in the face of a gradual disenchantment among the Poles surrounding him, that spurred him on.

The news that the Germans had unearthed mass graves in Eastern Poland's Katyn Forest[6] in April 1943 had been suppressed, leaking out only slowly, and for a long time was disbelieved as Nazi propaganda, at least by the British. The Polish Government in Exile under General Sikorski were certain that the Russians were responsible, as too many Polish officers were unaccounted for when General Anders was forming his army in Tashkent, then Tehran.

The Poles had long suspected that Stalin had made sure that the Polish government and command structure was emasculated long before the Germans invaded Russia. Their best efforts at blaming Hitler found no echoes at all among the Poles, so Stalin promptly cut diplomatic relations with Sikorski, leaving Churchill and Roosevelt with a problem.

By mid-1943, they needed a Mediterranean-based Polish Army to be an effective and committed force to distract the Germans away from the likely site of a major European invasion already in planning for northern

France. Also, the several Polish Air Force squadrons based in the UK and North Africa were an integral part of the war in the air. They could not afford for any of them to become disenchanted, feeling that the USA and UK were not wholly committed to Poland's own war aims, while the major part of US forces, both land and air, had yet to arrive, be fully trained and become the overwhelming force they needed to be if Germany were to be utterly defeated.

The isolation of the Polish Government in Exile was not a feasible option and somehow Churchill and Roosevelt had to do a very carefully choreographed dance to keep both their Russian and Polish partners on side.

Stalin was all for throwing all the Polish divisions into a thrust through still neutral Turkey into the Balkans or up through Georgia to maintain access to the major European oilfields, bringing them all firmly into his orbit once Germany was defeated. To that end he was determined that all Polish Air Force resources should be under his ultimate control.

Churchill, in particular, wanted the Polish Army under General Anders to help invade what he called 'the Underbelly of Europe', following an invasion of Sicily and Italy.[7]

Some Polish squadrons had done a brief tour in North Africa in order to improve their understanding of how air-to-ground operations would work once a new front was opened in northern France. RAF planners had already earmarked the Polish fighter squadrons to be included in the 2nd Tactical Air Force,[8] which would ensure critical air superiority over the beachhead once it had been established.

Somehow they had to keep the Polish Government in Exile onside without upsetting Stalin, but Sikorski was an adamant and an irritating thorn in the flesh, resistant to all suggestions of compromise. It was only a matter of time before the full impact of the Katyn massacres was felt and there was a real fear that Stalin might negotiate a separate peace with Hitler, dooming the USA and UK to a much longer drawn-out war in the west. Something had to be done.

The solution came unexpectedly in Gibraltar on 4 July 1943, at 2307 hours, when, following a tour inspecting the Polish forces in the Middle East, the Liberator transport carrying Sikorski,[9] several officers and his chief of staff crashed after take-off. Only the Czech pilot survived. For many Poles this 'accident' would for many years seem a little too convenient. The sad fact was that they had lost their only effective and charismatic leader.[10]

The official cause was a pack left at the rear of the fuselage that slipped back when the Liberator rotated at take-off, jamming the elevator controls. The fact that only the pilot was wearing a lifejacket and stories that furs, jewels and black-market contraband were found in the sunken wreckage only increased most Poles' scepticism that this was not really an accident.

Tomek was already deeply involved in his advanced training while these great matters of historical import took place. By late July rumours were circulating, but as he had discovered many times before, rumours were unreliable and he was far better off concentrating on the job in hand, which was to become an effective pilot. Angela had become a fixture in his life and by means of letters, boosted by odd visits, she had come to accept him as a possible husband.

He had little idea as to how his flying career, wartime politics and his hoped-for marriage would collide. He became a little resentful when a couple of his mates, then a few of the instructors, and finally officers, started to issue warnings about not making any long-term plans. He could not see how anything could possibly interfere with his progress towards flying a Spitfire, winning a war and settling back in Poland in a matter of months.

As autumn declined into winter, instrument flying became critical to survival. Often Tomek went up above the clouds to carry out that day's scheduled exercise, which could include recovery from unusual attitudes, spinning, aerobatics and occasional formation flying with another Miles Master. It was getting back below the cloud that caused problems. He mastered pretty quickly how to keep his aircraft on an even keel and pointing in what he hoped was the right direction, until he popped out underneath. The problems invariably began after that, as in the frequent murky drizzle, it was very difficult to be sure of where he was.

Several of the student pilots had got lost, overshot Nottingham and found themselves over the Peak District, with high ground merging into low cloud. Some of the lucky ones bailed out at that point, provided that they were high enough for their parachutes to work. Then they faced the inevitable problem of being found before they died of exposure. They would then be transported back to RAF Newton to face an inevitable enquiry into what went wrong, was it their fault and could they have redeemed the situation. In some cases the student pilot was so badly affected that they asked to be reassigned to other duties or even washed out of the course entirely. There was little room for failure as the wartime training machine ground on.

Where possible Tomek would observe, on dual-instruction flights, how his instructor found their way back and try to emulate their techniques. If he was assigned a non-navigational exercise, he had to fly due east until he was well over the North Sea before attempting that sortie's assigned task. That way he was sure that he had no pylons, chimneys or high ground lying in wait for him.

He often noted that with a westerly wind the smoke plume from the industrial East Midlands and Nottingham in particular would be blown well out to sea. If he took his oxygen mask off, he could often smell the sulphur. By staying in the thick of the plume with the increasingly unpleasant smell, he was certain that he could navigate his way back to the approximate location of RAF Newton and find some familiar landmarks.

He was fortunate that there was no active balloon barrage out to catch him in its wires, but the risk of collision with another aircraft was very real and he developed the habit of keeping his head moving the whole time, scanning in every direction – a habit that stood him in good stead.

He had a couple of close encounters but nothing that really constituted a near miss, save one occasion when he nearly touched wings with another Master in the circuit. Some of his colleagues were not so lucky. The number of funeral parades went up steadily.

His assessments were good, and kept him moving towards his goal of flying a Spitfire. His other assessments in terms of being a team player and potential officer were not so good. He never really understood that flying abilities alone would not guarantee him a place in an operational Spitfire squadron.

One surprisingly clear day shortly before Christmas 1943, he saw an unusual Spitfire with contra-rotating propellers take off from Hucknall and almost aim straight up, passing a few hundred yards in front of his Master II at a rate he could hardly believe. By now he had seen a number of Spitfires take off and land but this was something extraordinary. In all probability it was one of the prototype Spitfire Mk. 21s, but of course any later enquiries were met with a wall of silence. Whatever it was, it had to remain a secret.

16

Marriage and Disappointment

By Christmas 1943 there was little doubt that Germany could not win the war. The Allied campaign in the Mediterranean was going to plan, with Rommel's Afrika Korps now out of North Africa. The following successful invasion of Sicily, then the landing in Salerno, Italy, involved the total commitment of Polish forces based in the Mediterranean. All of this was under way without any wobbles since the death of General Sikorski.

Operation Overlord, the invasion of Normandy, was planned for the late spring of 1944 despite strong urging from Stalin to bring it forward. Both Roosevelt, who by now was ailing, and Churchill had to be pretty agile in their negotiations, effectively parking any mention of what would happen to Poland after the war was won.

The tide of battle in the Pacific was turning and both Roosevelt and Stalin had acknowledged that Britain would be an almost bankrupt, declining world power with a shrinking empire after the war. Many British sources were well aware of this thinking, even though their boss Churchill did not want to contemplate such an outcome. However, there was recognition, even by him, that pressure was building and that he had to face the fact that Stalin was in a position to call many of the shots.

The question of a democratic Polish nation was sliding down the agenda and the official attitude was to keep quiet in front of any Poles. Slowly, this gradual acceptance of wartime 'Realpolitik' was percolating down to the Polish squadrons and it is significant that any urgency in getting them re-equipped with more up-to-date equipment, such as the new and very fast Spitfire XIV or the Hawker Tempest V, had pretty well calmed down. Similarly, there was recognition that keeping the Polish squadrons in reserve until the invasion was under way, and thereby maintaining a lower rate of attrition, might be a good move.

Although it was never discussed openly, many Polish airmen were beginning to wonder if the Polish Air Force element was deliberately held back from expanding, as many more potential front-line pilots found themselves assigned to other less-demanding roles. Years later the author heard many former Polish aircrew wonder if there had been a fear that the Poles would have transferred their hostilities to fighting the Russians once Germany was defeated.

It is difficult to document the truth behind this impression, but anecdotal evidence suggests that by early 1944 many Poles had the feeling that the British upper echelons were beginning to have reservations about how much operational autonomy the Polish squadrons should have once Operation Overlord was under way.

Tomek was not looking forward to Christmas. A gloom had settled over him as he had the feeling that the Polish *Wigilia* (Christmas Eve) was going to be a thing of the past. His only consolation was meeting his beloved Angela again at her mother's house. Propriety meant that he would be staying with neighbours, which was just as well as he had no idea how hard up his future mother-in-law was and how cold the little bungalow at 91 Vale Avenue in Patcham was likely to be.

Angela was beginning to realise that Tomek was still carrying the burden of his experiences in Siberia, and had decided that she would do her best to help him lead a more peaceful life, when she received a brief note: 'My Mummy have died'. This hit her hard as she had just realised that her own mother was keeping to herself the fact she had breast cancer and that would mean some major operations.

The news about Tomek's mother had come via the Polish Government in Exile from General Anders' staff in Palestine. There were few details beyond that she had died of a fever and had been buried in an unmarked grave. Subsequent and persistent enquiries did not help at all. The usual reaction was one of a sympathetic smile and a shrug of the shoulders. It was war after all, and people were dying in their thousands everywhere.

The immediate effect was to throw Angela and Tomek together even more closely than before. She was becoming both charmed and amused by his quaint command of English, such as the time he was watching her brush her long hair that stretched down past her shoulders. She caught sight of him in the mirror over her mother's mantelpiece looking on with adoration. Arlene came in just in time to hear him say, 'Oh Ania, I do so like the hairs on your back side.' He was puzzled by their laughter. Arlene hugged him and kissed his cheek. She looked over to Angela and nodded in approval. Surprised, he asked, 'May I call you Mummy?' It was as much as she could do not to burst into tears.

As they got to know him better, they indulged his odd phrases like, 'He's too late for a gate!' without understanding exactly who he was and why a gate?

Angela decided to have some Polish lessons organised by the Polish chaplain in Brighton. She could only get to them on those odd weekends when she wasn't working. Very occasionally Tomek was off as well and decided, by way of encouragement, to come as an observer. All went well until she heard a loud whoosh and turned to see him with singed hair and blackened face. In the absence of an ashtray he had used an open box of Swan Vesta matches as a repository for his cigarette ash, with some explosive consequences. That very human error finally persuaded Angela to accept his proposal of marriage and let her family know what was already quite obvious to them all.

He managed to get a few days off over Christmas to meet Angela's war correspondent father, Arthur Oakeshott,[1] in London and ask his permission to marry Angela, which, as she was not yet 21, was a legal requirement before he could apply for permission to marry and also satisfy the necessary paperwork demanded by the registrar.

With Tomek in RAF Newton and Angela working at Bletchley Park, the load fell on Arlene and their parish priest at St Mary's Preston Park. This would have consequences as Tomek had very little idea as to how the formalities worked.

Marriage and Disappointment

The meeting with Angela's estranged father went well, as he wrote to his daughter saying that Tomek was a nice bloke, barely understandable but 'he sounded a bit like a goat every time he laughed!'

Unbeknown to Tomek and Angela, Arlene would be recovering from her double mastectomy by the time they both had some Christmas leave. Inevitably things were busy as they arranged the wedding schedule, with the big day set for 15 April 1944. In many ways the planning was a blessing as it raised Tomek's spirits after the loss of his mother added to his usual Christmas gloom, and the effects of Arlene's operation.

Tomek was back flying again within a couple of days. Details such as where they would live together were postponed and barely addressed as their respective workloads eclipsed any sense of celebration.

His logbook by 3 January 1944 shows that he had completed a total of around 190 hours flying with an increasing number of dual night-flying navigation exercises. It was then the realisation was beginning to bite that he was barely halfway on his journey to flying a Spitfire. By his own admission, the endless hours of practice and the steady attrition among his contemporaries was taking its toll. He was hopeful of having his wings presented before his wedding day, but was beginning to have doubts. His instructors were not encouraging. The weather was frequently bad and they were unwilling to speed up his training in light of recent accidents.

Angela came to visit, staying in a one-room B&B on the outskirts of Nottingham. She was disappointed as, having missed a number of training sorties through bad weather, Tomek's workload had gone up once the cold and frosty weather set in. Instead of having a few hours' downtime after the day's training, on some days he was going from lectures to training flights and even a night-time sortie before reporting back and being released to his billet. There was absolutely no question, given the social and sexual mores of the time, of the couple spending an evening, let alone a night, together in her B&B.

One afternoon, exhausted after some intensive flying, Tomek was released early as fog had rolled in, so he hitched a lift into Nottingham. He called on Angela and it was bitterly cold with no heating. She was sitting up in bed fully clothed with her overcoat on. Tomek simply got into bed beside her still wearing his RAF issue duffle coat and fell fast asleep while she sat up writing letters. Typically, her landlady, fearing that her miserable digs were being turned into a house of ill repute, opened the door without knocking and registered disappointment at the modesty of the scene. Angela asked if there was anything she wanted, to which the good woman simply sniffed and slammed the door shut. Tomek did not even stir.

Angela had a sizeable autograph book, which contained a number of poems and sentiments written by old school friends and servicemen who had spent afternoons with the girls in Patcham, one of which really tickled Tomek:

Across the stile he stole
And many a wink he wunk
And many a weary smile he smole
As many a think he thunk.

He loved quoting it, often trying to use it as an exercise in pronunciation, much to Angela and her family's amusement.

The other one that struck a chord with both Angela and Tomek, even to the point of bringing tears to their eyes given the uncertainty of fate during the war, was a verse by Christina Rosetti:

Should one of us remember,
And one of us forget,
I wish I knew what each will do –
But who can tell as yet?

Should one of us remember,
And one of us forget,
I promise you what I will do –
And I'm content to wait for you,
And not be sure as yet.

Marriage and Disappointment

In order to lighten the mood after reading that once again, Tomek drew a cartoon of himself riding a baby's bottle with a propeller on the front and a farting cow's behind, while an obviously pregnant figure with two small children beside her waved from the globe below.

Everyone who saw that cartoon in Angela's book commented that it was obvious what Tomek wanted out of life. He was determined to leave his mark on posterity and Angela was to be the means of achieving it.

What Angela had not realised at the time was the sheer risk faced by Tomek when it came to flying training. The wartime censor made sure that no figures were published on training accidents, or indeed other losses, for fear of spreading despondency. That said, anyone living near high ground could attest to the number of crashes that happened in bad weather.

Things sped up in February and March with his first introduction to practice bombing and aerial gunnery. Interception was not yet part of Tomek's training regime.

When it came to deciding on how to conduct the war, the Allies recognised that the Luftwaffe was a spent force in France. Most German fighter units had been either assigned to the Eastern Front or on home defence against the ever-increasing, round-the-clock bombing raids. Hitler may have unleashed the concept of 'Blitzkrieg' on Poland and France with close co-operation between tactical air power and ground forces, but the lesson had been well learned and the Allies were about to pay him back in the same coin.

This would be a disappointment for Tomek and his fellow trainees. There would be little chance of emulating the heroic air battles of the earlier Polish Spitfire and Hurricane squadrons in 1940–41. RAF emphasis was now on close support and interdiction behind enemy lines, as tactics evolved for supporting Operation Overlord.

By the spring of 1944 it was obvious to everyone that an invasion was coming, but the where was still a very closely guarded secret. Many new satellite airfields had sprung up across the countryside. Many more aeroplanes were seen in the air. Tents sprung up like mushrooms overnight and there were American GIs everywhere, on top of the British, Canadians, South African, Free French and Polish servicemen who had already become a familiar sight.

This impacted on Angela and her family as ever more GIs were entertained in Patcham and, to her surprise, she came across attitudes of discrimination towards Black servicemen, especially from those who had been brought up in the Deep South. She was grateful that Tomek was less able to have enough time off to visit, as she felt sure that her fiancé would start a fight.

Her sisters were finding American overconfidence irksome, as there was an assumption that all English girls were fair game. Often there was no hint of delicate romance, just an immediate attempt at quick seduction. Her young sister Maureen found a GI sitting next to her in the cinema, despite it being almost empty. Without any warning, he promptly exposed himself. With the sort of *sang froid* that belied her 16 years and convent upbringing, she sighed in a bored seen-it-all-before fashion and replied: 'No thanks, I don't smoke woodbines.'

Angela, her mother and sisters agreed that they all preferred the gentler, more courtly approach of the Poles.

If she had any doubts about her Polish future husband, those and similar experiences strengthened her resolve to be the wife he obviously needed, especially after he had started, albeit haltingly, to talk about his experiences in Siberia, much to their shock.

When she confided this to her war correspondent father, who by now had covered several convoys to Murmansk in northern Russia, he simply smiled, nodded and said: 'I know kid, we're told not to report at all anything about what the Russians are really like. It's total war and we need all the allies we can get.'

Tomek found that there were now lectures on what their roles might be in fighting the Germans. The effectiveness of their training was emphasised and occasional intelligence reports were included that talked up the effectiveness of the Allied bombing campaign, the attrition among Luftwaffe pilots and the fact that they were now fighting on three fronts against air forces coming from the west over France, the south over Italy and the east over Russia and Ukraine. Germany was bound to lose the war and they would be at the forefront of the coming invasion.

All of this positive talk made him feel that he was making progress to a front-line squadron, when finally, on 19 March 1944, he was signed off having completed a navigation test in the dreaded Anson. His permission to marry was finally sent off by the station adjutant to the Brighton registrar ten days later.[2]

That was the last of the good news. He was posted with immediate effect to Ipswich to fly the Miles Martinet target tug with 679 Squadron.[3] The Spitfire seemed as far away as ever. He might have been awarded his coveted Polish Air Force eagle in place of the RAF wings, but operational flying was still a distant prospect.

On 7 April, barely eight days before his wedding day, he took off for the first time to familiarise himself with the local area, followed by a few days spent on sorties over the anti-aircraft guns at Clacton, minus a drogue target towed behind while the guns tracked him without firing. There were bets made as to how good the gunners' aircraft recognition was, as on previous occasions a few rounds had been loosened off against Martinets flying without a drogue in the mistaken belief that they were German Focke-Wulf Fw 190s.

He was allowed four days to cover getting down to his own wedding, the great day itself and subsequent honeymoon. What he did not know was that Angela had been told that she was not to work at Bletchley Park any more as she would automatically have Polish citizenship upon marrying Tomek and was henceforth to be regarded as a security risk. What was even more galling was that any small benefits that might have accrued during her service at Bletchley Park were now voided as she was the responsibility of the Polish Government in Exile! The final catch-all was that, having signed the Official Secrets Act, she was not to mention her previous work, or indeed the terms of her sudden unemployment.

Among the many things not explained to Tomek was that he was not getting married at St Mary Magdalene's, the one Catholic church he was familiar with in Brighton, but at St Mary's Preston Park about 2 miles away across town.

Somehow a bouquet of daffodils and freesias had been found for Angela and by some miracle, probably involving parachute silk and the best efforts of the local black market, she had been fitted with a white wedding dress, veil and stockings.

What was missing, however, when Mr Elphick, the local taxi driver, conveyed her to the church, was the bridegroom. After two circuits around the neighbourhood, by which time Angela thought she had been jilted, a good friend who was taking the place of her absent father, away reporting on efforts to sink the German pocket battleship *Tirpitz* in Norway, suggested that maybe Tomek was at the wrong church with his best man!

Two young men were despatched on motorcycles, arriving back within twenty minutes with a pair of very confused Poles, who had no real idea of what was going on. Fortunately the rest of the day went well and that evening Angela found herself on the train with several changes en route before reaching Ipswich for a very brief honeymoon.

In common with many of his contemporaries, Tomek was beginning to wonder if, along with other Polish airmen, he was being what the Americans called sidelined. It was obvious from the sheer weight of numbers building up, particularly of Americans, that the Poles were no longer regarded as being of any serious relevance to the war effort as a whole. They had held Churchill in high regard as a friend of Poland, but as concerns post Sikorski's death were being voiced out loud when flying was slow or postponed, Tomek realised that Mikołajczyk's government in London had none of the gravitas or influence enjoyed by Sikorski.

Tomek was torn. He had got on well with his future father-in-law Arthur and his brother Wulstan Oakeshott, who had told him in confidence what they knew about the Tehran Conference that previous December, which was not published in any detail. Tomek did not want to believe that Poland had been betrayed and to some extent he had been buoyed up by the prospect of marriage to Angela. However, now that was a sealed deal, his sense of abandonment and misery was growing into resentment. This had been noted and may have played some part in his new posting.

Others had gone directly into 61 Operational Training Unit (OTU) based at Rednal in Shropshire, where they learned the arts of air-to-air firing, practice bombing and conversion onto front-line fighters such as the Spitfire. Tomek felt, with some justification, that he had been posted into a backwater. This was reinforced when two Brazilian pilots arrived to join the pool of pilots in Ipswich, especially as Tomek had no idea that Brazil was actively engaged in the war!

The Brazilians' lack of urgency communicated itself to some of the other pilots and their winch operators, leading to an inevitable decline in standards, with predictable results. Tomek felt he was being let down on all sides and did not have sufficient rank to do anything about it. His efforts simply caused resentment and isolation as plainly he was not one of the boys.

Several times he had to cut short a sortie when a winch was u/s (unserviceable), leaving the drogue to stream out just under the fuselage with the risk of wrapping round the rudder and elevator. Engines ran rough or cut out and the British winch operators were becoming sloppy, frequently behaving as if they could not, or more likely would not, understand any of the Polish airmen.

The endless routines of flying the Martinet on either a low tow or high tow became tedious, each day consisting of a very careful pre-flight inspection, watching as the propeller was pulled through to check for any oil that had pooled in the bottom cylinders of the radial engine. Tomek then clambered up awkwardly into the cockpit while a fitter checked his harness and parachute straps. The pilot passed them forward over his shoulders, plugged in his microphone and headset leads, checked the fuel contents, set the prop, checked the cooling gills, taking care to prime correctly, then pushed the booster coil and starter buttons. There was a whine as the propeller blades flicked across his field of vision, followed by a puff of grey smoke as the engine rumbled into life.

He set the gyrocompass: were all the instruments performing as they should? Then a quick check on the intercom that the winchman was all set, and the slow waddle out to the holding point, opening the throttle, cycling the propeller from fine to coarse and back to fine. Then he checked the magnetos, switching left and right: was the drop in revs within limits? Check mixture, temperatures and pressures, check flap setting, check brakes released, creep forward, check that no other planes were on final approach, and look towards the control tower. A green light, then line up, check the windsock, then open the throttle to be deafened and shaken to bits as the Martinet slowly gained speed.[4]

He could almost do it in his sleep, and the climb out was slow and boring. He checked the undercarriage and trim, throttle friction, mixture, revs, temperatures, oil pressure, then set course across the landscape towards Clacton. Progress was slow, loud, occasionally painful and the flight strictly straight and level.

He was aloft on 6 June 1944. He had had an unusually thorough briefing. He had to stick to a particular course and check the weather. There were to be no live firings that day. He had never seen so many aircraft. There were Dakotas, Spitfires, Thunderbolts, Mustangs, even Stirlings, Halifaxes and Lancasters all with black and white stripes painted on their wings. Some of the heavy bombers were towing gliders. There were some aircraft he did not recognise, but they were all headed in the same direction. Below, the sea was churned up by hundreds of ships, their wakes making broad 'S' shapes over the grey sea as they zigzagged to make any intruding U-boat's task more difficult.

He's been advised to stay well away from any Royal Navy ship as they would be nervous and trigger happy. D-Day had arrived and the invasion of France had begun. Impressed though he was, he felt once more that he was missing out on the action. At this rate the war would be over before he ever sat in a Spitfire.

There were occasional compensations such as when, having read the manual and been talked through all the switches and buttons, he was allowed to fly the Hurricane. At last a single-seat fighter, albeit without loaded guns. At first he did a short cross-country, before a couple of silent exercises with the Clacton anti-aircraft guns, which simply tracked him at a much higher speed than the pedestrian Martinet could manage. He liked the Hurricane: the view was good, it was fully aerobatic with a reserve of power, and although it was obsolete as a front-line fighter, it felt potent.

He managed a couple of forty-eight-hour passes, taking a beaten-up Ariel motorcycle that had seen better days to Brighton. His only route lay through a blacked-out London as the V1 Blitz was under way. V1 Doodlebugs[5] were coming over every few minutes with their distinctive rasping burble, before cutting out and diving down to end in a massive explosion.

These were the precursors of the cruise missile drones that have featured in the war in Ukraine. They had sufficient fuel to take them from Pas-de-Calais to London powered by a primitive yet effective Argus pulse jet, which sat like a long stovepipe atop the tiny pilotless plane. Compared to Ukrainian war drones, they were very fast, flying between 2,000 and 5,000ft. The latest Spitfires, Mustangs and Tempests were capable of catching them, but as they had a very large explosive warhead, there was considerable risk in shooting them down at close range.

Unlike the drones of today, the V1 was incapable of manoeuvring and only had a gyrocompass and timer to determine where they came down, having been aimed in the direction of London. They were, in reality, an unguided terror weapon, soon to be followed by the supersonic and stratospheric V2 strategic rocket, which was too fast and too high for even the faintest possibility of interception.

Tomek's silencer had long taken leave of the Ariel's exhaust system and it wasn't long before he was pulled over by a policeman. Just then another V1 rasped overhead. Tomek simply looked quizzically at the constable, who agreed that the motorcycle was no worse than a Doodlebug and sent him on his way.

On 8 August he took a Hurricane to Castle Bromwich, where he was astonished at the number of Spitfires lined up for test flying then delivery. He dearly would have loved to get his hands on one, but had no time to talk to any of the many test pilots, who seemed to hand over notes, talk to some engineers, then jump into another one and take it up. He had seen for the first time how the industrial war machine churned out what was needed. It impressed him mightily and he vowed that once the war was over he would surely work in the aviation industry. He wanted to be part of it.

He had one unauthorised flight that he dare not log. A Fairey Barracuda had arrived. This ungainly yet effective carrier-borne torpedo bomber had been assigned to the Ipswich flight and tried as a target tug, a role it took to with few problems. The Fleet Air Arm pilot was pretty relaxed at showing Tomek what was what and occupying the observer's seat while Tomek took it up for some local flying. He found the flap arrangement very different and, despite having the same engine as the Hurricane, much slower and noisier. Even so, it struck Tomek as a proper fighting aeroplane.

The day 30 August 1944 almost ended his flying career. He was scheduled to take a Martinet over to Clacton and tow a drogue for the local guns. His winchman, LAC Weller, was one he had not flown with before and Tomek had fallen into the trap of assuming that he knew what he was doing. This winchman did not.

Having set up for a low tow, the engine cut and they were well offshore beyond easy gliding distance of the beach. Tomek announced they would have to bail out, LAC Weller replied he had forgotten his parachute! The next option was ditching: Weller couldn't swim. What about his Mae West lifejacket and personal dinghy? He had left them behind as well. Tomek was far from impressed and realised that he could not leave Weller in the lurch. By now smoke was billowing from his stopped engine.[6]

Fortunately, he had put the propeller into coarse pitch, which cut down a lot of the drag from it windmilling. His pre-war gliding experience helped a bit here and after stretching the glide as much as he could, he just scraped the nose and wings over the cliffs at Frinton. By now the plane was burning merrily and Weller had jumped out, running away like a hare.

Tomek managed to get as far as the fuel-filled wing when he was pulled up short. His dinghy that was attached on the end of a lanyard was caught up in the cockpit, which was now filling with smoke. The port wing beneath his feet was beginning to feel very hot through his flying boots and the Martinet was rocking with its rear fuselage and tail hanging over the edge of a cliff.

The smoke was choking and he could not see to undo the clip to his dinghy's lanyard. He fiddled with it frantically, afraid to take his gloves off for fear of burning his hands. More by luck than judgement, it parted and he threw himself off just as the wing caught fire. His gloves, goggles and helmet were scorched but fortunately he was still alive.

Angela was staying in Ipswich at the time and was getting worried when her new husband wasn't back in the evening. She had seen oily black smoke rolling up into the sky, possibly caused by another crash or maybe an airfield fire truck practising on a condemned aircraft hulk. She was already nervous before two young Polish airmen arrived and in broken English said that Tomek had had an accident.

Tearful and resigned to early widowhood, she was both relieved and angry when a very tired Tomek finally appeared at around 10 p.m. She was even more distressed, wanting him to stay with her for a few hours more, when he was detailed to fly a Hurricane the next day. There was no room at all for pity or domestic harmony. He had to get back into the cockpit and prove he was still a capable flyer.

It was with a very heavy heart that Angela made the onerous train journey back to Brighton. By the time she reached the Patcham bungalow she was feeling poorly and running a temperature. Her mother put her to bed and called the family doctor, Dr O'Mahoney, who had known Angela since childhood and later diagnosed German measles. He did not have the heart to tell her then that she was probably pregnant.

Tomek was not told that his wife was expecting their first child and certainly not what German measles in the first few weeks of pregnancy almost inevitably meant in terms of a baby born with many congenital problems.

That tragedy lay in the future.

For the moment Tomek was, in common with many other Polish airmen, feeling an ever-growing resentment towards the British Government. It was obvious that their initial fears about being sold out to the Russians were being realised. Their distrust of what Britain and the USA would do after the war became ever more deep-seated. Rumours had begun that flights to relieve the horrors and desperate fighting of the Warsaw Uprising were being held back in order not to annoy the Russians.

All the Poles had hoped that this was the beginning of an independent Poland, capable of liberating itself from the Germans. The response was furious and overwhelming. Warsaw was about to become one of the worst casualties of the war with no building left undamaged and a massive loss of life. The city centre was totally destroyed and the resistance took to the sewers, hoping that somehow the Allies would come to their aid. It was a vain hope.

By the end of August the stories had increased in intensity, with Tomek being assured that some of the Polish bomber boys from 301 Squadron had been intercepted by Russian night fighters. Certainly some Liberator bombers had been lost and that only fuelled even more rumours.

Tomek felt demoralised and powerless. He described his almost daily target tug flights as footling and pointless. When in fact news did filter through that the Americans had finally been allowed to make a supply drop to Warsaw, he was convinced that the Russians had deliberately stalled to ensure that all non-communist Poles had been wiped out by the Germans.

Whereas there may have been some truth in those opinions at the time, the reality was more nuanced. The Russian General Rokossovsky was certainly unwilling to take on the besieging Germans by crossing the River Vistula, although some elements of the Polish 1st Army under Zygmunt Berling, who was now a general promoted by the Russians, did make contact with the Polish Land Army in Warsaw, but there was no follow-up.

The Russians estimated that 96 per cent of all the air drops aimed at helping the Warsaw Uprising fell into German hands. Meanwhile, the systematic destruction of Warsaw went on, along with such barbarities as giving Polish children booby-trapped sweets.

Marriage and Disappointment

Warsaw, by October 1944, was probably the most destroyed capital city in percentage terms of all Europe and possibly the world. What is beyond any question is that the ineffective Polish Government in Exile, now under Tomasz Arciszewski, had no influence whatsoever on decisions made in London and Washington, let alone Moscow. They were being left behind by events, and Polish airmen such as Tomek knew this.

The news that slowly escaped Warsaw was depressing. The Poles in Britain really did not want to consider the prospect of a Russian-dominated Poland, and it was noticeable that at first quite a few who had escaped via Rumania in 1939 still regarded Germany as the main enemy. Those who had flown against them before Poland was overrun were now firmly embedded in the officer elite and disinclined to listen to the late arrivals who had escaped Siberia following the amnesty in 1941.

There was probably a twofold reason: the Poles from the original fighter squadrons such as 303, who had fought in France[7] before their sterling efforts in the Battle of Britain, had been fighting the Germans for five years and understandably, having lost friends and colleagues, would have found it too painful to consider that their sacrifices had been in vain. The second probable reason would have involved rank. Few of the later escapees would have been commissioned officers, and in the nature of military hierarchies there would not have been much opportunity for the sergeant pilots to become familiar enough with their senior officers to share opinions freely enough to contradict them.

There was a relatively short distance from the home-based squadrons and the Polish Government in Exile based in London, which meant that there were frequent visits and encounters; therefore the operational service side knew what was going on politically and the senior government figures had their fingers on the front-line pulse. Nobody really wanted to accept the reality of being outmanoeuvred by the pragmatism of impending postwar politics and the necessary shift in strategic alliances.

The majority of escapees from Siberia were now numbered among General Anders' forces fighting in the Mediterranean. There was some interchange of information and ideas up to the death of General Sikorski, but that had all but evaporated after D-Day as any face-to-face communication between Anders and the Poles based in London was increasingly dependent upon the permissions and resources of the Supreme Allied Command and, inevitably, Polish wishes and priorities were now pretty low down the list.

Finally, some of these late arrivals did not quite seem as 'Polish' as those from old families around Warsaw and Kraków. Their accents were different and some, particularly among Anders' forces, sounded like Ukrainians, Belarusians, Ruthenes and Jews.

17

Spitfires at Last!

Finally, Tomek was sent to report for training on the Spitfire and that meant a lot of ground school first. As so often happened in wartime, a few days were spent trudging around from one wooden cabin to another for lectures, then tests in the intricacies of the Spitfire's systems followed by yet another written exam. On 7 September 1944, he was put through an intense written and oral examination of his R/T procedures, fluency and terminology by a very English flying officer named David Southwood, rather than a Polish instructor who may have been a bit more indulgent and inclined to let the odd mistake slip through.[1]

He felt pretty confident about all the tests on the Spitfire Mk. V[2] cockpit drill but was completely unprepared for the use of oxygen test in a decompression chamber.[3] He and about ten or eleven others were lined up on two long benches inside the chamber, which looked to Tomek's eyes like the inside of a submarine. They were all wearing leather helmets and oxygen masks. The large barometer dial showed a fairly rapid equivalent climb to 12,000ft, where the sound of Tomek's breathing was only interrupted by the instructor's tinny voice over the earphones telling all the students to start writing their names on a slate, which they continued to do, even after being ordered to remove their masks.

Tomek felt confident that he would have no problems, having flown the Martinet to over 10,000ft with no ill effects …

13,000 … No problem. 14,000 … and one of the other students had slumped over, before the instructor leaned forward and reattached his mask. 15,000 … now several students had passed out or dropped their slates and Tomek was sure that the instructor's eyes were smiling encouragingly behind his own oxygen mask …

Feeling very confident, now with his mask on, Tomek wondered what all the fuss was about. He alone had carried on with no problem … That was until the instructor showed him, after the test was over, how his writing had become more and more of a scrawl, ending with just a chalk line before he passed out. It was only the evidence on the slate that eventually convinced Tomek that he was no superman. As the instructor explained to all of them, there was no warning of oxygen failure. The usual symptom was overconfidence. They must always check their oxygen flow gauge and be sure to get to a lower altitude if they ran out, or the flow was stopped through malfunction or battle damage.

His next stop was 61 OTU RAF Rednal in Shropshire,[4] where Tomek had to learn the business of air fighting, before being posted to an operational squadron.

He was disappointed to find that his first flight at Rednal was in a Miles Master III, being checked out by W/O Trybulec. Tomek had to prove that he was both confident and consistent in local navigation. It was critical that, whatever the weather, he could always find his way back. The emphasis was on staying in the local area, as the Welsh mountains were only a few minutes' flying time away, with cloud-capped summits only too ready to claw the inexperienced from the sky.

Once his instructor was satisfied with Tomek after only a twenty-minute flight, he was allowed to sit for some time in a Spitfire cockpit and familiarise himself with all the dials and buttons, being talked through the start-up procedure, which was not too dissimilar from the Hurricane he had been flying before.

Once strapped in, the view ahead of that long Merlin engine was not brilliant and he had to weave left and right to make sure that were no obstructions ahead. The narrow undercarriage felt a bit sensitive – a lot

Spitfires at Last!

less forgiving than the Hurricane. Lined up and pointing into the wind, with the throttle opened progressively, he matched the right rudder pedal against the increasing torque that could cause him to swerve to the left. As the tail came up at 40mph he increased rudder pressure with slight right aileron to keep the Spit pointing along the runway.

Now a lot started to happen at the same time, threatening to catch him out.

He pushed the throttle forward as he eased the control column back. Then he pushed the throttle all the way forward and the Spitfire took to the air at over 85mph. He let her accelerate to 140mph as he changed hands to lift the undercarriage lever marked 'chassis' and touched the brakes to stop the still rotating wheels, then checked as the lights turned from red to green. He felt the plane was now turning to the right, so he eased off the rudder.

A quick check of the temperatures showed they were all in the right place, so Tomek closed the radiator shutter, uncaged the gyros, made sure everything was pointing in the right direction before dropping his seat slightly and sliding the canopy forward. Happy that everything was doing what the pilots' notes had told him, he now climbed out at 180mph. When he looked down, Tomek was surprised to see he was already over the Welsh hills. Everything happened so much quicker than in the Hurricane!

To his delight, he did not so much turn the Spitfire around in the direction of Rednal but thought to point it back to the safety of lower ground beneath him. The plane was already part of him, almost anticipating his every move. He had never found flying such an instinctive experience before. He had been told, many times, that you wore a Spitfire rather sat in it and now he came to understand what they meant. It was in some strange way an extension of his thought processes. Tomek now knew, as he would relate many times later in life, this was what he was born to do. All the evils and stresses he had endured so far were simply painful steps to this single experience. For the first time in many years, he felt elated.

Coming back over the airfield, he eased everything back as he curved down to line up for his first landing. As he later said, he was determined to show his instructor that he knew how it was done. He slid the canopy back and pumped his seat up to improve visibility over the nose. Throttled back, the Merlin's battering roar was now reduced to a series of crackles. With his flaps down, perfectly lined up, over the perimeter track, he held the nose up and up as the Spitfire felt its way to the ground ... nothing! It just floated on and on and he was now more than halfway down the field.

Kicking in a little right rudder, he eased the throttle forward and aimed back to a safer altitude. The Spitfire was a creature designed for the air, not the ground, but Tomek's fuel supply was by no means inexhaustible. He knew, at best, he was good for an hour and a half, so he spent the best part of an hour practising landings on an obliging sheet of stratocumulus, until he was quite sure that the plane would do what he wanted when he got near the ground.

Finally, after one hour and ten minutes in the air, he made a sideslipping curved approach to round out with his wheels just inches above the runway. This time she behaved and, finally down, he taxied back to park, shut down, report and fill in his logbook. He was now, at very long last, a Spitfire pilot!

If Tomek thought this was pretty much the end of his training, he was to be sorely disappointed. There was now urgency in his hopes of becoming operational. Operation Market Garden was under way with landings at Arnhem, which sounded as if the Allies were about to cross into Germany. The shared opinion was the Nazi Germany was only weeks away from total collapse, and here he was with only ten or so Spitfire hours under his belt and those were on the obsolete Mk. V. He had yet to fly a front-line Spitfire such as the Mk. IX or XVI, and even those were somewhat pedestrian compared to the sleek, powerful and deadly Mk. XIV with its snorting Griffon engine producing more than 2,000hp – 400 more than the Mk. IX's Merlin.

He admitted to being very impatient and at times almost insubordinate, probably as a result of frustration that the war was moving on without him. He had got used to the Spitfire Mk. V with its sweet handling and good manners.

This all changed when finally he was introduced to the Mk. IX. The increase in acceleration shocked him; it was brutal and the torque was such that keeping the Spit straight was a major exercise in kicking in right rudder. He saw several accidents when trainees opened the throttle too hard and too soon. Few kept the Mk. IX straight down the runway until they had got a feel for it. Power management was now the priority. Before the issue was keeping temperatures down on the Mk. V with its single radiator, but the Mk. IX's twin radiators allowed it to taxi longer without overheating on the ground. That extra power meant it positively leaped into the air before the pilot was ready for it. Tomek described feeling his head slammed back when accelerating down the runway adding more and more power, or his shoulders, cheeks and eyes dragged down in a sustained tight turn as he tried deflection shooting at over 300mph. The engine did not so much roar as surround him with an impenetrable wall of noise.

He was briefed time and again about breaking the wire for emergency boost that would mean an engine overhaul before it was used again. The perils of exceeding maximum permitted speed, high-speed buffeting and even structural failure were all emphasised, yet all the time Tomek felt sure that his body would give out before the Spitfire failed him; if anything he was becoming overconfident.

There was a lot of formation flying, at which Tomek felt he excelled, tucking his wingtip between the wing and tailplane of whoever was flying alongside.

There followed a brief posting to 84 GSU (Group Support Unit) at Lasham, Hampshire, but any thoughts of delivering a new Spitfire from this overcrowded base to a front-line squadron in Europe were dashed as the weather was too bad to risk a new pilot and valuable aircraft on an unfamiliar route across the Channel or North Sea. If he drifted too far north he would encounter balloon barrages and flak. His opportunities for flying a Spitfire were limited as he sat around in a state of jumpy frustration while low cloud rolled over the hangars, trailing the misery of drizzle and rain.

When the weather brightened sufficiently to allow some flying, instead of taking a shiny new Spitfire to Belgium, he flew in the opposite direction to South Wales in another dreaded, noisy, smelly, rattling Anson, as it buffeted its way across the Downs and Salisbury Plain. He was sitting on a very uncomfortable sideways-facing seat opposite a couple of other new pilots he had never met before. Over the racket he was able to make out that they too were posted to 317 (Polish) Squadron. The experience was miserable. As he later recalled, the Anson's wings seemed barely held together with gaps between ailerons, flaps and wing. He described it as a collection of flapping fabric, aluminium bits and pieces flying in loose formation behind a pair of dodgy-looking engines that spouted soot, smoke and oil. He hated being a passenger and admitted to being almost constantly airsick.

Upon arrival, Squadron Leader Chelmecki told him he would be assigned to 'A' Flight. Tomek's job was to be his leader's wing man and to cover their rear from any attacks. He was to follow his flight commander's orders to the letter and report any potential target on the ground, or other aircraft to him. On no account was he to go off on his own initiative.

It was the flight leader's job to decide if a target was worth attacking and how to go about it. Every mission was planned and specific areas were allotted to each flight. Good communication and discipline in the air were critical if they were to survive long enough to be of any use. It was all too easy to be shot down by your own side by being in the wrong place at the wrong time. In conditions of poor visibility and low cloud, anti-aircraft batteries often opened fire on any unidentified aircraft in an area where no friendlies were expected.

Tomek remembered what had happened to the Mosquito over Brighton, and the weather then was pretty clear by comparison with these dreary autumn conditions. He had no intention of becoming a friendly fire statistic.

The squadron leader then gave the new arrivals a quick talk about how the squadron worked and what they were expected to do. He explained that following a very exhausting tour of duty with almost daily action and more than a few losses, 317 had been withdrawn from its operational airfield with 131 Wing at airfield B61 (Sint-Denijs-Westrem) near Ghent and based temporarily at RAF Fairwood Common (now Swansea Airport) for a rest and regroup. It was the perfect opportunity for refresher training in dive bombing, and live-firing exercises off Swansea Bay, while the new pilots worked up to full operational efficiency alongside veterans who had already had their skills forged in the heat of battle.

This time he was warned that once the squadron was back in Belgium there would be little time to shepherd him along. The squadron would be immediately operational at a very busy airfield within easy reach of the front line, and every pilot had to be on their toes all the time. He was also warned not to waste his downtime sightseeing, playing cards or writing letters. Sleep was the most important commodity as they could find themselves flying two or three sorties a day. Debriefing, evaluation, intelligence reports and logbooks must be completed before the operational pilot could rest. Exhaustion was as dangerous an enemy as flak and German fighters. Missions must be accomplished, ammunition not wasted.

He was warned that the Spitfires were often overloaded with one 500lb bomb and two 250lb bombs. Take-off runs would be longer and the aircraft would not behave the same way in the air. They were not to try to land with any unused bombs or overload fuel tanks still attached. There would be designated areas to dump them. If any bomb failed to release (he called them 'hang ups'), then they should try a series of rapid negative and positive 'G' manoeuvres to get rid of it. If that failed then they should carry out a very gentle landing. Bombs had been known to drop off and explode after a hard landing or even skip along a runway and hit a building, or worse still, an ammunition dump.

Tomek realised that flying the Spitfire was probably the easy part. It was emphasised time and again that their main enemies were flak, exhaustion and weather. After that came enemy fighters (rarely seen), flying into someone else's bomb blast (don't get too low or too close) and, most of all, running out of fuel. The faster they flew, the more the Merlin engine behaved like a drunkard on a Saturday night.

For the moment, their major challenge was the Welsh weather. Late November and early December were not renowned for their sunny days and limitless visibility. What surprised Tomek and the others was that the squadron often flew in weather that would have grounded any training unit. There was a no-nonsense approach with the chances of operational success being the only criteria. They had to hone their flying skills, but they were only judged by the number of hits on the target.

Once they began air-to-ground firing exercises, simulated deflection shooting and dive bombing, Tomek tried to take risks in proving he was a cut above the rest. It failed to impress and as a result he was very frustrated by the tough, unimpressed approach of the flight leaders, who would insist on discipline and teamwork. After leading the exercise, they would compare results and debrief with faint praise even if everything had gone to plan.

All the time it was emphasised that they were not here to enjoy the flying. The sole object was always to destroy the briefed target as quickly and as efficiently as possible, then bring their valuable aeroplane back in one piece. They were now part of a relentless fighting machine that used flying as a means to an end. The flight leaders' comments were never flattering, so Tomek went even further out of his way to show that he was capable, tending, as before, to be competitive almost to the point of being a one-man show. This frequently led to him being dressed down by a senior officer. Tomek hated criticism, especially if in bending the rules he had succeeded in hitting the target where others had failed.

So far there had not been any tragedies until a friend of his, newly married, seemed a bit unfocused before they took off. Others joked that he was suffering the effects of a honeymoon.

Out over the bay at around 10,000ft, his mate briefly touched wings with Tomek, whose reflexes were instant. He was able to correct a sudden and violent snatch to the right before it developed, while the other Spitfire reared up in a tight wingover, then headed down to the sea. Tomek could not see what happened next but heard the shouts of the other pilots over the R/T, all to no avail. Flying straight and level to check that his own Spitfire had not been damaged, Tomek then looked down, where he could see a circle of white foam and spreading ripples far below where the other Spit had gone in.

The exercise was scrubbed, bombs were jettisoned over the sea, and back on the ground there was an intense debrief. The pilots that followed the pilot down said that they could see he was looking round to see who had hit him and was not responding to their R/T calls. Significantly, one pilot said they could see that he was not wearing his oxygen mask. The death was recorded as oxygen failure. It was hit home to all of them that oxygen must be used at all times with the canopy closed, as even at low altitude there was always a risk of carbon monoxide fumes getting into the cockpit.

Unusually, permissions had been given for wives and fiancées to join them. Angela was by now showing quite a bump and Tomek felt a sense of proprietorship over his impending family. He was convinced it would be a baby boy. On the trams running along the seaside, he and Angela felt they stuck out like a pair of thumbs as local women would engage them in conversation, in quite a friendly manner, before turning to a friend and then conversing in Welsh.

Angela, who had not told Tomek about the dangers of German measles, was already feeling insecure. She had tried to joke about how she had upset her mother after returning from a previous visit to Nottingham by pretending to come back with a northern accent. She was now suggesting she would try a Welsh one instead, but Tomek was tense and didn't see the funny side. He was facing a real war, with real risks and inevitable casualties. He knew with a deep and irretrievably sinking feeling that 1944 would be the one Christmas he would definitely spend away from his wife. Angela did not seem to take it in and later admitted that she was trying to shield Tomek from her own fear about the baby. What made it worse was his insistence that they call his son Andrzej after a particular friend of his. Angela wasn't inclined to argue, she just hoped against hope she would have a healthy baby.

Now faced with the real prospect of flying to the fighting over Europe, Tomek was noticing the lack of enthusiasm among his squadron colleagues for getting back into the fray. Those who were being posted back for a tour at an out, or even being confined to ground duties for senior admin or even staff positions, did not seem too upset about not flying operationally. There was little or no crusading spirit, just a fatalistic acceptance that they still had a job to do and everyone had bloody well better get on with it.

There was desultory talk about what would happen post-war, with none of them having any idea of what their prospects would be. Most had accepted that the Russians would control Poland's fate and some had suggested that there was no longer any enthusiasm among the British for the Polish Government in Exile. The older, more experienced officers who had arrived in 1940 had been heard to mutter that they no longer enjoyed the red carpet of being greeted as heroes, but instead were beginning to encounter resentment from the British, who had seen rations cut and were embittered by the long, grim and colourless grind of total war. They no longer felt welcome the nearer that an inevitable victory approached from over the distant horizon.

Even so, Arnhem had been a disaster and Tomek felt that the advancing winter had stalled the European war as a result. Now it seemed less likely that the war would end without him.

Sadly, General Stanisław Sosabowski was made a scapegoat for the many failures of Operation Market Garden.[5] He was highly critical of the way his Polish forces were deployed late and inefficiently during the airborne landings at Arnhem. Some of the stories circulated bathed the surviving British officers in a favourable light while dismissing the sterling efforts of the Poles under circumstances that were already doomed.

Considerable pressure was put on the Polish Government in Exile to have him removed from the 1st Independent Parachute Brigade, in some part to cover up British intelligence, communication and command failures. It was not long before the understandable hurt and resentment felt by the senior Poles filtered down through to all Polish ranks. This only heightened the considerable unease felt by many Polish forces, including the fighter-bomber squadrons of the 2nd Tactical Air Force, that they were being sold out by the British.

It was bitterly cold and the weather was atrocious on the afternoon of 13 December, when the squadron arrived back in Belgium. Tomek was briefed for a sector reconnaissance as soon as the weather allowed. It was critical that he could identify local landmarks if he were to get back to his base in poor visibility and snow showers.

Tomek did not settle in well, as it was now obvious that he was regarded as just another new arrival. He had had a brief meeting with Group Captain Gabszewicz, who plainly didn't have much time for the latest recruits to his wing. In common with many of the more senior officers, he had been fighting a lot longer, had many tours of duty behind him, been rotated back to a training unit and in all probability was wondering what the hell he had been fighting for, as the one thing almost every senior officer knew was the Poland they had fought for was not going to be post-war Poland.

Most of Tomek's subsequent sorties were what he recorded as 'Armed Recco', where he didn't even record the amount of flak encountered. His whole attitude was one of frustrated disappointment. His dive-bombing skills had been noted. The critical thing was to survive those first few weeks and become an effective member of the squadron. As he gained in experience he would find himself occasionally acting as wingman for the flight or squadron leader.

Usually armed reconnaissance missions comprised just shooting at targets of opportunity behind a carefully briefed 'bomb line' beyond where the latest Allied incursions were reported. The situation was fluid and, as far as was possible, this was updated after each mission based upon what the pilots had seen.

Dive-bombing missions were different. This time a specific target was identified, map references cross-checked, flak and other hazards assessed and, as far as possible, weather conditions forecast. Wind was a critical factor if bombs were to land in the right place, civilian casualties were to be avoided at all costs and the mission would be scrubbed if the cloud cover was too bad for positive identification of the target. By this stage of the war, they were very unlikely to encounter any opposition from the Luftwaffe, whose efforts against Allied strategic bombing and the perils of trying to hold back the Eastern Front were hamstrung by the lack of fully trained and experienced pilots, a lack of spares and fuel, and hampered even further by the selfless and dangerous acts of sabotage by the slave labour force.

The Spitfire was designed as an interceptor and dogfighter, but by this stage of the war it had been pressed into service as a fighter-bomber. Its mission was to harass German transport by strafing and dive bombing those vital soft targets that delivered fuel, ammunition and spares to the German front line. The Germans were employing every vehicle imaginable, from requisitioned lorries and horse-drawn transport, via often well-defended trains, to barges. To this end, bomb racks had been fitted and it was not uncommon for the Spitfire Mk. IX to carry one 500lb and two 250lb bombs.

The four .303 machine guns were being replaced by the larger .50-calibre weapon to back up the two 20mm cannon. The wings were frequently clipped, losing the Spitfire's iconic ellipsoidal wingtips, to improve rate of roll and speed at low level. The intention was for these later marks of Merlin-powered Spitfires to be effective in any air-to-ground mission, yet still be capable of fighting their way back home against any aerial opposition.

Unfortunately, compared, for instance, with the heavily armoured, air-cooled, radial-engined American P-47 Thunderbolt, the Spitfire's liquid-cooled Merlin engine's underwing radiators were vulnerable to ground fire. Its new air-to-ground mission would bring it into the effective range of German rapid-firing light flak. This would be reflected in aircraft and pilot losses at this late stage of the war.

The other typical mission would have been bomber escort. Compared to the P-51 Mustang and P-47 Thunderbolt, the Spitfire had no significant operational range and was only used for escorting tactical bombers such as the Douglas Boston, North American Mitchell and Martin Marauder over short distances. Although the Spitfire Mk. IX was significantly faster than all of these, its economical cruise speed was lower. That could be a problem when escorting the Marauder and later Douglas Invader that made an appearance during the last weeks of the war. Fortunately, tactical bombers were not considered a worthwhile target for the German Messerschmitt Me 262 jets, which were over 100mph faster but had an engine life of around ten hours! These were too few, too late and too unreliable to make much of an impact, and Tomek would never see a single one of them in the air.

If a squadron was tasked with attacking a specific target, the routine was the same: a safe course was plotted between areas of intense flak, often Allied, as nerves were taut the nearer they flew to the front line. Spitfires usually flew at 10–12,000ft and would fly past the briefed target until it was just aft of the leader's port wing, at which point he would pitch up and over into a 60-degree dive, with the others following at three-second intervals unless otherwise briefed. Bomb release was at 2,500ft, usually accompanied by a two-second burst of machine-gun and cannon fire to discourage any accurate light flak. It did not always work and sometimes the whole squadron would come back with their Spitfires peppered with small holes.

Inevitably, some pilots did not return, which may have explained why firm friendships did not often develop. There was also a surprising turnover among the officers, with a regular rotation for leave, reassignment or promotion.

Tomek described the situation in late 1944 and early 1945 as being like a permanent state of anticipated removal where he knew that they would move, but not where or when. Living conditions were not brilliant with some local billeting, and a lot of activities, such as rearming and basic servicing, were carried out in the open or under canvas despite the bitter weather. Where possible the aircraft were dispersed around the airfield with sandbag revetments as a precaution against providing multiple targets for any enemy strafing run.

Sometimes this didn't work, as other aircraft diverted in as a result of flak damage or bad weather and it could get chaotic with aircraft scattered or clustered, dictated by the availability of space and hard standings. Sometimes there was no transport available and Tomek could face a long bicycle ride around the perimeter track to reach his assigned Spitfire. He had to get to dispersal early as sometimes the Spitfire had gone u/s through some late-discovered malfunction. That meant another long ride, explanation and hurried discussion before another serviceable Spitfire was found.

When arrangements fell apart, as they inevitably did in wartime, Tomek would be damp with sweat from the cycling and feeling tired before he began. The perspiration would trickle down his back, then freeze, or if he did get airborne, his goggles would mist over, then ice up. The flying suit was well made but, unlike many American outfits, was not electrically heated. He often described shivering uncontrollably while trying to keep his aircraft straight and level.

Sometimes it was so bad that his leg would tremble or even bounce up and down, to the extent that he could not keep his feet on the rudder bar. He even became adept at using the rudder trim to prevent the Spitfire from yawing and flying out of balance. There was a cockpit heater, but often it was ineffective or only raised the temperature slightly in time for Tomek to slide back the canopy, pump up his seat and remove his goggles to see the runway, gelid tears streaming back in the slipstream. He consoled himself with the thought that it was not anywhere as bad as Siberia, but nevertheless it felt bitterly cold and depressing.

The ground was either frozen hard or churned up into mud, despite acres of pierced steel planking being used over the softest ground. Tomek quickly learned that he should not taxi with his flaps down as the propeller blew up loose stones, mud and frozen sods of earth, coating the underside of his fuselage, radiators, control surfaces and flaps with brown slime, dents and occasional holes.

It can be seen from his logbook that he rarely got to use the same Spitfire with any consistency. Some of the pilots had adorned their planes with the names of wives, mothers or girlfriends, but inevitably whichever Spitfire was assigned depended entirely on serviceability. A number of the more senior officers had been in the habit of having mascots or cartoon characters painted on 'their' Spitfires, although the results were never as colourful or voluptuous as those the Americans had adorned on their Flying Fortresses, Liberators, Thunderbolts and Mustangs. By 1944, in the 2nd TAF, such artistic individualism was discouraged. The most Tomek ever achieved was to write *Stefa*, his mother's name, underneath his cockpit.

There was one exception to this. The group captain's aircraft was unofficially sacrosanct, but even so it could, on occasion, be assigned for a mission if no other was available. The pressure, particularly on any junior sergeant pilot, to bring it home unscathed was enormous.

Tomek heard of one pilot from neighbouring 308 Squadron who, upon being upbraided by Group Captain Gabszewicz[6] for the sorry condition of his personal mount, replied that perhaps 'Sir' should have advised the Germans not to shoot at his special Spitfire. Tomek had no idea what, if any, consequences followed.

Squadron Leader Chelmecki tried to lead from the front whenever possible. Of all the officers, Tomek found him the most sympathetic and approachable. Even so, as Tomek later said, he could be a strict disciplinarian if he felt any of his NCO pilots were tugging too hard at the reins.

As Christmas approached, the weather worsened, which meant that any breaks in the dismal low cloud and snow showers were stuffed with as many operations as could possibly be flown, in order to deter any German advances while Allied fighters were grounded. On these few occasions Tomek found himself flying up to three operations in one day, with occasional sorties into Germany instead of the more usual sweeps and armed reconnaissance over the Netherlands. Germany meant even more intense flak as they flew over the Rhine.

18

Dogfights and Rockets

There was absolutely no chance of getting time off for Christmas. It was obvious that the next great push was going to be across the Rhine and into Germany. Now there was a tangible anxiety that permeated 131 Wing. Tomek could feel it even at his very junior level. His results so far were above average and he had shown a talent for bombing accuracy, almost sensing the wind and allowing for drift.

He rarely trimmed his Spitfire for a dive, preferring to push the joystick forward and hold it there against the pressure, reasoning that as soon as he relaxed it his plane would automatically nose up into a climb. He had seen other Spitfires maintain their dives right into the ever-increasing density of light flak and small arms fire, even to the point of crashing just behind the target.

Rolling the elevator trim wheel forward as the speed increased in a dive, then rolling it back to climb away was, to Tomek's mind, an unnecessary fiddle and distraction from sighting properly and releasing his bombs at the right point. He suggested to his squadron mates that if he were wounded at least the Spitfire would climb away to a safe altitude, giving him a chance to revive and, if necessary, bail out. That habit would save his life within a few weeks.

Angela's letters to Tomek were still arriving in bundles up to two weeks late on occasion. As she had left Bletchley Park upon marrying Tomek, she had been forced, like so many others, to take up

Polish citizenship. For reasons best known to the censor, her letters occasionally had the notorious blue pencil obliterate whole lines of endearment.

To her dying day, Angela could not work out what possible information she could have given that would, in any way, be a security risk. Tomek's painfully composed, halting English was similarly treated, though of course there could have easily been sensitive material about missions flown and targets attacked, especially when it came to V2 launch sites, as many details of these ballistic missiles were kept secret for fear of both dismaying those on the Home Front and giving German intelligence some slight insight into RAF efforts to prevent their launch.

There was one thing that Angela had kept to herself. She made no mention of German measles and the growing fear that it would mean a baby born with some deformity or loss, such as blindness or brain damage. Her mother told her that all may still be well and there was no point in upsetting Tomek (whom by now she called the more affectionate Tomczu). She knew that he would be gloomy enough spending Christmas away from her.

They made the best of a few days' leave granted shortly before he had to return to his squadron. There had not really been much preparation for Christmas; rationing took care of that and there was very little income for his mother-in-law to lavish on the family. He was both itching to get back and miserable at the prospect. Angela tried to comfort him but there was something missing; she was not showing much joy at the prospect of becoming a mother. Tomek put it down to pregnancy blues. He had heard of such things from some of the married men in the squadron; in any case, this war had gone on far too long and he knew that his young wife would be glad when it was all over.

He was not at all happy flying back to Belgium, once again as a passenger in a vindictively bouncing Anson.

If Tomek thought that the war would end soon and before he had much impact on it, he was rudely awakened on 16 December 1944. The weather was poor and a number of operations had been curtailed or scrubbed completely. Frustration was building up and Tomek had a cold. His sinuses had filled up before and the medical officer had simply put a hefty dose of menthol crystals in a bowl of boiling water, and told him to put a towel over his head and breathe deeply. The menthol made his eyes smart and the steam made him sweat. This rather basic treatment sometimes worked sufficiently to allow flying, but not always. Blocked sinuses became so painful with the reduced pressure at altitude that a pilot could be literally blinded in absolute agony and suffer permanent damage to his eardrums.

This time there was no possibility of a quick fix and Tomek was taken off flying duties. If he developed a high temperature then he was to be ordered off base and spend a couple of days in bed. He had not got to that stage, so had been given some other duties off the base. There was not much else to do. For all of one day he was detached to a radar unit on the outskirts of Antwerp as part of a co-ordination exercise.

The radar network relayed information to the guns, who would anticipate the height and course of an incoming V1 and concentrate their fire. Concentric semicircles had been laid, with a mixture of heavy and light flak covering the most likely V1 routes. The whole process was becoming more automated, with a reaction time that was so much more deadly than that he had seen over Brighton more than a year before.

He was surprised to hear the distinctive throaty, rasping warble of a Doodlebug flying over, while the other men took no notice. Tomek had heard many going over in the distance before, but not directly overhead. It made sense as, to be effective, this outpost was positioned underneath their flightpath and their new target, the port of Antwerp. He asked if this was unsettling, only to be told that they had got used to it. They had an important job to do as the Germans were doing everything in their power to stop Allied ships resupplying friendly forces through the port. He was told in no uncertain terms that as the cloud base was often too low to identify friendly aircraft, they had instructions to shoot first and ask questions afterwards. All Allied aircraft units had been warned to stay well away.

Tomek began to understand what lay even deeper behind Squadron Leader Chelmecki's warning about sightseeing. Any airborne excursions into this zone would be very hazardous to health given the intense barrage protecting the docks. He made a mental note to stay well away from flying over Antwerp, a message that he was expected to take back, reinforcing the squadron leader's warnings.

There was one dividend to this experience, as now he did not feel so bad about the one time he had been directed to look out for a V1. By the time he spotted it, he had no chance of catching it up as it disappeared into the murk and low cloud over Antwerp. He now fully understood the dangers of chasing any Doodlebug over Antwerp. The guns were radar directed and the flak they could put up was intense. Any straying Spitfire wouldn't stand a chance. The Doodlebugs, though, were a much smaller target and some always got through.

One of the men had seen the damage to Antwerp at first hand. The city was being reduced to rubble, not only by the V1 attacks, but V2s[1] were beginning to find the target as well and they had no means of stopping them. The only hope was to push the launch sites ever further back into Germany, putting Antwerp out of range. As if to emphasise the point, another two Doodlebugs rasped over in quick succession.

Tomek was allowed to make a quick detour on the way back and see how the city was coping. There was rubble everywhere and he photographed a child with a hose beside a heap of bricks. He could not see why, but later he realised that the child was probably hosing away bloodstains on the cobbles. It was plain that what the aircraftsman had said about Antwerp suffering so badly was true: there would not be much to see if he went further into the city.

It was now blindingly obvious why Antwerp was really a no-go area on the ground as well. He could see that there was a serious risk of losing valuable aircrew to a Doodlebug or V2. It wasn't worth taking any chances.

By the time he got back, there was a bit of a flap on as news was filtering through about a German breakthrough in the Ardennes.[2] Tomek later learned that there had been urgent requests for air cover, but the weather was too bad. Fortunately, if the Germans had hoped to become masters of the air over the battlefront, they were every bit as grounded by the snow showers and low cloud as were the Allies.

Tomek began to feel a bit anxious when he was called to a briefing. The squadron leaders of all the units based at B61 were there, along with the group captain. The intelligence report was stark and clear. The German objective had to be to cut off Antwerp. The only problem was that B61 near Ghent lay directly in the path of any German encircling manoeuvre from the Ardennes.

The tension was ramped up once again. As a tactical air force unit they were near the ebb and flow of the ground battle and they were playing by very different rules to the home-based squadrons.

The squadron was flying again on 22 December but without Tomek. It was not a particularly notable operation as low cloud and snow showers saw to that. He was chafing, his cold had developed and he was feeling very low as he had not heard from Angela. He hated ground duties and felt he was being punished unnecessarily. The reality was that he was not fit enough to fly, a designation that left him very resentful.

There was now an urgency to get aircraft into the air and 317 had to take up the challenge despite bad weather keeping most aircraft on the ground. He took part in a fighter sweep on Christmas Eve. This time fewer aircraft went aloft, the intention being that each section would rotate just to keep some sort of presence in the air, making the movement of any enemy traffic difficult. Weather was still the major factor keeping flights at low level, with no chance of dive bombing through the layers of icy cloud.

Other than a Mass, where a few Polish carols were sung, there was little or no evidence of the Polish *Wigilia* where twelve dishes would be served on a table strewn with straw. This made Tomek even more introspective and uncommunicative. He knew that many of the other pilots felt the same. He sincerely hoped that this would be his last miserable wartime Christmas.

Christmas Day dawned clear enough for some dive bombing over the Netherlands with no distinguishable results and another fighter sweep in the afternoon. Total war took precedence over the season of goodwill. The weather closed in again, grounding everyone until clearing enough for some bombing and strafing of motor transport trying to sneak their way through Holland.

Over the front of what was to become known as the Battle of the Bulge, the German advance had run out of steam and the weather overhead was still poor. There was a lot of pressure to get the Spitfires into the air as most of Holland was still under German occupation, and the fear was that German forces breaking out of the Ardennes would link up with resupplied troops in Holland and cut the supply line from Antwerp to the Allied forces still trying to cross the Rhine into Germany. The V1 and V2 attacks on that unfortunate city were relentless the longer Allied air forces were grounded, allowing a greater number of launch sites that could be used for longer to sustain the attacks without interruption.

The Germans were still attacking London and targets along the Thames Estuary with V1 Doodlebugs launched from occupied Holland and a few air-launched examples using modified Heinkel He 111s. By this stage in the war, attacks on London were more of nuisance value, but still tied up resources as well as adding to the stress and war weariness among the civilian population.

The frustration felt among the aircrew who had to sit twiddling their thumbs while Doodlebugs burbled overhead, powerless to mount any interceptions, was tangible. In common with all fighting men, inaction and waiting led to low morale and frayed tempers.

The Allies desperately needed the cloud to lift and visibility to improve. Their prayers were sort of answered on 1 January 1945. Planes all across Belgium were warmed up and launched as dawn broke to take advantage of this long-awaited clearance.

Unfortunately the Germans had been hoping for the same opportunity to launch Operation Bodenplatte, a chance for a mass surprise attack against all front-line Allied airfields intended to destroy their air superiority. This had been planned to coincide with the Ardennes offensive, but as both sides had learned, the weather had other ideas.[3]

New Year's Day was to turn out to be the first real opportunity for both sides getting aircraft into the air. Up till that point, the only way that the Germans could ensure anything resembling air superiority was by intense flak over high-value targets, a lesson that is being played out even today over Ukraine as drones are used in the face of very effective anti-aircraft missiles and artillery. Ultimately, as 1945 was to show, a combination of superior equipment and highly co-ordinated air-to-ground forces always decides the outcome. The advent of better-trained pilots ensured the success enjoyed by the Spitfires, Tempests and Thunderbolts over Belgium, Holland and north Germany. These are lessons that will apply to any modern war.

Tomek was up early that New Year's Day. The previous night's forecast proved to be accurate, allowing an early start for a dive-bombing sortie. Even so the results, as was so often the case, were difficult to confirm, so Squadron Leader Chelmecki ordered 317 to form up and return home.

Ground control radar then reported over the R/T that German aircraft were forming up near Ghent, which was a totally unexpected development. This was shortly followed by radio chatter as 308 Squadron became entangled in a dogfight over Sint-Denijs-Westrem.

Chelmecki ordered all pilots to dump any remaining bombs and head back independently. The problem was that waiting to form up into formation meant both delay and more fuel burned. As it was, the squadron had already been aloft for more than an hour and a high-speed dash would only give them minutes of fuel remaining. This was far from ideal.

Tomek felt a knot in his stomach as he turned off the gun safety and selected 'Fw 190' below his gyro gunsight. The glowing circle of diamonds sprang to life. Now if he could frame the enemy aircraft inside that circle, he would be in range. The gunsight display with its central pipper slewed right as he turned left and opened the throttle.

In a turning fight he would have to pull hard, so the gyro adjusted to where his bullets would land. At last his training was going to pay off.

As he nosed down towards Ghent, Tomek could see smoke rising in the distance and hear urgent messages over his R/T. At full throttle, he arrived over the airfield at about 2,000ft. Far below him he saw a red-nosed Focke-Wulf Fw 190 lining up for a strafing run. He rolled over to the left, closing the distance rapidly. His gunsight stubbornly slewed off to the bottom right of the display as he pulled and pulled on his control column. He was desperate to get that circle to catch up and frame the enemy as he closed the distance, certain that the Fw 190 would sense him and roll away before it was caught in the net of his gunsight. The more he pulled, the heavier he felt as his cheeks sagged under the G force until, there it was, framed by that circle of deadly diamonds, pipper holding between the Fw 190's fuselage and wing. Almost as a reflex, he pressed the firing tit. He kept pressing as a long burst from his cannon and machine guns scored multiple hits across the wings and fuselage.

The German plane reared up and cartwheeled, both wings on fire like some sort of fiery cross, an image that for decades afterwards would sear across Tomek's brain as he fell asleep, sometimes causing him to wake up screaming.

He had no idea at the time that the teenage Latvian Luftwaffe pilot was thrown clear as he shed his canopy and soared up with sufficient height to deploy his parachute. The Fw 190 plunged into a flower shop in the town centre of Ghent. Fortunately, the shopkeeper survived.

Tomek had made a bad mistake; in his determination he had forgotten the first rule of air combat: save your ammo! He had kept spraying bullets longer than necessary, and his total firing time was measured in seconds not minutes. He converted the energy from his dive into a zoom back up, gaining altitude he could trade for airspeed. Now three more Fw 190s were crossing below him. Instinctively, he rolled almost onto his back and pulled through, as he pushed his throttle through the wire. The instant jolt of acceleration from the emergency boost allowed him to pull tighter and tighter in his efforts to catch to catch up with the rearmost Fw 190.

He was barely making up the distance as the dancing image of the Fw 190 was finally caught in the vibrating frame of his gunsight as he used up the remainder of his ammunition on this new target. To his astonishment, the Fw 190 accelerated away, its superior rate of roll twisting it from side to side – a manoeuvre that the slower-rolling Spitfire could not emulate. Helpless, he watched as his target drew ahead, now well out of range of his empty guns. His momentary frustration evaporated as the black smoke trail from the escaping Fw 190's exhaust turned to thicker smoke and maybe a flicker of flame. As he broke away, unable to follow, he saw another Fw 190 firing on a Spitfire.[4]

Without thinking, once more he pulled tightly into the German in a classic interception, giving every impression that he was waiting until the last second before opening fire. Tomek's aggressive manoeuvre tricked the Fw 190 as it broke off its attack and dived away. Tomek followed, his over-boosted Merlin engine screaming in protest. Again the Fw 190 outdistanced him, rolling from side to side; the German fighter's one party trick as it could not out-turn a Spitfire. Another half-roll, then the enemy flicked away before Tomek could follow him.

Despite the bitter cold, Tomek was drenched in sweat and felt utterly drained, his head turning, his eyes anxiously scanning the sky above, knowing full well that it was the enemy you didn't see who would kill you. Suddenly, apart from the oily columns of smoke from burning aircraft and fuel dumps spreading above, the sky looked empty. Where was everybody? At 400mph both Spitfire and Fw 190 could cover a lot of ground in a few seconds.

Tomek was running out of options as he was dangerously low on fuel. Hoping that the attack had moved on, he risked pulling into a very tight turn over the airfield, killing his speed as he throttled back. He rounded out with his wingtip a few feet off the ground, aiming to land between two burning Spitfires and an almost gutted Shorts Stirling lying as a hulk off to one side. He used his brakes sparingly, allowing his coughing and spluttering engine to taxi clear of other landing Spitfires before coming to a stop and climbing out.

There was smoke everywhere and ammunition was going off from a burning B-17 Flying Fortress that had made an emergency landing a few days before. However, the nearest danger was a burning Mosquito whose tracers were flying overhead as he bent down and followed a mechanic between the burned-out remains of Spitfires marked by lines of ashes and the crossed arms of propellers marking their graves.[5]

There were no more German planes in the sky, so Tomek decided to remain safely behind the dispersal's sandbags until the explosions and crackle of cooked off ammunition had ended. The intense action had seemed to last almost a lifetime but to his astonishment, when he checked his watch to note times for his logbook, the whole engagement from the first calls on the R/T to landing was just over ten minutes!

This day would be etched on his memory for the rest of his life as any remaining adrenaline drained away. An Fw 190 had clipped the Stirling, then skidded across the airfield before hitting a tree. As Tomek approached he saw that the dead German pilot had been laid out on the frozen ground. A couple of ground crew were going through his wallet and papers. One of them handed over a photo of a young, fair-haired Luftwaffe officer with presumably his wife and baby. To his horror, Tomek noticed that the pilot's ring finger had been hacked off and was found a short distance away, minus a wedding ring. He knew that looting of dead bodies was rife despite being officially frowned upon, but this was the first time he had seen it up close in all its meanness.

He felt tired and sick.

The debriefing was long and complex as assessments were made of casualties and claims of kills verified. Nobody was in any mood for congratulations and it was obvious that something had gone seriously wrong for the Germans to have mounted such a comprehensive attack. Reports were coming in from other airfields of similar damage. It was plain that the first order of business would be to replace all the lost aircraft and make sure that all aircrew were accounted for.

By the end of the afternoon they knew they had lost a flight lieutenant and some other pilots were unaccounted for but could have pulled off forced landings in the countryside or at other airfields. It would be some time before the situation was fully understood.

One pilot, who had run out of fuel, pulled off an emergency landing just as two Fw 190s appeared underneath him. Snapping right and left to avoid him, they both stalled and crashed on either side of the shocked pilot, who later claimed two victories even though the patches over his guns were still in place, not having fired a single bullet. Tomek doubted that claim would be allowed.

After his debrief, Tomek was credited with one Fw 190 destroyed and another damaged,[6] although it was unlikely that it had got away back into Germany. The developed gun camera footage would confirm the claims.[7]

By evening many reports were coming in of more crashed Luftwaffe aircraft than either pilots or anti-aircraft gun crews were claiming. This caused a great deal of speculation and quite a lot of intelligence effort. Eventually the Allies gleaned through radio intercepts and interrogation of downed German aircrew that what became known as Bodenplatte ('baseplate' in English) had been conceived and assembled in such secrecy that German anti-aircraft units knew nothing of it. In the darkness of the winter's early morning and cloud, they were shooting at all aircraft flying across the Rhine, including their own. This was a disaster, as the Germans could ill afford such friendly fire losses.

At the time, Allied staff could not understand what the Luftwaffe hoped to achieve by such an expensive attack that had squandered pilots, aircraft and fuel to so little effect. Had they but known it, that opinion was shared by Luftwaffe General Adolf Galland, who was effectively demoted for being too robust in his criticism of the operation. It was later learned that at the highest level, senior German officers hoped that by inflicting severe losses on the Allied air forces they would accept a negotiated peace rather than carry on with an expensive and wearying all-out war. That outcome was never going to happen and Bodenplatte was nothing more than a hiccup in the Allied war effort. By the next day many of the losses were already being replaced, thanks to the Allies' vast superiority in logistics and available reserves.[8]

Most of the Luftwaffe pilots were not well trained, with significant numbers coming from the Baltic states as their fear of Russia eclipsed any misgivings they had about Hitler's Germany. Discipline and communication skills were poor, with many having the barest minimum of training on front-line aircraft.

The last few months of the war were increasingly disordered, messy and confused, which only added to the Poles' growing sense of disillusionment. It will surprise many to learn that, far from slackening off, the endgame in the European war would result in fearsome casualties on both sides as 1945 advanced towards the ultimate goal of Germany's unconditional surrender.

19

The Sting in the Tail

If Tomek thought there would be some respite, he was to be disappointed. No. 302 Squadron's Spitfire Mk. IXs were redeployed to make up 317 and 308's losses[1] while they re-equipped with the new LF Mk. XVI. Some of the latest versions were already equipped with bubble canopies together with cut-down rear fuselages to improve the all-round view, American Packard-built Merlin engines optimised for low-level speed and clipped wings to improve the rate of roll. No. 317 were due to receive theirs in a few weeks. There was no more pretence at being interceptors; they were fighter-bombers first and foremost with most of their future targets being on the ground.

Tomek was also beginning to hit targets where others had failed. Barges were a favoured method of getting supplies around Holland and it was 317's job to make sure that didn't happen. Tomek was now being credited with direct hits in the squadron's combat reports.[2] The whole squadron had performed pretty poorly on one mission, with a lot of bombs dropped wide of a line of barges moored up alongside a canal bank. There was some light flak from an emplacement a short distance away, and in their efforts to avoid it, Squadron Leader Chelmecki had erred on the side of caution.

He ordered the Spitfires to report if any still had any unused bombs. Tomek was the only one to answer. He alone had a single

The Sting in the Tail

500lb centreline bomb left. He could almost hear the impatience in Chelmecki's voice as he told Tomek to get rid of it.

He did, but not as the squadron leader expected. Pulling round and approaching steeply with the wind behind him, he guessed that the flak predictor would lag behind him. It did, allowing him to concentrate on the leading barge, releasing his bomb from lower than the optimal 2,500ft. As he released it, he pulled his Spitfire into a gut-wrenching climb, his vision becoming a narrow grey tunnel as the G force steadily dragged the blood from his head. He thought he heard an exclamation over the R/T. Upon recovering to join up with the rest of the formation, he glanced down to see that all the barges had blown up and were burning fiercely.

Chelmecki made no other comment than to set the course for Ghent.

That evening Tomek was called in to see Group Captain Gabszewicz. Without more ado and with no ceremony, he told Tomek that he had been awarded the Polish Cross of Valour. Tomek finally felt he had arrived.

Two days later the squadron was ordered to pack up as they would now be operating from Airfield B60 (Grimbergen). There would need to be a period of local flying to get familiar with the terrain before more operational sorties. Some of the pilots, Tomek included, were tasked with flying spare Spitfires to Courtrai for allocation to other squadrons after depot maintenance.

Tomek was now becoming an experienced Spitfire pilot, occasionally tasked with carrying out a met reconnaissance flight, or weather check. These were not in any way straightforward. Often he would enter cloud within a few hundred feet, climbing at the Spitfire's maximum rate in order to cut down exposure to icing. Severe icing could build up on the propeller, wing leading edge and control surfaces, making the aeroplane unflyable.

On one such flight, Tomek burst out into bright winter sunshine with clear blue sky above and a dazzling white undulating carpet of cloud beneath him. In his mind he composed a lyrical account of the experience. He was in no hurry to end the flight and report back to the met officer. He looped and rolled, cut through wisps of cloud with his elegant elliptical wingtip and for once left all thoughts of war behind him. Relieved of its usual bombload, this is what the Spitfire was designed for: a powerful thoroughbred, with masses of acceleration and thrust, capable of going straight up aiming towards Heaven. Unusually for him, Tomek whooped with joy.

All too soon he had to descend into the gloom and emerge into the misty, cold greyness only a few hundred feet above the flat countryside and pick his way back, squinting for familiar landmarks before his fuel ran out. War may have provided him with the perfect aeroplane, but it still demanded a very high price.

The move to Grimbergen, not far from Brussels, brought even more German territory into the Spitfire's bomb-carrying range. The Rhine was in reach but they had all been warned off from doing any freelance armed reconnaissance unless otherwise briefed, as the high density of flak was bad for their health.

Tomek had already had one sortie over the German border but had not gone as far as the heavily defended Rhine. Now the pace quickened as the weather improved slightly, allowing more dive-bombing missions over Holland. The risks were not just from flak, as snowstorms towards the end of January frequently blotted out targets halfway through a dive-bombing attack, or worse still, just as a Spitfire was coming in to land. Sometimes someone did not return and it would be several days before their wreckage was spotted, or occasionally the pilot returned having been picked up by friendly forces.

Even when bailing out, it was not all over after the parachute opened, as landing in a flooded field, river or icy canal, of which there were many, was very much the same death sentence as being shot down.

Tomek's friend, Józef Hajduk of 302 Squadron, was lost after being hit by flak trying to crash land in a snowstorm, adding to the steady stream of casualties that mounted up inexorably as the winter months dragged on.

The schedule was relentless and wearing. Tomek, in common with many others, became almost indifferent to his fate. He felt that skill

The Sting in the Tail

had very little to do with survival, it was just one great roulette wheel in the sky and you had no idea if the ball would fall into the slot with your number on it. At least Angela was due soon. He was convinced it would be a boy, Andrzej, who would continue the Hubert name, his legacy to the post-war world.

Now the emphasis was increasingly on stopping railway transport, which was probably the fastest and most reliable means for the Germans to resupply their forces in the west and north of Holland. As long as they remained there, V2s and V1s would rain down on London, Antwerp and Brussels.

No. 131 Wing had adopted the strategy of sending aloft pairs of Spitfires before dawn to disrupt this flow by attacking any locomotives, leaving them stranded for others to come along in broad daylight to finish the job. Tomek's undoubted skill in scoring direct hits on railway lines, bridges and choke points was employed to the full, delaying rail traffic even further, and on 5 February he helped destroy a trainload of ammunition.

Weather then grounded the squadron. After that, close support was the order of the day as the Allies attempted to break through the Siegfried Line. No. 317 were now operating during the day from forward Airfield B85 (Schijndel), which was much nearer the front line. Tomek was taken off flying and sent up nearer the fighting close to Nijmegen. He was supposed to act as a forward air controller, helping his mates identify specific targets by R/T embedded among the forward command posts. He was horrified by the carnage and the smell. He described seeing human remains that had been blasted up into the trees, the horror of seeing Crocodile tanks in the distance at night, their flamethrowers lighting up the countryside, and the screech and crunch of artillery. After a week of this, Tomek's nerves were even more frayed than before. The responsibility of getting it right weighed heavily on him. He knew how difficult it was to identify a potential target from over 5,000ft and the near impossibility of describing accurately from the ground where a Spitfire should place its bombs, often within a few hundred yards of friendly troops. The consequences of getting it wrong were plain to see, especially when Allied troops made an unexpected advance only to be hit by friendly fire.

He was pulled out for a few days on compassionate grounds as Angela had given birth to a baby boy. It was slightly premature, but that wasn't the problem. During a very long and painful labour, the baby had been strangled by the umbilical cord and was still born. She never saw the poor little mite as he was taken away for incineration. She was inconsolable. Tomek was not really in any fit state to console her as his own pain and disappointment went too deep.

By way of consolation, Angela was offered an operation to straighten out her womb, but she would have a long wait. As she often said many years later, it was a bit too successful as she eventually had six children. All that was to lie in the future; now, for both of them, early 1945 was a tragedy.

Once back at Grimbergen it was straight out on armed reconnaissance missions harassing German military traffic. On 25 February he destroyed a staff car, which although being a soft target was small and easily missed. Now most of the missions were over the German homeland with an increased risk from intense light flak. Few aircraft returned undamaged.

There was little respite once back at their base, as an unpleasant surprise was to find themselves under the flightpath of V1s on their way to Brussels. This had an unexpected consequence when one Doodlebug landed on the roof of the barracks holding ground crew. It rolled off and blocked the exit, meaning that they had to scramble over the flying bomb, which was making a threatening ticking noise. Fortunately it did not go off.

By the time February had given way to March, with some improvement in the weather, Tomek had racked up more than thirty hours of operational missions, which compared to a bomber crew does not sound much. In terms of sorties, however, mostly flown low and passing within minutes over targets well protected by rapid-firing light flak, it meant seeing curtains of tracer rounds saturating the airspace above the target through which any attacking Spitfire had to fly. Given how vulnerable the liquid-cooled Merlin engine was to any punctured radiators or oil system, Tomek lived an extremely charmed life. His plane may have been peppered with holes, but the engine never let him down and, extraordinarily, he was not injured by shrapnel or bullets, unlike many of his squadron mates. Some of them had even suffered damage and injury from the blast of their own bombs, or more often those from the plane in front going off despite a built-in two-second delay in their fuzing.

Some targets blew up in front of them as their cannon rounds hit arms or fuel dumps, and some unfortunate pilots never emerged from the explosion. It was by now a wearying war of attrition with no let-up. Tomek felt no joy at a successful strike and watched in horror when strafing a line of vehicles to see he had not corrected enough for drift as his rounds hit bushes at the side of the road and a figure tumbled out, bowled along by the force of bullets hitting his body. Yet another nightmare to torment him for years to come.

The incidents began to pile in on each other, and sleep was at a premium. Tomek collapsed exhausted, his body taut with nerves and his eyes dry and painful, his throat dry and sore from the forced breathing of oxygen, his brain rerunning the incidents of the day. These included the anxiety of watching the fuel gauge inch its way down to empty as he tried to keep up escorting a formation of Martin B-26 Marauders as they cruised nonchalantly along well above any Spitfire's best endurance speed, and the sight of a V2 standing on a column of flame and smoke and not even seeing where it had been launched from a few seconds before. Then there was being told off by ground crew after diving after what might have been an Arado jet bomber, only to be buffeted as he went past the Spitfire's never-exceed speed and his wings ballooned up, its panels detached by the extreme loads. He was lucky to get away with that one. And, most recently, he had nearly been shot down over the Rhine.

It had been an almost routine armed reconnaissance over Germany, looking for any targets of opportunity to report back. At over 10,000ft, just above the effective range of the light flak, he saw two enormous mounds far below. He reported them and rolled over to investigate, as usual not trimming for the dive. He had no recollection of the bright flash and explosion immediately in front of him. All he could recall is seeing blue sky ahead of him as his Spitfire, having climbed naturally when Tomek's grip relaxed, ran out of energy. It was vibrating fit to shake the engine loose from its mountings. Gingerly, he nosed over and throttled back. Part of his propeller was missing. At just under 180mph the vibration lessened and the aeroplane was controllable but losing height slowly. Ahead of him was the Rhine, with its inevitable curtain of tracer and this time large black eruptions of smoke as the heavier flak joined in. He had no chance of avoiding it and could smell the acrid sulphurous smell of the explosions as he flew helplessly through them.

By now he was down to less than 5,000ft and it seemed that every gun along the Rhine had him in their sights. He was only vaguely aware of his squadron mates side-slipping under him in the hopes of either drawing their fire or shielding his Spitfire.

By the time he barely limped over the boundary at Grimbergen, his plane resembled a colander. At least it was carted away for spares and scrap. He had no such respite, he was up for yet another mission after a restless night of bad dreams and cold sweats.

He had flown a new Spitfire LF Mk. XVI and liked it, but to his and the squadron's disappointment their losses were made up with yet more Mk. IXs, some of which had obviously been patched up after battle damage with other squadrons. No. 317 was beginning to feel neglected.

The latest bomber escort had resulted in a massive explosion that rocked Tomek at 5,000ft and some distance away. A massive rolling column of smoke mushroomed above them and he could see secondary explosions going off around a huge crater that appeared in what had been a pristine field. Someone had called it correctly. Intelligence gathering was really on the ball as they had hit an underground V2 assembly plant, but Tomek also knew that the workers were mostly forced slaves living in hellish conditions not unlike Vorkuta. No doubt the German scientists and technicians had got away in time, leaving the other poor sods to bear the brunt of the attack.

The Sting in the Tail

He fell foul of the group captain when, after an armed reconnaissance over Holland well beyond the reported furthest Allied advance, he saw a vehicle scurrying along a road leaving a column of dust. As he rolled in to attack, it braked suddenly, spoiling his aim as the bullets flew over what he now saw to be a jeep with a large white star on its bonnet.

He screamed over the R/T, 'Don't attack, they're on our side!' first in English, then Polish, until Squadron Leader Chelmecki ordered him to shut up. Tomek felt aggrieved.

Once he landed, a furious Chelmecki told him to say nothing, then marched him in to Gabszewicz. Tomek stood there fuming while his squadron leader explained what had happened. Wordlessly the group captain went over to a large map on the wall.

'Sergeant Hubert you are mistaken, this is where the front line is at present. Are you telling me you know best?'

'Yes sir, it was a jeep with a white star!'

The group captain sniffed and dismissed him. Tomek was tired and angry.

'Don't you believe me?' The group captain ignored him, so Tomek tore off his brass Polish eagle and threw it on the desk.

'I'm not mistaken, I don't lie and those men's safety demands you take me seriously!' With that he stormed out and got a lift back to his billet, still trembling with rage.

That evening he was woken by Chelmecki bringing back his Polish eagle. He said nothing other than to comment, 'This was still in the group captain's drawer. Don't worry about those American soldiers.' He handed over a small cardboard box in which lay Tomek's Polish Cross of Valour.[3]

He smiled. 'Let's say the group captain's been very busy and forgot to give it to you after the award.'

Nothing more was said, but from that time on, there was little doubt in Tomek's mind that Group Captain Gabszewicz had very little time for him.

Chelmecki left soon after that and a new squadron leader was appointed.

The pace of operations accelerated through March, with sorties over Germany becoming ever more frequent. Often the German installations were so very well camouflaged that it was only through very good intelligence and detailed analysis of photo reconnaissance that Tomek and the other squadron pilots could be sure that they were over any target at all! It would only be when they began either diving onto a target or a strafing run when all the flak opened up that they were certain there was any worthwhile target there. The Germans would frequently delay shooting in the hope of not drawing attention to themselves. It was a game of cat and mouse.

Tomek became particularly good at calling their bluff, sometimes with spectacular results. On 20 March 1945 he surpassed himself with two direct hits on the German 88th Corps headquarters, which was utterly destroyed. Many fires were burning fiercely as the squadron left the scene.

The next day, by both bombing and strafing he destroyed two vehicle columns, a German Army camp and finished by attacking a local factory, despite a great deal of very accurate return fire. He had a knack of going in low and sensing any crosswind, laying off his drift then opening fire with great accuracy at the last moment at a range of less than 300 yards. This was both brave and possibly foolhardy.

By now he described flying almost like an automaton: up early, briefing, out to dispersal, walk round checks, making sure that all holes had been patched, control surfaces had free movement and covers and gust locks had been removed. He would then push and shake the bombload, making sure the latches were secure and nothing would drop off as he taxied out. Finally, he would check that the windscreen and canopy were clean. Impaired visibility was frequently a death sentence.

He would then start his Merlin engine, making sure he didn't over-prime, two or three blades flicking past in the morning's grey half-light, a puff of smoke, a lick of flame from the exhaust stubs, then the familiar rumble that shivered up through his legs as he checked full and free movement of the control column and rudder pedals. He would make sure all temperatures and pressures were where they

The Sting in the Tail

should be, turn the gunsight on and illuminated, then off again, and cycle the prop from coarse to fine with the change in note from the prop blare. He would look round, a thumbs up from the ground crew showing the chocks had been removed, then open the throttle, bouncing a bit out of dispersal, checking right and left weaving slightly, no obstacles. He would follow his leader out to the holding point, check brakes, control column full back, open the throttle until he felt the tail buffet in trying to lift against his up elevator, as the Spitfire made every attempt to creep forward, sliding on the wet grass that peeped through the pierced steel planking. He would throttle back, then line up behind and to the left of his leader as others slotted themselves, staggered behind right and left back down the runway, quick R/T check, now waiting for the green light from the flying control van, stomach knotted …

A green! Leader bounces away, his tail coming up already. Tomek's gloved hand pushes his throttle forward as he picks up speed, the acceleration more sluggish as he is weighed down by one 500lb and two 250lb bombs. His tail is up and the grass and runway marker boards shoot past. He holds it down, 100, 110, 120 … he's airborne. Hold it down, 140, 150 … he would have no recollection of touching the brakes or moving the chassis lever forward, it's all instinct and muscle memory. 160, 180 … his leader is climbing now, silhouetted against the brightening sky as the sun starts to break through. A half turn to the left, the R/T clicks, 'Form up!' No other chatter and the day's work has begun.

On 23 March, after another mind-numbing bomber escort, Tomek had flown one of 308's LF Mk. XVIs from Grimbergen to Airfield B77, Gilze-Rijen in Holland, which had until recently been a very well-equipped Luftwaffe base. The camouflage, seen from a distance, was very effective, with only a radar reflector betraying its presence. They had to stay in tents at first while any booby traps were located and defused. All the pilots and ground crew had been told stories of what could happen if they tried to help themselves by 'liberating' cameras, binoculars, even coffee pots, which could have pressure pads underneath them wired to explosives.

This all only served in adding to the tension. As always, sleep was craved desperately.

If anything, the pace increased as 24 March was marked with real progress and masses of air activity as Allied forces crossed the Rhine. The briefing was clear, they needed eyes in the back of their head as massive Curtiss C-46 Commandos, C-47 Dakotas, parachutes and flak would be everywhere. Tomek's squadron was to steer clear of the drop zone, ranging instead well beyond the perimeter, tasked, along with almost everyone else in 131 Wing, with preventing German reinforcements getting anywhere near the Allied forces on the ground. It was exhausting flying two intense sorties where the progress of the war would really be affected if they got it wrong.

Tomek saw, in the distance, a C-46 roll over trailing smoke and flame from one wing. He lost sight of it before it hit the ground, praying that the paratroopers and crew got out beforehand. There were parachutes looking like dandelion seeds in the distance. He could not see any flak bursts or tracer, but knew they had to be there. If anything, that spurred him on to shoot at anything moving towards the melee. In effect they were holding the line.

The pilots were told, at the end of a cruelly exhausting and mind-numbing day, that there had been messages of congratulation and appreciation for a job well done both from the commanders on the ground and Eisenhower's staff. However, in common with all the other pilots, Tomek was just too tired to take it in.

There was no let-up, the next day he left for a raid on the Dutch SS[4] headquarters in Amersfoort. He felt very worried seeing lines of ambulances with crosses painted on their roofs queued up outside and it took several R/T messages to convince him that the SS were deliberately using them to disguise their real purpose.

Tomek felt no enthusiasm for the task and avoided shooting at the ambulances, concentrating on the building instead. He had little doubt that the SS would have had no compunction in commandeering the vehicles and forcing civilian drivers to man them.

He aimed at putting all three bombs through the walls and windows of the first floor by flying lower than briefed as others followed suit. Later the SS headquarters was officially recorded as being totally destroyed, with a German general killed.

Given the operation's success, it seemed odd to be tasked with bombing practice in the afternoon. It did not occur to Tomek at the time that 317 was being considered for other precision attacks.

B101 Nordheim meant a grass field, tents and dust. It was a very poor site, which meant that the Spitfires could not take off and land in the same direction as there were high pine trees at one end of the field. This was temporary and very unsatisfactory. The planes landed towards the trees and took off away from them, which meant that traffic movements had to be choreographed very carefully.

Rashly, Tomek offered to take an Auster light liaison and artillery spotter off to where it belonged. He would also take the young mechanic who had fixed it after some engine trouble had forced its landing at B101.

Assuming that such a light aeroplane would get off easily, Tomek faced it into the wind (and the trees), only to find that he had hardly left the ground when the power failed once more and he was left bouncing among the treetops, eventually halting and swinging to and fro with one wing impaled some 20ft off the ground. They were stuck at a crazy angle a little way into the forest.

The mechanic unbuckled his seat belt and promptly fell through the starboard door, hitting the ground with a groan followed by a lot of cursing. Tomek tried a more dignified exit, only to land on the unfortunate mechanic, who had two cracked ribs.

It was later agreed that Tomek did not need to log this flight as it was barely two minutes from the wheels leaving the ground.

It was obvious that Germany had to surrender soon, but Tomek was surprised when 308 Squadron went back to Fairwood Common in Swansea for a five-week refresher course. That put an extra load on 317 and 302 Squadrons.[5]

Attacks on German airfields had been added to the mix as a lack of fuel had kept almost all Luftwaffe aircraft on the ground. The light flak defending them was such that Tomek, in common with many others, felt that in some ways they should be credited with aircraft destroyed in the same way that aerial victories were. His own ground score now included a Messerschmitt Bf 109 and two Junkers Ju 188s. Once again, his Spitfire had been damaged but he was unscathed.

The weather warmed up in May as they moved to B113 at Varrelbusch in Germany. They were the first squadron to be based on German soil, but there was still no let-up. German resistance was uncoordinated but still dangerous.

This was rammed home on 4 May when 302 and 317 were briefed to attack a 500-ton ship moored off the heavily defended island of Wangerooge. It seemed as if all 317's bombs had missed, so Sergeant Lasław Szczebiński of 302 Squadron began a strafing run. Tomek recalled that he did not even see a single tracer round from his guns before the ship blew up, taking his Spitfire with it.[6]

Years later, Tomek subscribed to the belief that some of 317's bombs had found their target and were either on a longer-delay fuse than briefed or had started fires below. The loss upset Tomek greatly as he felt by that stage of the war it was an utterly pointless death.

As they were due to re-equip with their long-awaited Spitfire LF Mk. XVIes, 317 were stood down at 0800 the next day. They did not even fly another patrol, despite their sister squadron 302 flying two more without any action. Germany was finished, despite odd pockets of resistance and the certain knowledge that high-ranking Nazis were already plotting their escapes through occupied Norway, which had yet to surrender formally, or neutral Sweden and Switzerland.

The final surrender on 8 May was not greeted with any enthusiasm at all among the Poles. As Tomek said: what had they been fighting for and why? He was certain of one thing. He was never going to see his hometown again.

Being told he had been awarded a bar to his Polish Cross of Valour was no compensation at all.

20

Aftermath

All enthusiasm for flying had gone. The squadron had taken on their new Spitfire LF Mk. XVIs, which were more optimised for low-level attack and dive bombing than their old Mk. IXs. Now they could play throttle and RPM against boost, giving a little extra range, and with clipped wings the rate of roll had improved, but those were modifications that helped when fighting a war. The question was, a war with whom?

Germany was utterly defeated. There was no doubt about that, but Russia? Given half a chance, many Poles would have bombed up and taken on the Russians immediately.

Stories were already filtering out about Russian behaviour to the Poles once the Germans had been forced out. Worse still, resentment had continued to grow over the way that the top brass had prevented a full-scale air drop of supplies to the beleaguered Poles in the Warsaw Uprising. There was now little doubt that Stalin and his puppets were determined to install a communist government in Warsaw. The Uprising had been the last desperate gasp for freedom and true independence. The Poland they had all left behind was now gone for good. They had little doubt that Churchill and Roosevelt were behind it as they did not want to antagonise Stalin.

The effect on morale was severe. By now all the Poles in the West were convinced that Marshal Rokosovsky[1] had deliberately paused on the far side of the Vistula in order that the Germans would do his dirty work for him in Warsaw and eliminate all non-communist resistance. What made it worse was that Rokosovsky had a long line of Polish patriots on his father's side whose fortunes had improved under the old Russian Empire. Along with recently promoted General Berlinger, he was now regarded as a traitor by the Polish Government in Exile, not that it made the slightest bit of difference.

A handful of Polish officers who had only fought the Germans since 1939 would not be convinced that they had no chance of influencing matters in a Poland now dominated by Stalin's forces. They would all meet unfortunate fates, with some perishing in jail for being 'traitors' despite their heroic efforts fighting the Nazis.

Sadly, the news that a few well-known officers were going back to Poland only helped to muddy the waters for the majority, who knew that they had no future in the post-war Poland under Russian rule. There was now a growing realisation that almost 100,000 Poles and their families would need housing and assimilating into British society and that was likely to feed a growing resentment among those British who would be looking for their pre-war jobs once they had been demobbed.

Added to that, British society had changed with a largely female domestic workforce, many of whom had acquired skills and did not want to go back to the pre-war status quo of domestic servitude in the kitchen or domestic service for their 'betters'.

Even before the shooting had stopped, the mechanisms of government were considering what was to be done about the Poles. They were an effective fighting force, but would they be useful in any other context?

Tomek and his squadron mates knew that a brand-new set of problems were rearing up ahead of them. If they thought they were going to be instantly demobbed and find their way back to a heroes' welcome in the bosom of their families, they were sadly mistaken. Tomek was among the many who had married British girls, but had not really got to know their brides or their background.

War had inevitably pressured them into short courtships and rushed marriages, and few had any idea as to what life would be away from their air force units. Tomek wanted a future in flying but had had enough of service life. He was not a natural fit for service in a peacetime RAF.

Any decision was taken out of their hands as they were now based in north Germany and given a number of formation training sorties to impress upon the locals as to who were the winners.

Occasionally the squadron flew to another airfield and back again, keeping skills alive that they were unlikely to use any more. The flights became less intense and more infrequent, so almost inevitably accidents started to happen.

One that remained with Tomek until his dying day happened as a result of sheer showing off. It had become a point of honour to side-slip in on a curved approach, then round out at the last possible moment with the wingtip almost touching the grass. Tomek, as usual, had risked everything, polishing his performance to the point where he could see individual blades of grass bending in his wingtip vortices. He rounded out to make a perfect three-point landing and taxied off the runway to watch how the others fared.

One of his mates left it too late, catching a wingtip, and performed what Tomek called a *capotage*, rolling over and sliding upside down along the grass. In common with all the others, the pilot had pumped his seat up to improve visibility. Tomek was convinced that he had been beheaded. He leaped out of his own Spitfire and ran over, fearing the worst. Two mechanics were lifting the tail as Tomek slid underneath. The pilot was stretched back over the open canopy but appeared to be breathing.

Frantically, Tomek punched his quick release and the pilot fell out, allowing Tomek and another to ease him out from under his Spitfire. Where his face had been was a bloody mess of flapping skin torn back from his jaw and over his eyes. It was a horrible sight.

An ambulance was on hand almost immediately and the pilot's head was dressed as soon as he was laid out on the stretcher. Tomek looked on numbly as he was taken off at high speed to the nearest hospital.

A day later he was allowed to visit. To his astonishment, the pilot's face had been pulled back down and stitched into place. He looked bloodied and severely bruised, but could see and, despite painkillers, was talking quite lucidly. The prognosis looked good.

Two days later he was dead. The cause was internal bleeding. He had had major bruising to the abdomen and Tomek feared that he had triggered it by hitting the quick-release disc on the pilot's harness. He felt doubly responsible for the death, both by pulling off a silly stunt and by trying to release him from the cockpit. He admitted to feeling very guilty afterwards and often talked about it with anyone who would listen.

Another entirely avoidable accident happened when Tomek went for an air test in an Auster that had just had some necessary maintenance and then been inspected prior to being signed off as airworthy. He had already had one bad experience with hitting trees on take-off as related earlier, but as the only pilot available who had some slight experience of the Auster, he had been detailed for the task. He had been very cautious during the run-up, magneto checks and subsequent take-off. This time there were no obvious snags. The Auster behaved itself, no engine hiccups and everything seemed to be working. After satisfying himself that the Auster was flying safely, he risked a few steep turns before returning to his base near Cloppenburg in north Germany.

He landed a little fast before realising that he was still carrying a bit too much airspeed. He looked for the brakes, not realising that they were operated by his heels below the rudder bar – an utterly different system from the Spitfire. He was running out of available runway, so he slewed off onto the grass, only to be confronted with a Spitfire with a windmilling propeller. He managed to hop over it but slammed into the wing of another, thereby ending his second Auster sortie.

A few weeks later he was told to lead a team looking for a Gestapo officer who had not been accounted for. Intelligence said that he had family nearby and they were to search a farmhouse belonging to his parents. They were issued with an assortment of handguns, but told only to use them if they were fired on first. This was not a duty that Tomek relished as he was reliant on one of the engine fitters who claimed to speak good German.

Aftermath

As it turned out, the man spoke excellent German, to such an extent that the matriarch of the family shouted at him that he was a traitor working with these useless Poles. They did not find the Gestapo officer, who had probably been tipped off, but they found plenty of evidence that someone had been hiding in an attic room. There was also a set of motorcycle tyre tracks leading out of a barn. As petrol was severely rationed and there was not only a local curfew but a movement restriction on Germans in the area, it was a reasonable guess that the man they sought was either having a lot of help or had blackmailed others into assisting his flight. The head of the household was also missing and several in the area said he had been a local *Gauleiter* who had been very keen on rounding up Jews. Before they left empty handed, the Poles removed all the furniture throughout the house and piled it up in one room, floor to ceiling. They were not popular with the farmer's wife. It was small enough revenge.

Throughout the summer of 1945, the disillusionment grew. Stories had filtered back of conditions in post-war Poland and the fates of the few that had decided to go back. Most of 317 Squadron were marking time, flying when post-war austerity allowed, playing volleyball and taking the advantage of there being more opportunities for leave back in England.

Tomek was polishing his photographic skills using a small Zeiss 20mm cine camera he had adapted for stills photography. The lens was far too slow to allow good air-to-air shots as the vibration in the cockpit was too great. However, he had some success taking shots around the camp – one could hardly call it a base as many were still living under canvas. He was developing his photos under a blanket in place of a darkroom. Having no enlarger, the contact prints were miniscule.

Back in Brighton, he investigated the possibility of courses to further this new career, but the clouds of distrust were gathering as the new Atlee Labour Government showed little enthusiasm for criticising Stalin's Russia, even to the point of invoking them, at least from Tomek's perspective, as the saviours of Eastern Europe.

Discontent was rife throughout the squadron and some saw little point in obeying any rules, even to the point of criminality. One scheme was the smuggling of gold coins in tins of boot polish as the Spitfires flew back to the UK!

There was a contrast between the noises coming from the newly formed Polish Resettlement Corps and what the Poles themselves felt on a day-to-day basis. The rules for non-commissioned pilots were likely to change. Tomek was told that prior to discharge he would have the substantive rank of warrant officer, as that would ensure a better gratuity, but as the station and its flying activity wound down, the rumour mill began again. They would only get a £30 gratuity and one demob (civilian) suit. After that they were on their own.

Worse still, there was talk of them only being allowed to re-enlist in the post-war RAF as ground crew with the rank of AC2. There was no chance of flying the new Gloster Meteor or De Havilland Vampire jet fighters. This sounded like the greatest betrayal of all.

It was now a very tense Tomek who spent time with his young wife Angela, causing her a great deal of distress, compounded by the knowledge that her mother Arlene was facing even more operations for breast cancer. Her own surgery to improve the chances of a healthy pregnancy going to full term was scheduled before the end of the year.

Tomek's last Spitfire flight was on 1 October 1945 from RAF Hethel near Norwich.[2] Elements of 317 Squadron had been sent back in dribs and drabs. There was no ceremony. They had been undertaking pointless squadron formation flying and navigation exercises across the flat Norfolk countryside for a while. Some, Tomek included, had managed to get their wives into local accommodation, but it was obvious that once flying pay had stopped there was little chance of him being able to afford rent for any reasonably comfortable accommodation.

He handed over his Spitfire and was told to take some leave. Everything was dependent upon actions elsewhere and nobody seemed to know what was going to happen. Tomek was not going to stick around, as some of the Nissen huts beyond the perimeter track had already been used by the Polish Resettlement Corps and Tomek had no desire for his wife to move into one of those.

Angela went back to her mother's bungalow in Patcham and Tomek followed a few days later. There was some assistance in terms of travel warrants and the promise that any civilian training courses would be paid for, but there was very little in terms of paperwork that made any sense or carried any weight.

In November, still in uniform, Tomek was best man to his new brother-in-law Alec Smirnoff, who married Angela's 19-year-old sister Agnes. As the youngest, Maureen was still at home. It was obvious that the bungalow was getting too crowded.

Through the local parish and a lot of personal recommendations, Angela and Tomek found local rented accommodation that they could just about afford. Tomek by now had realised that his Polish Air Force uniform did not guarantee him much consideration and he was beginning to hear off-colour comments such as 'Why don't you go back to Poland' in the long queues for the post office or the National Assistance office.

He enrolled in a photography and printing course at the Brighton Technical College night school. During the day he tried any job he could, as the basic wage from the RAF covered very little. In desperation he even drove for a local undertaker but found it far too depressing.

He made enquiries about re-enlisting, but as he was still officially in the Polish Air Force, he was told that no decision had yet been made as to how that could be achieved. Effectively he was stranded between service and civilian life.

He managed to get some freelance work with a local photographer, Frank Dobinson, usually taking masses of photographs at civic functions and business dinners, developing and proofing them, before getting them back for approval and eventual sale. However, the takings rarely justified the effort.

He was lucky enough to be assigned as one of the photographers for two royal visits, those of Queen Mary, then Princess Elizabeth. The results were good and published in a local paper, the *Brighton and Hove Herald*. The money was helpful but still not great and did not lead to much other work as there were now so many returning servicemen, some better qualified and others looking to claw back their pre-war jobs.

It was going to be a lean Christmas.

His brother-in-law made a slightly rude suggestion that they should surprise their mother-in-law Arlene by rounding up all the RAF-issued condoms they could find and fill them with the ghastly chicory mixture that passed for instant coffee. At first Tomek thought he was going to use them as decorations, but instead Alec produced a dartboard and hung them in front of it. The idea was to puncture them with thrown darts. An old curtain was laid down to catch the inevitable messy results. In some way it was a protest against everything that had happened to them. Tomek had taught himself to blow glass Christmas decorations, but few had sold, while Alec had acquired a lathe from somewhere and had used old aluminium bar stock, possibly stolen from a crashed aeroplane or a black market dealer, to make fishing reels.

Neither venture had brought much money, nor future sales prospects. Everyone was too hard up. Tomek, in particular, was feeling morose and rejected. He had photographed some very wealthy men getting absolutely plastered at various functions and had heard rumours of war profiteering. This had made him very resentful. He applied, without telling Angela, for emigration to the USA, hoping that prospects would be better there. He was to be disappointed as no reply would arrive for another twelve years! Alec tried to persuade him that Argentina was a good bet and that they should go into partnership in an engineering business he would set up over there.

By now, it was obvious that Arlene was very seriously ill and that Angela had no intention of leaving her mother. There was a lot of consultation and argument, but in the end it was agreed that her sister Agnes would go to Argentina, if they were granted residency; teenage Maureen, their younger sister, would study and work in France, taking advantage of a kind offer made by a family friend; while Angela and Tomek would try to make their way in England, on hand to return should Arlene's double mastectomy not stop the cancer from developing further.

The year 1946 arrived with even worse prospects as rationing was tightened. Tomek was becoming very irritable and isolated from everyone, the knowledge that not one Polish pilot would be taking part in the victory fly-past and march-past scheduled for 8 June only adding to his sense of abandonment and misery.[3]

Angela was by now fearing for both his and her sanity. She said at the time that it was as if Tomek was suffering from shell shock. The term Post Traumatic Stress Disorder was not in common usage then. The nightmares had started and, if anything, the distance from front-line flying was making Tomek worse.

He would erupt into bouts of violence, smashing crockery then storming out of the house. She tried desperately to understand what was wrong and spoke to Father Wojtas, the Polish priest at St Mary Magdalene's in Brighton. His advice was simple. Tomek had lost everything in Poland: his home had gone and his home town of Lwów was no longer included in Poland. He had effectively been betrayed and Father Wojtas understood what was happening, as many Poles in his parish were deteriorating in the same way. He put it bluntly. They had all been betrayed! The fact that they were still nominally in uniform in service to an exiled government that was no longer recognised by the British made things even worse. He suggested that Tomek should get out of uniform officially, and soon.

Angela was encouraged to do as much as she could to try to build little customs, such as adopting the Polish *Wigila* (Christmas Eve), just to salve the wounds. Father Wojtas warned her that it would be hard and at times she would feel like giving up.

For a while they attended the Polish Mass but even that did not have any long-term effect. Communications from the Polish Resettlement Corps were usually skim read, then torn up. Angela attempted to improve her basic knowledge of the Polish language in the hopes of understanding what was really going on, but her efforts were in vain.

The only bright spot was the sheer love and consideration Tomek showed for her mother's suffering. Without saying much, it was as if Arlene and Tomek had developed a bond based on pain and distress.

The final blow fell when Tomek was told that if he was to stand any chance of transferring fully to the Royal Air Force as a career, he would have to report to RAF Hethel on a particular date at his own expense. There was no way he could afford it and he knew nobody who was in a position to lend him the money.

That was the last blow, severing his link with 317 (Polish) Squadron and the Spitfire.

Postscript

In early 1975 Tomek was invited to Ghent as the sole survivor who had flown on 1 January 1945 from Sint-Denijs-Westrem. A street had been named after the Poles and the good citizens of that town wanted something of a gala to celebrate the thirtieth anniversary of that event.

My sister Stephanie was studying music at the Brussels conservatoire, and it had taken some persuasion by my mother Angela for Stef to make the journey and support her father. Tomek had never really understood how to bring up a daughter, especially through the more liberal 1960s.

He was so fearful of communism and, to him, the certainty of a nuclear war that he had joined civil defence and regarded even the Co-op as part of a Russian takeover. He was still licking his wounds over being fined for possessing a wartime Mauser pistol he had kept in case of the need to fight a way to safety for his wife and six children. It had not helped that one of my brothers had found it and accidentally discharged it, wounding a friend in the arm.

Angela felt very strongly that some family support at the event in Belgium would give Tomek a sense of worth. He had successfully blagged his way into engineering and been promoted on sheer ability without any qualification, but nevertheless felt undervalued and irrelevant on top of his worsening PTSD and several brain injuries through a series of motorcycle and other accidents.

The celebration went well; that is, right up to the time when, to Stef's horror, Tomek was invited to fly a local flying club's new French-built Cessna 150 Aerobat. After a brief explanation of where was what, and this time taking great note of how the brakes worked, he decided that he had to impress upon his daughter that he was once a young man with real flying abilities.

Despite the passage of years, he said it all felt so familiar. He was determined to make some sort of impression and show these civilians what real wartime flying was really about. This was no Spitfire, but it had a full aerobatic harness, was new, better powered than the Auster and he had been assured it was vice free in its flying characteristics.

There was no way he would be able to climb to any height but he made best use of what he had been given. He lifted off at 45mph, held it down well past its best climbing speed of 70mph, then zoomed up at 100mph, half rolling as it ran out of steam in a perfect Immelmann turn at about 500ft. He checked left and right, raising each high wing in turn just to make sure that there were no other aircraft in the sky. Visibility was good, with broken cloud at about 2,000ft.

Rather than pushing the nose down, he half rolled, then dived towards the crowd – something that was usually forbidden for air displays. He had narrowly avoided being a spectator in the decimated crowd at the 1952 Farnborough Airshow disaster, where John Derry was killed as his DH 110 broke up, its engines flying into the crowd and killing twenty-nine people and injuring sixty.

Such safety concerns did not occur to Tomek as he felt invincible. Without any second thought for his or the crowd's safety, he gave the aerobatic display of his life, rolling, looping, performing a brief inverted pass just above the crowd, stall turns and a very slow roll, testing the little Cessna's abilities to the limits. He side-slipped into a curved approach and landed in true Spitfire manner. The crowd went wild with applause. Stef, terrified of the consequences, slipped away.

It was only after shutting down the engine, hearing the sound of the gyros whirring down and the ticking of the engine as it cooled that, after a short, nostalgic pause, he opened the door and admitted he had not flown any plane since 1945!

Postscript

We still don't know what was said by the flying club's CFI. Was Tomek dressed down in the same way as he was at a certain Polish gliding club in August 1939? Tomek would just smile. He knew he had had the last laugh.

Tomek dined out on the memory of this flight right up until his death in 2006.

Appendix

In His Own Words

I knew about an account my father had written some years ago about flying, but never knew the sense or context.

To my delight, a cousin in Poland had a copy that she sent me shortly after I had completed the bulk of this manuscript. Reproduced below is a careful translation from my father's fairly classical Polish in a style that is rarely seen or heard in modern Poland.

Although the fuel level is low the aircraft is behaving very well, but it feels cold. The airfield can already be seen clearly. Petrol bowsers and aircraft are on fire. On the left, something larger is ablaze. There are black patches where our aircraft usually stand. But, beyond the largest hangar, something big is moving. A bowser is hiding behind the brick wall. In the centre of the white airfield there are black patches. One couldn't land there.

The radio calls: 'It's flying on the right' – 'Two of them – I'm going after the second one!'

Continuing to observe, searching, I see a small cross moving in my direction! That's one of them. Very low. The surrounding sky is clear. I throw the aircraft over onto its back and continue after him! I'm gaining speed. I'm trying to fly in such a way that my engine doesn't obscure my view, flying as I am, at maximum speed, in order to catch him! There is no one behind him. Is the safety released on my cannon?

Could I try a quick burst? But we're over a town and I've already fired at the bowser, so I shouldn't. Is there anyone behind me? [Unreadable phrase.] I remember how Pieniążek was killed in a collision at Swansea. The thought flashed through my mind: 'Lord, let me bring up my son, myself.'

He's closer now. Get him into the aiming circle! And press! But he's getting away. More speed. Mother, help me. He's there again! No, he turned away. He's fleeing upwards using half-loops! I'm using all my strength on the control column in order to copy what he's doing because, if I don't succeed, he might get away from me in a sudden turn. He's in the circle! Suddenly, the small silhouette of the Focke-Wulf is transformed into a large, flat shape just in front of me! Two bursts and there appear two sheets of flame from both his wings. He turns over and falls! He's hit a building. I can't see him any more. Up, up! Quickly! No one behind me? Nobody. That was for Poland! That was for Lwów! Yet those poor people have lost their home.

Fuel? I must land. But where? Two thousand, three, four. Good. That's high. I look around the sky, at the ground, at my instruments.

Thank you, God. That wasn't like it was for the 'Lwowskie Dzieci' [the Children of Lwów] at Łyczaków [allusion to the Polish child soldiers who defended their city against the Ukrainians in 1918 and the Russians in 1920, who now lie in the Łyczaków cemetery]. I put my aircraft into a wide right turn. There are some aircraft milling around in that direction. But it's too far. Here's one behind another! Down! The first one has a cross and the other is too far. I have to catch the German! He's escaping very fast! He has a different engine to the previous one. A half-roll to the right, to the left, he's coming into my sights, once, twice, again. I fire. He's spun away! I chase after him on full power but he's receding! There he is again. I don't have any more power. I fire. Something fell away from him. He's really screwing around. I've lost him, can't see him. So, up, once more! And I'm searching. I can see two Spitfires in the distance and a German, in front of them. Already in flames. I make a turn to the left. My wings are vertical. There, there are aircraft circling around in front of me. One of them is fleeing, the other is giving chase. That first one isn't one of ours! So, after him! A large deflection! The sights are far to the left but I do open fire. A short burst. Is that the end of my ammunition? In that case – up, up! I turn to the west in order to catch sight of the airfield. The ground appears once more. Although there is much smoke over the airfield I can see it clearly from my position. There are fires on two sides. One can tell that it's aircraft that are on fire by the black propellers that stick out. A Spitfire flies over it, low and slow. The battle is over! The Germans have gone.

In between the dark patches and the flames on the airfield, a sufficiently long and free space can be found. I decrease the throttle and turn right, to the north, in order to position myself for a quick descent and landing.

The engine splutters. Flaps, undercarriage, OK … I open the canopy and reposition the aircraft to the left … We're close to the edge of the airstrip, so I go into a deep slide. Losing altitude, I'm aiming my wing at a precise spot so that I don't gain speed and so that I come out of the slide in the direction of the clear space beneath me.

Maybe it'll work out well and I'll return safely, as say the words of the song that's playing in my head [allusion to the last verse of the 'March of the Children of Lwów', 'Marsz Lwowskich Dzieci']. Now you can discern individual clumps of earth [presumably because it's so close to the ground]. I come out of the slide with my wing just clear of the ground and all at once I can feel that my wheels are on even ground. 'Ignition off – Brakes'.

I roll only for a short distance and immediately restart my engine in order to make room for others. Someone is running and giving me hand signals so I move in his direction. The engine splutters and dies and the man indicates that I should come to a stop. I release my buckles and jump out onto the ground. I can hear firing … People are running, bent double. I can see tracers and flying rounds. They're making signs that I should also bend over … On the right there is a burning Mosquito and its cannon are firing across the airfield. I run beneath the missiles. Someone grabs me by the shoulder and begins patting me on the back, saying [in a Lwów accent]: 'I saw you. You were like a hawk, from above. Hubert, you're from Lwów and I'm from Złoczów, which is not far.' We made our way along the line of engines that were held up by their propellers. That's all that was left of our aircraft that had been on the ground. Apart from the buildings, everything on the airfield had been destroyed. There were no anti-aircraft guns. They had all been taken away for use against the German forces that were concentrated at the Rhine river.

Later on, in the afternoon, we worked out that our six pilots had been credited with eighteen German aircraft shot down, although twenty-one had been found in the vicinity of the airfield. It was said that, of the forty Germans who had attacked there, only one, damaged, was able to return to the German lines. One of the pilots who had made a forced landing told us that he had not fired on those first Focke-Wulfs only that, when they saw him in their mirrors, they each went into a corkscrew out of fright. One of our number managed to take off and went into battle but the Germans shot him down and he perished.

One of the mechanics had been driving a petrol bowser across the airfield when the attack began, so he leapt out and hid underneath it. Wanting to escape from there, he jumped in again and drove it behind the hangar, where I saw it from above. He was lucky that they didn't hit him.

It's good that I wrote this up in 1947, as I don't remember it well now.

Tomek's account in original Polish:

Choć benzyny mało, maszyna zachowuje się wspaniale ale jest zimno. Już widać lotnisko dobrze. Palą się cysterny benzynowe, samoloty, po lewej, coś większego się pali. Czarne plamy tam, gdzie nasze samoloty normalnie stoją. Ale, styłu [sic] *z tyłu* największego hangaru, coś wielkiego się rusza. To poza ceglaną ścianą cysterna jest schowana! Po środku białego lotniska, czarne plamy. Tam lodować [sic] *lądować* lądować nie można.

Radio krzyczy; 'Leci na prawo' – 'To dwóch – ja za drogim [sic] *drugim*!'

Patrzę się nadal, szukam, i widzę maleńki krzyżyk posuwa się w moim kierunku! To jeden. Bardzo nisko. Niebo dookoła puste. Przerzucam maszynę na plecy i dalej, za nim! Szybkość [sic] *szybkości* nabieram. Staram się prowadzić maszynę w taki sposób by silnik mi nie zasłaniał lecąc na pełnym gazie, by go złapać! Nikt za nim nie leci. Armatki odbezpieczone? Czy spróbować krótką salwę? Ale to nad miastem i już strzelałem z nich na cysternę więc nie trzeba. Idzie ktoś za mną? *Biorę ???? O.* [Can't catch the meaning of this sentence.] Pamiętam jak Pieniążek w zderzeniu zginął, w Swansea. Boże, pozwól mi własnego syna wychować, przez myśl mi błyskawicznie przeszło.)

On już bliżej. W koło celownika go! I nacisnąć! Ale ucieka. Na szybkość. Matko dopomóż. Jest znowu! Nie, skręcił. Ucieka do góry, półbeczkami! Całą mą siłę używam na drążku by powtarzać co on robi, bo gdy nie zdołam, to mi może, w nagłym skręcie, uciec! Jest w kole! Naciskam. Jakby hamulse [sic] *hamulce* na mą maszynę ktoś założył! Me tracery lecą! Nagle, mała sylwetka focke-wolfa zmienia się w duży kształt-płaski, przedemną! Dwie salwy i dwie płachty płomieni z obu jego skrzydeł! Przewala się w lewo i spada! Uderzył w kamienicę! Już nie widzę. Do góry, do góry! Szybko! Nikogo za mną? Niema. Po za Polskę! To za Lwów! Ale biedni lodzi [sic] *ludzie*, *probably*, stracili mieszkanie.

Benzyna? Lądować. Ale gdzie? Dwa tysiące, trzy, cztery. Dobrze. To już wysoko. Patrzę się, po niebie, po ziemi, na zegary.

Dzięki Ci Boże. Nie tak jak Lwowskie Dzieci na Łyczakowie. Przekłądam maszynę w głęboki zakręt w prawo. Tam się jakieś samoloty kręcą. Ale za daleko. Tu jest jeden za drugim! Na dół! Pierwszy ma krzyżyk, a drugi jest za daleko. Muszę niemca złapać! Ucieka bardzo szybko! Inny ma silnik niż ten poprzedni. Pół beczki w prawo, w lewo, przechodzi przez mój celownik, raz, drugi, znowu. Strzelam.

Odkręcił się! Ciągnę za nim z całej siły, ale się oddala! Znowu jest. Gazu więcej nie mam. Strzelam. Coś od niego odleciało. Ale się zwina. Straciłem go, nie widzę.

Więc znowu, do góry! I szukam. Widzę w dali dwa spitfajery, a przed nimi, niemiec. Już w płomieniach. Skręcam w lewo. Me skrzydła są pionowo. Tam, kręcą się maszyny, przedemną. Ktoś ucieka, ktoś goni. Ten pierwszy, to nie nasz! Więc, za nim! Duża deflekcja! Celownik jest dużo na lewo, ale strzelam. Krótka salwa.

Amunicja skończona? Do góry, więc, do góry. Skręcam na zachód, by zobaczyć lotnisko. Ziemia pokazuje się na nowo. Choć dużo dymu nad lotniskiem, z mojej pozycji widzę je wyraźnie. Po dwóch stronach, ogień. Widać że palą się samoloty, bo stercz czarne śmigła. Jakiś spitfajer przelatuje nad nim nisko i wolno. Walki już nie ma! Niemców już nie ma.

Pomiędzy ciemnymi plamami i płomieniami na lotnisku, można znaleźć dość długą, wolną przestrzeń. Przymykam gas, skręcając na prawo, na północ, by przybrać pozycję do krótkiego schodu do lądowania.

Silnik kaszle. Flapy, podwozie, O.K. ... Otwieram kabinę i przeprowadzam maszynę na lewo... Już blisko skraju, więc wkładam w głęboki ślizg. Tracąc wysokość, celuję skrzydłem w wybrane miejsce, by nie nabrać szybkości, by wyjść ze ślizgu w kierunku wolnej przestrzeni tuż pod si?i??? Może uda się, i powrócę znów, piosenka mi się <u>gwiżdże</u> *(possibly)* ... Już widać pojedyńcze grodu ziemi. Wychodzę ze ślizgu ze skrzydłem tuż nad ziemią i natychmiast czuję me koła na nie równej ziemi. 'Ignition off – Hamulce'.

Toczę się bardzo krótko i natychmiast startuję silnik na nowo, by zrobić miejsce innym. Ktoś biegnie, dając mi znaki rękami, więc kieruję w jego stronę. Silnik, parskając, gaśnie, a człowiek daje mi znać bym stanął. Odpinam się i wyskakuję na ziemię. Słychać strzelaninę ... Ludzie biegną, zgięci w pół. Widzę tracery, pociski latają. Machają do mnie bym się także zgiął ... Na prawo, pali się 'Mosquito' i jego armatki strzelają ponad lotniskiem. Przebiegam pod pociskami. Ktoś mnie chwyta za ramię i klepie mnie po plecach, mówiąc: Ja cię widział. Tyś jak jastrząb, z góry. Hubercie, Tyś ze Lwowa, a ja ze Złoczowa, to nie daleko. Przechodziliśmy wzdłuż linji silników podpartych śmigłami. To wszystko, co zostało z naszych samolotów na ziemi. Za wyjątkiem budynków, wszystko, na lotnisku, było zniszczone. Artylerii przeciwlotniczej nie było. Wzięli ją by użyć na skoncentrowane niemieckie siły przed rzeką Rhine.

Później, po południu, doliczyliśmy się że nam sześciu pilotom przyznano osiemnaście niemieckich maszyn zniszczonych, choć koło lotniska znaleziono dwadzieścia jeden. Mówiono że od tych czterdziestu niemców, którzy tam atakowali, tylko jeden, uszkodzony, zdążył dotrzec do niemiecki [sic] *niemieckiej* linji. Ten pilot, który pierwszy przymusowo wylądował, powiedział nam że on do tych pierwszych focke-wolfów nie strzelał, tylko, gdy go w lustrach zobaczyli, obaj, ze strachu, w korkociągi wpadli. Jeden z naszych kolegów zdążył wystartować do walki, ale go niemcy zestrzelili i zginął.

Jeden z mechaników jechał cysterną benzynową przez lotnisko, gdy atak się zaczął, więc wyskoczył i schował się pod nią. Chcąc z tamtat [sic] *stamtąd* uciec, skoczył do niej na nowo i poprowadził ją poza hangar, gdzie ja ją z góry widziałem. Miał szczęście że go nie trafili.

Dobrze że napisałem to w 47mym roku, bo teraz o tym mało pamiętam.

Przepisane z maszynopisu – Marek Mrozek, Polski Instytut i Muzeum im. Gen. Sikorskiego.

Transcribed from the original by Marek Mrozek, Polish Institute and Sikorski Museum.

Acknowledgements

This book would not have been possible without the support of my entire family.

Kathy, for letting me read it to her *ad nauseam*, adding comments and urging me on. My nephew, young Christopher, who is an archivist and genealogist extraordinaire; my brothers, Simon and Christopher, with nephew Jonathan, who have kept and conserved artefacts and memorabilia of my late father; their wives and the greater family for providing necessary reminders when communications went astray; and not forgetting my remarkable daughter Emma, who kidnapped me and took me to Kraków, where I reconnected with my Polish roots.

Chris Nowakowski and Marek Mrozek, who arranged the translation of *In His Own Words*; Cousin Ania, who found a copy of the same; and the helpful staff at the Sikorski Museum.

Not forgetting my lovely commissioning editor Claire Hartley at The History Press for her faith in me, her enthusiasm, encouragement and sheer friendliness, which has made writing this sometimes harrowing account so worthwhile.

There are so many others who have helped in so many ways over many years, chief among these being my sainted mother Angela, who described herself as the mediatrix between the family and our sad, damaged, frustrated and yet courageous dad.

Thank you all!

Further Reading

A great deal of the background to pre-war Poland, the gulags, the wider influences on my father's experiences, in common with many others, the social history, the development of the Polish Air Force in the UK and the overall historical context may be found in the following excellent books:

Brown, Alan, *Flying For Freedom*, The History Press, 2011.
Cynk, Jerzy B., *The Polish Air Force at War: The Official History: 1939–43*, Schiffer Publishing, 1998.
Cynk, Jerzy B., *The Polish Air Force at War: The Official History: 1943–45*, Schiffer Publishing, 1998.
Davies, Norman, *Trail of Hope*, Osprey Publishing, 2015.
Franks, Norman, *Battle of the Airfields*, Grub Street, 2000.
Karski, Jan, *Story of a Secret State*, The Riverside Press, 1944.
Karta, Ośrodek, *Aresztowani w rejonie Lwowa i Drohobycza*, 1998.
Manley, Rebecca, *To the Tashkent Station: Evacuation and Survival in the Soviet Union at War*, Cornell University Press, 2009
Michta, Andrew, *Red Eagle: The Army in Polish Politics, 1944–1988*, Hoover Press, 1990, Stanford University, California,
Olson, Lynne, & Cloud, Stanley, *For Your Freedom and Ours*, Heinemann, 2003.
Sharp, Dan, *Spitfires Over Berlin*, Tempest Books, 2015.
Waydenfeld, Stefan, *The Ice Road*, Mainstream Publishing, 1999.
Zamoyski, Adam, *Warsaw 1920, Lenin's Failed Conquest of Europe*, HarperPress, 2008.

Notes

Prologue

1 Cynk, Jerzy B., 'Salamandra Glider', *Polish Aircraft 1893–1939*, 1971.
2 Jozef Piłsudski, 1867–1935. Regarded as the father of modern Poland.
3 Cynk, *Polish Aircraft 1893–1939*.

Chapter 1

1 Now Lviv in Ukraine.
2 Cynk, Jerzy B., 'Evacuation of CinC', *The Polish Air Force at War: The Official History: 1939–43*, Schiffer Publishing, 1998, p.86.
3 Karta, Ośrodek, *Aresztowani w rejonie Lwowa i Drohobycza*, 1998, p.120.

Chapter 2

1 *The Polish Review*, Volume LV, Polish Institute of Arts & Sciences, 2010.

Chapter 3

1 Vorkuta was a gulag 1932–62 in the Komi Autonomous Area of Russia.
2 Balmforth, Tom, 'Life in Stalin's Gulags', *The Atlantic*, 4 March 2013.

Chapter 5

1 'Gulag: Many Days, Many Lives', gulaghistory.org, p.4.

Chapter 6

1 Jan, Karski, *Story of a Secret State*, The Riverside Press, Cambridge, Mass., 1944.
2 Norman, Davies, *Trail of Hope*, Osprey Publishing, 2015, p.35.
3 www.archives.gov/research/foreign-policy/katyn-massacre#:~:text=From%20Record%20Group,at%20Katyn%20(1943).

Chapter 7

1 Olson, L. & Cloud, S., *For Your Freedom and Ours*, Heinemann, London, 2003, p.125.
2 *The Polish Air Force at War: The Official History: 1939–43*, pp.163–195.
3 Robert W., Thurston, *Life and Terror in Stalin's Russia, 1934–1941*, Yale University Press, 1998, p.139.
4 Waydenfeld, Stefan, *The Ice Road*, Mainstream Publishing, 1999, p.95.
5 *Aresztowani w rejonie Lwowa i Drohobycza*, p.120.

Chapter 8

1 Murphy, David E., *The Enigma of Barbarossa Intelligence in Recent Public Literature*, Yale University Press, 2005.
2 *Trail of Hope*, p.54.
3 www.military-history.org/articles/operation-barbarossa-map-1941.htm.
4 *Kolkhoz* were labour camps, often with family units, who worked on a collective project for a small wage.

Chapter 9

1 *Trail of Hope*, p.258.
2 Hubert, Henryk, *Cards with Memories of an Insurgent* (first published 1938, republished privately from the Hubert family archive by Marcus Hubert, 2023).
3 *Trail of Hope*, p.132.
4 Syg. Wydzielone Państwowe Archiwum SBU F. 16, Op. 23-sp, S. 20–24.
5 International Criminal Court, 17 March 2023.
6 Manley, Rebecca, *To the Tashkent Station: Evacuation and Survival in the Soviet Union at War*, Cornell University Press, 2009, pp.7–9.
7 *Trail of Hope*, pp.130–159.
8 Wheeler, Barry, *The Hamlyn Guide to Military Aircraft Markings*, Chancellor Press, 1994, p.73.

Notes

Chapter 10

1 *Trail of Hope*, pp.130–159.
2 www.americanoceans.org/facts/what-happened-to-the-aral-sea.

Chapter 11

1 *Trail of Hope*, p.190.
2 Michta, Andrew, *Red Eagle: The Army in Polish Politics, 1944–1988*, Hoover Press, 1990, Stanford University, California, p.33.
3 Bigg, Matthew Mpoke, *New York Times*, 6 June 2023.
4 www.vdh.virginia.gov/epidemiology/epidemiology-fact-sheets/epidemic-typhus-fever-louse-borne/.

Chapter 12

1 *Trail of Hope*, p.234.
2 The *Polish Air Force at War: The Official History: 1939–43*, pp.163–167.
3 Ibid., pp.464–467.
4 Ibid., pp.580–583.
5 Ibid., pp.243–244.
6 Ibid., pp.263–265.
7 Ibid., p.623.
8 Ibid., p.625.
9 *Oxford Companion to Ships and the Sea*, www.oxfordreference.com.

Chapter 13

1 Tomek's service record documentation.
2 *Story of a Secret State*, pp.345–350.
3 The Avalon Project: Casablanca Conference 1943 (yale.edu).
4 Churchill, Winston Spencer, *The Second World War: Closing the Ring*, The Houghton Mifflin Company, Boston, 1951, p.642.
5 Tomek's pilot's logbook entries.
6 The Focke-Wulf Fw 190A was a very effective German fighter in 1942–45.
7 The Junkers Ju 88 was a twin-engine German bomber that flew throughout the Second World War.
8 The De Havilland Mosquito was an exceptionally fast twin-engine fighter-bomber in 1942–45.

Chapter 14

1 Tomek's pilot's logbook entries.
2 Ibid.

Chapter 15

1. Ibid.
2. The Miles Master 2 was a radial engine training aircraft in service from 1941 to 1946.
3. Tomek's pilot's logbook entries.
4. Ibid.
5. The Avro Anson was used as a twin-engine trainer aircraft and transport in 1938-50.
6. 'Le Paradis Sous Terre', German propaganda leaflet released in Vichy France, 1943, Imperial War Museum Collection.
7. *The Second World War: Closing the Ring*.
8. *The Polish Air Force at War: The Official History: 1939-45*, p.357.
9. Ibid., p.350.
10. Ibid., p.348.

Chapter 16

1. Arthur Morris Oakeshott 1899-1957, Reuters, embedded with the Home Fleet 1942-44.
2. Hubert family archives.
3. Tomek's pilot's logbook entries.
4. Miles Martinet pilot's notes.
5. The Fieseler Fi-103, known by the Germans as V1 (Vergeltungswaffen 1), was the first 'revenge weapon' deployed in 1944 as a reprisal for the twenty-four-hour mass bombing of Germany. It was known colloquially by the British as the Doodlebug.
6. Tomek's pilot's logbook entries.
7. Cynk, Jerzy B., *The Polish Air Force at War: The Official History: 1943-45*, Schiffer Publishing, 1998, p.94.

Chapter 17

1. Tomek's pilot's logbook entries.
2. Spitfire pilot's notes.
3. Tomek's pilot's logbook entries.
4. Tomek's RAF service record.
5. Sosabowski Stanisław, Encyklopedia PWN: źródło wiarygodnej i rzetelnej wiedzy.
6. *The Polish Air Force at War: The Official History: 1943-45*, p.402.

Notes

Chapter 18

1 The V2, which was initially being used to attack London from northern France, was by late 1944 being deployed from mobile launchers. It was the first ballistic missile to be deployed in both a strategic and tactical role. Its exceptional high speed and trajectory through the stratosphere meant it was impossible to intercept.
2 Caddick-Adams, Peter, *Snow and Steel: The Battle of the Bulge, 1944–45*, Oxford University Press, 2014, p.649.
3 Franks, Norman, *Battle of the Airfields*, Grub Street, 1994, p.87.
4 Ibid.
5 See 'In His Own Words'.
6 Tomek's pilot's logbook entries.
7 Raporty Bojowe Z Lotow, Polish Institute Sikorski Museum Lot AV 45/16.
8 Sharp, Dan, *Spitfires Over Berlin*, Tempest Books, 2015, p.37.

Chapter 19

1 *Polish Air Force at War*, Volume 2, p.406.
2 Raporty Bojowe Z Lotow.
3 Tomek was eventually awarded a bar to his Polish Cross of Valour (Polish: Krzyż Walecznych). This was confirmed by the Sikorski Institute in 2023.
4 *The Polish Air Force at War: The Official History: 1943–45*, p.407.
5 Ibid., p.408.
6 Ibid., p.409.

Chapter 20

1 rokossowski.com/bio.htm.
2 Tomek's pilot's logbook entries.
3 *For Your Freedom and Ours*, p.5.

You may also enjoy …

978 1 80399 719 3